Conversations
with David Foster Wallace

Literary Conversations Series
Peggy Whitman Prenshaw
General Editor

Conversations with
David Foster Wallace

Edited by Stephen J. Burn

University Press of Mississippi   Jackson

Books by David Foster Wallace
The Broom of the System. New York: Viking-Penguin, 1987.
Girl with Curious Hair. New York: Norton, 1989.
With Mark Costello. *Signifying Rappers.* New York: Ecco, 1990.
Infinite Jest. Boston: Little, 1996.
A Supposedly Fun Thing I'll Never Do Again. Boston: Little, 1997.
Brief Interviews with Hideous Men. Boston: Little, 1999.
Up, Simba! Seven Days on the Trail of an Anticandidate. Boston: Little, 2000.
Everything and More: A Compact History of ∞. New York: Norton, 2003.
Oblivion. Boston: Little, 2004.
Consider the Lobster. Boston: Little, 2005.
McCain's Promise: Aboard the Straight Talk Express with John McCain and a Whole Bunch of Actual Reporters, Thinking about Hope. Fwd. Jacob Weisberg. Boston: Back-Little, 2008.
This Is Water. Boston: Little, 2009.
Fate, Time, and Language: An Essay on Free Will. Ed. Steven M. Cahn and Maureen Eckert. Introd. James Ryerson New York: Columbia UP 2011.
The Pale King. Ed. Michael Pietsch. Boston: Little, 2011.

www.upress.state.ms.us
The University Press of Mississippi is a member of the Association of American University Presses.

"Approaching Infinity," an interview with David Foster Wallace conducted by Caleb Crain, originally published in *The Boston Globe*, Copyright © 2003 by Caleb Crain, used with permission of The Wylie Agency LLC.

Library of Congress Cataloging-in-Publication Data
Conversations with David Foster Wallace / edited by Stephen J. Burn.
    p. cm. — (Literary conversations series)
    Includes index.
    ISBN 978-1-61703-226-4 (cloth : alk. paper) — ISBN 978-1-61703-227-1 (pbk. : alk. paper) — ISBN 978-1-61703-228-8 (ebook) 1. Wallace, David Foster—Interviews. 2. Authors, American—20th century—Interviews. I. Burn, Stephen.
    PS3573.A425635Z66 2012
813'.54—dc23   2011027372

British Library Cataloging-in-Publication Data available

Contents

Introduction

"I'm wretched at interviews," David Foster Wallace told me in a letter sent late in the summer of 2007, "and will do them only under big duress."[1] Wallace's discomfort with interviews makes sense on multiple levels. His concern about public revelation is reasonable in terms of the overall arc of his career, which shuttled between what Wallace called the "schizophrenia of attention" and the despondency of private torment (Stein). Equally, his thematic obsessions—self consciousness, the difficult exchange economy that exists between characters' interior landscapes and the world around them—draw on the same energies that might be located in the interview process. Finally, one of Wallace's signature techniques for revealing character through dialogue—the one-sided conversation, which we might call the *belled interview*, after a term coined for Nabokov's critique of telephone conversations where the reader hears only one speaker[2]—turned the mechanics of an interview into a central focus of Wallace's middle-period fiction (*Infinite Jest* [1996] and *Brief Interviews* [1999]). This nexus of imaginative activity made the set-piece of an interview something more than a polite formality for Wallace, a pursuit that could not be coolly divorced from creative practice. But there were clearly more personal reasons why Wallace became reticent about interviews. After he became engulfed in the media storm surrounding *Infinite Jest*, Wallace wrote to Don DeLillo about the experience:

> If you try to be unpretentious and candid, a reporter comments on the unpretentious, candid persona you've adopted for the interview. It ends up being lonely and wildly depressing. And strange. I had guys in my *house* (a tactical error). . . . The guy from the *Post* . . . who's become a friend because he was my first interview and I was wildly indiscreet about stuff like drug histories . . . and he stopped me in the middle and patiently explained certain rules about what to tell reporters . . .[3]

Yet good advice might only lessen, not eradicate, personal intrusion. When Frank Bruni interviewed Wallace for *New York Times Magazine*, he felt obliged to chronicle the contents of the novelist's medicine cabinet ("his bathroom contains special tooth polish to combat the effects of the tobacco he chews. There's also a special acne medication to keep his skin unblemished"[4]), a move that outraged the novelist. Drawing this cluster of concerns together, Wallace came to the overarching conclusion that there were structural flaws that eroded the epistemological aspirations of the interview format, telling *Amherst* magazine in 1999 that the problem with interviews was "that no truly interesting question can be satisfactorily answered within the formal constraints (*viz.* magazine-space, radio-time, public decorum) of an interview."[5]

Why, then, gather a collection of interviews with Wallace? On a basic level, it's notable that in the years since Wallace's death, Wallace-the-person (as opposed to purely the stylistic or thematic specter of Wallace-the-writer) has become an increasing presence in contemporary American literature—in Jeffrey Eugenides's "Extreme Solitude" (2010), Richard Powers's *Generosity* (2009), and most directly in Jonathan Franzen's *Freedom* (2010), Wallace's biography seems to be recast and diffused through each narrative. While his technical influence is certainly still widely in evidence—Wallace's nested narration is playfully parodied in Jennifer Egan's *A Visit from the Goon Squad* (2010)—because a good interview or profile illuminates both the writer and the work, it's easier to objectively ask questions about the parallels between Wallace's biography and such fictions—and hence, to measure Wallace's personal impact on American letters—after reading these interviews.[6] What does it mean, for instance, to note David Lipsky's revelation that Wallace painted his bedroom black and was fascinated by Margaret Thatcher, and then register that such details overlap with Richard Katz's biography in *Freedom*?

Equally, while Wallace entertained few illusions about the interview's formal limitations, it doesn't necessarily follow that his own interviews were failures. His acute sensitivity to the medium's boundaries made the interview a productive haven for Wallace's remarkable articulacy. As Jonathan Franzen has argued, "the structure of interviews" provided a formal enclosure in which Wallace "could safely draw on his enormous native store of kindness and wisdom and expertise."[7] It's not surprising, then, that one of most quoted sources in Wallace criticism is an interview—Larry McCaffery's essential *Review of Contemporary Fiction* conversation with Wallace—and, beyond biographical correspondences, Wallace's interviews are important for more intensive textual study of his work. Though Wallace was alert to the interviewees tendency to reverse-engineer explanations of a completed work,[8] his comments on his themes and techniques are often penetrating. The subjects which have magnetically attracted Wallace criticism for fifteen years—irony, his relationship to other writers—are widely represented in this collection. Equally there are also revealing statements about his attitude to MFA programs (especially in the interview by Hugh Kennedy and Geoffrey Polk), his negotiations with religious belief (particularly in the pieces by Streitfeld, Gilbert, and Arden), the role of footnotes in his writing (again, the Gilbert interview is illuminating), and his multifaceted conception of his novels' architecture. Wallace explains to Mark Caro, for example, that *Infinite Jest* is patterned like "a very pretty pane of glass that had been dropped off the twentieth story of a building," and then tells Anne Marie Donahue that the same novel is also "really designed more like a piece of music than like a book."

Across the body of the interviews, it's also notable that patterns begin to emerge that give some indications of Wallace's shifting preoccupations. While Wallace deflects attention from *Brief Interviews with Hideous Men*, describing its agenda as "technical, formal stuff that I don't know if I want to talk about" (Arden), in interviews accompanying *Oblivion*, by contrast, he repeatedly takes care to contextualize quotations from the stories by drawing attention to the book's hybrid narratorial perspectives. Discussing "Mister Squishy" with Michael Goldfarb, for example, Wallace notes that the narrator's perspective shuttles "in and out of a more omniscient third-person narrator into the consciousness of . . . Terry Schmidt." Similarly, when reading a section from "The Soul Is Not a Smithy," Wallace highlights another variegated lens when he tells Steve Paulson that his narrator "is partly narrating as a child and partly as an adult." In addition to such technical matters, it's also possible to map out larger, more general, alterations in Wallace's working life that unfold across two decades of talking to interviewers. In early 1987, for instance, when Helen Dudar profiled Wallace for the *Wall Street Journal*, the young novelist's comments on his work habits sound positively breezy. Thirteen years later—in conversation with John O'Brien and Richard Powers—Wallace is considerably more solemn on the same subject.

Assembling a book such as this depends upon interviewers and copyright holders agreeing that their work may be reprinted. Working within this constraint, I have tried to select the interviews so that the book traces the full curve of his career—from the earliest pieces by Katovsky and Dudar to what I believe to be Wallace's last formal interview, which was given to the *Wall Street Journal*[9]—while also acknowledging the total spectrum of Wallace's omnivorous writing talent. The interviews gathered here, then, touch on each of his major fictional works, while pieces by Tom Scocca, Caleb Crain, and Christopher John Farley address different aspects of Wallace's nonfiction. Some of the interviews included here are available online from their original publishers—the excellent archives at Dalkey's website, for example, stand out as a particularly valuable resource for readers not just of Wallace's work, but of the contemporary field as a whole. Yet relative accessibility has been a lesser concern than quality—and especially sustained quality of insight—when I selected the interviews for this collection. Out of the more than seventy interviews that Wallace gave, it's rare to find any that do not have insightful moments, but Wallace rarely submitted to long, academic-style interviews, so there are many pieces that lack the sustained momentum that makes others worth including here. An online chat at *Word*, for example, is too chaotic to quote in full, yet it nevertheless has valuable moments where Wallace notes his distaste for Joseph McElroy's 1987 novel *Women and Men* ("I thought that book sucked canal-water"), but draws attention to affinities between *Infinite Jest* and McElroy's earlier novel, *Lookout Cartridge* (1974).[10] Wallace was, in a non-trivial sense, an American writer—engaged with cultural, social, and political issues thrown up by his nation state—and his artistic inheritance draws heavily on American arts. In addition to McElroy, he talks about DeLillo, Pynchon, Gaddis, and other national arts. In an interview not included in this volume, for instance, the evolution of Blues leads him to a revealing account of his technical development:

> there was a thing . . . called *Within the Context of No Context* by George W. S. Trow . . . where he talks about awkwardness versus sort of smoothness, and he's talking about a certain moment in Blues . . . I think for my generation . . . a certain kind of awkwardness . . . we associate not with naïveté or clumsiness so much as with sincerity . . . being real-homemade, versus being . . . like a corporate product.[11]

For Wallace, a writer such as Gaddis, whose work was strategically "very messy" and challenging, would become a major "stylistic influence." The sense of "roughness" he inherits from Gaddis is manifest in Wallace's work in multiple ways—particularly in his first two novels' disdain for neat resolution, what he calls in his interview with Michael Goldfarb his plan to have *Infinite Jest* resolve "outside the right-frame of the picture." Yet as time passes, Wallace's interviews provide an index for the mobile coordinates of his engagement with American fiction. While Wallace distanced himself from what he called (in an interview with Donn Fry) the "backyard-barbecue and three-martini" school of contemporary American realism, his relationship to "Nabokov's children" was clearly more ambivalent. While he championed Gaddis as a technical influence, there are also moments where he dismisses both Gaddis and Pynchon as "commercial avant-garde" in conversation with Donahue. At the same time, he also recognized that some realist work, as he told Michael Goldfarb, was "really . . . vibrant."

Yet while it's useful to note the American genealogy that emerges from Wallace's interviews, his imagination was not delimited by national boundaries and a list of significant European influences that Wallace criticism has yet to consider would include Albert Camus, Craig Raine's criticism, as well as Georges Perec and other Oulipo writers. While Wallace rarely traveled abroad—he visited France in 2001, and Italy and England in 2006—he was interviewed by a number of European publications, with interviews appearing in Italy, in *La Republicca* and *Il Sole 24Ore*, and in Germany, in *Die Ziet* and *Die Welt*. I have, however, not included these interviews because the original recordings for the select European profiles that I wanted to anthologize were no longer available, and the nuanced word choices of a writer as careful as Wallace make it undesirable to create the movie-with-subtitles quality that would surely result from translating Italian into English that has already been translated into Italian.

Some interviews tell the story of their own construction, but interviewing Wallace was evidently a memorable enough experience to spawn its own shadowy subgenre—an interview's photographic negative, where an author generates a kind of meta-essay about the process of trying to interview Wallace. The chief example of this genre is Joe Woodward's "In Search of David Foster Wallace," describing an unsuccessful "odyssey to interview DFW," though also notable is Fritz Lanham's account of trying to interview Wallace in 1996 despite only having read a hundred pages of *Infinite Jest* (the interview doesn't go well: "Wallace looked at me as though I'd lost my mind," Lanham writes of a response to one question). The most intriguing essay about a Wallace interview, however, is surely Joshua Ferris's "The World According to Wallace," which describes a meeting between the two novelists when Ferris—then an undergraduate at the University of Iowa—interviewed Wallace for the student newspaper.[12] The interviews gathered in this book evolved in different ways. Some took place according to standard journalistic protocols—Laura Miller's *Salon* interview, for example, took place at San Francisco's Prescott Hotel during the 1996 promotional tour for *Infinite Jest*. Taped and then transcribed and edited by Miller, the piece appeared without any further input from Wallace. Other pieces had a more collaborative birth, emerging following the give-and-take of drafts, something like the process that underlies a *Paris Review* interview. Larry McCaffery's interview with Wallace merits more discussion in this respect, partly because of the piece's intrinsic importance to Wallace studies and partly because the discussion had a long collaborative gestation.

The McCaffery-Wallace exchange took place at a pregnant moment for both interviewer and subject. Wallace at this point had not yet fully begun *Infinite Jest*, though he was clearly formulating where he wanted his work to go next. McCaffery recalls that he seemed very anxious to talk seriously with an academic about the current state of fiction, and kept referring to two writers who he felt represented the opposing poles of contemporary novelistic achievement: William T. Vollmann, who represented the serious literary artist, and Mark Leyner, who symbolized the flashy writer whose unusual and eye-catching skill-set incorporated aspects of the modern mediascape. Wallace evidently worried that his own work was closer to Leyner's example. For his part, McCaffery was eager to talk about generational shifts. He was at work on interviews with Leyner and Vollmann for his collection of interviews with innovative American authors (*Some Other Frequency* [1996]), and was immersed in the process of formulating his concept of "Avant-Pop," a successor movement to postmodernism that more accurately registered the late-twentieth century's media explosion. McCaffery dates the interview as having taken place in April 1991, when he drove to Massachusetts to meet Wallace at a run-down home where the novelist was living like a graduate student (at one point Wallace draws McCaffery's attention to the "palatial surroundings I'm currently ensconced in"). After going out for dinner, they returned to Wallace's house where they talked deep into the night, exhausting three ninety-minute cassettes that ultimately yielded a 140-page transcript. The free-wheeling conversation ranges from what Wallace called "the land-locked, self-locked reader," through a whole host of writers ("there's a click about *Madame Bovary* and damn it, if you don't feel it, there's something wrong with you" Wallace says), to conclude with a long discussion about American literature's relationship to freedom and the American dream. Amongst the most interesting sections are those where Wallace negotiates his relationship to Pynchon:

> The only time I've ever seen anybody . . . really show us where a transcendence might lead is Pynchon in *Gravity's Rainbow* . . . paranoia is a natural response to solipsism, alright, but Pynchon's transcendence is, boy, is a lot like Milton's Satan. You realize the problem and you rally what remains. Damn it, if I'm alone and metaphysical structures are primarily threatening and I am paranoid, then para-

noia is a central metaphor, damn it, I'm going to make this as beautifully ordered and complex as I can . . . but anyway, I've lost a lot of my interest in Pynchon because it seems to me that there's a different way to transcend it. That instead of a satanic way of transcending it, there's an angelic way of transcending it and for me—again I can't be articulate about this—it somehow has to do with where the click is.

The final version of the interview that appeared in the *Review of Contemporary Fiction* was the product of a long editing process, where Wallace and McCaffery exchanged drafts as they refined their discussion down to its more compressed current form. The version included here is about two thousand words longer than the interview published in the *Review of Contemporary Fiction*, and draws on material from the penultimate draft that McCaffery and Wallace had worked upon.[13]

The house rules for volumes in the Literary Conversations Series require that interviews be reprinted in their entirety, so there is inevitably some (often revealing) repetition in this collection. It's notable, for instance, that Wallace stresses the difference between communicative and expressive writing to both Donn Fry and John O'Brien, while the frequency with which he recounts his early defense of the pop and media elements in his work indicates the longevity of his resistance to some aspects of the creative writing instruction he received at Arizona. Where an obvious error exists in an interview—say, the date of a book's publication, or the name of Wallace's employer—I have made a silent correction. Otherwise, the only alterations involve trimming audio interviews (shortening long sentences, deleting stock comments about, say, a radio station's phone number by the interviewer, and so on) and changing the title of two interviews.[14]

In addition to individual copyright holders, I'm grateful to the David Foster Wallace Literary Trust for giving me permission to quote from Wallace's letters, while I would also like to thank Julie and Chloe Burn, Caroline Dieterle, Charles B. Harris, Didier Jacob, Larry McCaffery, Steven Moore, and my international spies, Andreas Kubik, Roberto Natalini, and Toon Staes.

SJB

Notes

1. David Foster Wallace, letter to the author. 30 August 2007. MS.

2. Peter Lubin produced the descriptive term "belled chat" to elucidate the scene in *Pnin* where Nabokov reflects on "the narrator's art of integrating telephone conversations." See, Peter Lubin, "Kickshaws and Motley." *TriQuarterly* 17 (1970): 187–208. Print. The Chris Wright interview in this volume plays with the form Wallace developed, while one ancestor of Wallace's technique may be such interview-based fictions as Donald Barthelme's "The Explanation."

3. David Foster Wallace, letter to Don DeLillo. 16 March 1996. TS. Don DeLillo's Papers. Harry Ransom Humanities Research Center, The University of Texas at Austin.

4. Frank Bruni, "The Grunge American Novel." *New York Times Magazine* 24 March 1996, sec. 6: 41. Print.

5. David Foster Wallace, "Brief Interview with a Five Draft Man." Interview with Stacey Schmeidel. *Amherst.* Amherst Magazine, Spring 1999. Web. 17 December 2010.

6. Partly because Wallace's nonfiction (as he told Tom Scocca) included "the occasional bit of embellishment," writing about Wallace's life has often contained errors. Charles B. Harris addresses this matter in "David Foster Wallace's Hometown: A Correction." *Critique* 51.3 (2010): 185–86. Print.

7. Jonathan Franzen, Wallace tribute. *Five Dials: Celebrating the Life and Work of David Foster Wallace 1962–2008.* London: Hamish, 2008. 16. Print.

8. "Engaging in critical discourse" post-publication, Wallace told Steve Paulson, is "very different" to the "boneheaded and practical" process of actually creating the work

9. In his *New Yorker* profile, D. T. Max suggests that Didier Jacob's piece was "his final major interview, given to *Le Nouvel Observateur* in August 2007" (60). In actual fact, the interview took place in 2005, and Jacob tells me that his piece was never published. It therefore appears here for the first time. See, D. T. Max, "The Unfinished." *New Yorker* 9 March 2009: 48+. Print.

Wallace, of course, gave no interviews directly devoted to *The Pale King,* but since *Oblivion*'s "The Soul Is Not a Smithy" was at one point a projected chapter for his posthumous novel, Wallace's discussion with Steve Paulson serves the dual purpose of addressing the central themes of *Oblivion* and *The Pale King.*

10. David Foster Wallace, "Live Online with David Foster Wallace." *Word.* Infinite Jest: Reviews, Articles, and Miscellany, 17 May 1996. Web. 16 December 1997.

11. David Foster Wallace, "David Foster Wallace." Interview with Michael Silverblatt. *Bookworm.* National Public Radio. KCRW, Santa Monica, 3 August 2000. Radio.

12. See, Joe Woodward, "In Search of David Foster Wallace." *Poets and Writers.* Poets and Writers, January–February 2006. Web. 10 May 2010; Fritz Lanham, "Unhappy Encounter." *Houston Chronicle* 21 September 2008: 8; Joshua Ferris, "The World According to Wallace." *Observer.* Guardian, 21 September 2008. Web. 10 May 2010. Ferris's article tantalizingly notes

that his "interview ran in the *Daily Iowan* a few days before Wallace came to Iowa City to give a reading as part of his book tour." The status of this piece is, however, unclear: Wallace read at the Prairie Lights bookstore in Iowa City on 28 February 1996, and the *Daily Iowan*'s librarian searched the February and March 1996 issues of the newspaper to try to locate the interview, with no success. I then contacted Ferris's agent, who reported that Ferris is actually unsure whether the interview ultimately ran.

13. The "new" material in the McCaffery interview is important on several levels—aside from simply expanding our understanding of Wallace, there are also significant comparisons to Franzen's work that deepen our sense of the overlaps between the two writers. In the discussion of "Forever Overhead," for instance, the emphasis on self-hiding and shame seem to be echoed in Franzen's later discussion of masks and the "shame of exposing yourself" (50) in the *Paris Review*. See, Jonathan Franzen, "The Art of Fiction 207: Jonathan Franzen." Interview with Stephen J. Burn. *Paris Review* 195 (2010): 38–79. The version of Mark Shechner's interview included here is also slightly longer than the edition that ran in the *Buffalo News*.

14. The title of McCaffery's interview has been changed, to distinguish it from the published version, while the title of the first interview in this book also needs some explanation. When Bill Katovsky interviewed Wallace in early 1987, for *Arrival*, several things were not yet in play: David had yet to be known by his three initials; and the appearance of "Lyndon" in *Arrival* represented his first exposure in a national publication (Wallace evidently repudiated his earlier college publications as juvenilia, omitting them from his CV as early as 1993). A fan of Clint Eastwood spaghetti westerns, Katovsky came up with a photo shoot idea of David standing by a saguarro cactus outside Tucson. Katovsky titled the interview profile "Hang 'im High," in homage to Eastwood's movie—albeit using "'im" and not "'em"—to what he saw as future accolades coming David's way. But, as Katovsky says today, he certainly couldn't foresee that David would one day take his own life by hanging. "That *Arrival* profile headline, in retrospect, is like something you'd come across in a Phillip K. Dick short story."

Chronology

1962   Born February 21, in Ithaca, New York, to James D. Wallace and Sally Foster Wallace. Six months later, the Wallace family moves to Urbana, Illinois. Wallace attends Urbana High School.

1980   In the fall, Wallace enrolls at Amherst College, where he rooms with Mark Costello. Seminal experiences at the college include his discovery of fiction by Don DeLillo and Manuel Puig (both recommended by his professor, Andrew Parker). Graduation is delayed by a year after Wallace takes two semesters off (spring '82 and fall '83), and spends the hiatus driving a school bus and reading voraciously.

1985   Graduates summa cum laude in English and Philosophy. Following the example of Costello, who completed a novel as his graduating thesis the year before, Wallace studied under Dale Peterson and submits a draft of *The Broom of the System* as his English thesis. His philosophy thesis—*Richard Taylor's Fatalism and the Semantics of Physical Modality*—wins the department's Gail Kennedy Memorial Prize in Philosophy. Enters M.F.A. program at the University of Arizona.

1987   *The Broom of the System* published in January. Graduates in August, and is named Teaching Assistant of the Year by the University of Arizona. Apart from juvenilia, Wallace's first journal publication—"Lyndon"—appears in *Arrival* in April 1987. After winning a residency fellowship spends the summer at the Yaddo artists' colony, and then takes a position as a visiting instructor at Amherst.

1988   *Girl with Curious Hair* is scheduled for a fall 1988 publication date, but the book's release is delayed as Wallace is caught up in legal battles over references to real people in the stories. "Little Expressionless Animals" wins a John Traine Humor Prize from the *Paris Review*. Publishes first critical essay—"Fictional Futures and the Conspicuously Young"—which appears in the fall issue of the *Review of Contemporary Fiction*. Begins correspondence with Jonathan Franzen.

1989   After some revision, *Girl with Curious Hair* is finally published in

September. Receives a Writer's Fellowship from the National Endowment from the Arts, and an Illinois Arts Council Award for Non-Fiction. Moves to Somerville, Massachusetts, where he shares an apartment at 35 Houghton Street with Mark Costello, but spends August back at Yaddo. Enrolls at Harvard, intending to complete a Ph.D in philosophy, but withdraws after checking himself into campus health services. Enters AA in September.

1990   Though initially planned as an essay, *Signifying Rappers* (coauthored with Mark Costello) is published in October 1990, and nominated for a Pulitzer Prize. "Here and There" selected for inclusion in O. Henry Prize Stories. Wallace spends six months in Brighton's Granada House—a halfway house—and writes his first book review, which is published in *Washington Post Book World* in April 1990. Teaches at Boston's Emerson College. Contracted to write a "short piece" on TV and fiction for *Harper's* that becomes the template for his famous 1993 *Review of Contemporary Fiction* essay, "E Unibus Pluram."

1991   Though Wallace had made three false-starts on projects resembling *Infinite Jest* between 1986 and 1989, work on the novel begins in earnest in 1991–92.

1992   Moves to Syracuse, where he lives in an apartment on Miles Avenue. Begins correspondence with Don DeLillo.

1993   The *Review of Contemporary Fiction* devotes a third of its Younger Writers issue to Wallace. Hired by Illinois State University as an associate professor. Finishes draft manuscript of *Infinite Jest*, though the editing process continues through to the middle of 1995.

1996   Wallace's cruise-ship essay, "Shipping Out," appears in the January issue of *Harper's*. In February, *Infinite Jest* is published to great acclaim, and by early March the novel is in its sixth printing. Research for *The Pale King* is underway at least as early as this point: Wallace audits an elementary accounting class in the fall, and in the coming years takes more advanced classes and corresponds with tax professionals. Receives a Lannan Literary Award for Fiction and a Salon Book Award.

1997   *A Supposedly Fun Thing I'll Never Do Again* published in February. Awarded a MacArthur Foundation fellowship. "Brief Interviews with Hideous Men #6" wins the *Paris Review's* Aga Khan Prize for the best short story published that year in the magazine.

1999   In May, *Brief Interviews with Hideous Men* is published. Awarded an honorary doctor of letters degree from Amherst. "The Depressed Person" selected for inclusion in O. Henry Prize Stories.

2000   Receives a Lannan Writing Residency Fellowship to spend part of the summer in Marfa, Texas. Invited to write a volume on Georg Cantor for Atlas Books' Great Discoveries series, which (at the time) Wallace hopes he can complete in four months.

2002   "Good Old Neon" selected for inclusion in O. Henry Prize Stories. In late July, moves to California where he is appointed Roy E. Disney Professor of Creative Writing at Pomona College.

2003   *Everything and More* published in October.

2004   *Oblivion* published in June. Marries artist Karen Green in December.

2005   Wallace's second essay collection, *Consider the Lobster*, published in December. Gives the Kenyon College commencement address, later published as *This Is Water*.

2008   After a troubled year of failed treatments, commits suicide, September 12.

2010   Wallace's undergraduate philosophy thesis published under the title, *Fate, Time, and Language: An Essay on Free Will* in December.

2011   Wallace's posthumous novel, *The Pale King*, published.

Conversations
with David Foster Wallace

David Foster Wallace: A Profile

William R. Katovsky/1987

From *Arrival*, Summer 1987. © 1987 by William R. Katovsky. Reprinted by permission.

David Wallace is kneeling in the hallway, like a golfer lining up a putt. He taps a Marlboro Light on his gray cords, then lights it. Before the cigarette reaches his mouth again, one of his students, a sorority girl, tanned, chunky, with a thick mane of honey-blonde hair, approaches him.

"I can't take class Thursday," she says.

From his vantage point, he's eyeball to crotch, so he stands up, the cigarette still several inches from his lips. "Can you say that again?" he asks.

"I can't make it on Thursday. I think I've come down with bronchitis." The silver bracelets encircling both wrists jangle, clank unmusically, as she brushes her bangs off her forehead. English 210, Introduction to Writing Fiction, will start shortly.

"Yeah, I've not been feeling too good myself," he says. "I just got over viral pneumonia. Everyone seems to be coming down with Valley fever."

"What's that?"

"Valley fever—a fungus in the desert soil that's airborne." He coughs.

She fidgets, uncertain. She strokes her bangs again. "Will it hurt my grade if I don't show up for class?"

He stares at her, frowning.

"I'm s'posed to be at the airport real early the next day to catch a flight to Hawaii."

"Oh."

"It's a five-in-the-morning flight." She's holding a jumbo plastic tumbler filled with a cola. There's writing on one side of the cup: I'm a material girl— diamonds are a girl's best friend.

"I'm afraid I just don't understand. You're going to Hawaii? Talk to me inside the classroom." The Marlboro never makes it home to his lips. He pinches it cold and tosses it into the wastebasket as he walks into the room.

They talk quietly at his desk while the rest of the class straggles in. Desks are rearranged to form a semicircle. One student erases conjugations of French verbs from the blackboard.

It's mid-March and 85 degrees outside. Most of the students are dressed in shorts, T-shirts, sandals, tank-tops. Tall, pale, reed-thin, with a fledgling beard, David sports a long-sleeved red-striped Brooksgate button-down shirt and partially laced Timberland hunting boots—probably the only such pair in attendance at the University of Arizona.

He reads from his green roster book. "Stephanie here?"

No answer.

"Stephanie hasn't vanished? Stephanie has red hair?"

No answer.

"Brandon here?"

No answer.

"Where is everybody?"

Laughter.

"Cory here?"

"She should be here, she was in my poly-sci class," offers Material Girl.

"Jack here?"

"Here."

A murmur of relief washes through the room.

"I see George's AWOL—he'll get shit."

Twenty students are here, and for the next hour and a half they analyze two short stories written by their classmates. David guides the undergraduate workshop like a seasoned pro, dissecting, explicating, outlining the stories' failings and strong points. "When you write fiction," he explains as part of his critique of a story about a young girl, her uncle, and the evil eye, "you are telling a lie. It's a game, but you must get the facts straight. The reader doesn't want to be reminded that it's a lie. It must be convincing, or the story will never take off in the reader's mind."

Witty, engaging, thoughtful, and illuminating, David leads his charges through the brambles and thickets of literary theory. With the exception of Material Girl and George, who arrives late and is reprimanded for reading a newspaper, the students are enthralled, lively, paying rapt attention, for when it comes right down to assessing his teaching wizardry, the University of Arizona recently named the twenty-five-year-old instructor Teaching Assistant of the Year.

Towards the end of class, he looks spent, like a race car about to run out of fuel. He fishes a toothpick from his shirt pocket and lets it droop, unmoving, from the left corner of his mouth.

A bell in the hallway sputters.

"I usually puke my guts out in the bathroom when class ends," he later admits. We are in the cafeteria. "I guess I'm really a shy sort of person. I hate to be the center of attention." He decides on a thick wedge of Boston cream pie—speedballing with sugar.

We chat about other matters. Like being the author of *The Broom of the System*, which has spearheaded Viking's new series on contemporary American fiction. The novel, penned as his 1,100-page senior honors thesis at Amherst College, is the product of a wild and gifted imagination. Set in Cleveland, Ohio, in the year 1990, *The Broom* revolves around Lenore Beadsman, a confused twenty-four-year-old telephone operator and her desperate search for her great-grandmother, a protégé of Wittgenstein who has inexplicably vanished from the Shaker Heights nursing home owned by her father's baby food company. Along the way, we meet a cast of hilariously limned characters: an obese man, Norman Bombardini, whose sole mission in life is to fill the world with his corpulent self—which, of course, entails eating as much as he can; Lenore's foul-mouthed pet cockatiel; her one-legged brother, nicknamed the Antichrist, who hangs out at Amherst where he tutors friends on meaty subjects like Hegel in exchange for pot which he stashes in a drawer in his prosthesis; and her boyfriend, Rick Vigorous, an inveterate raconteur whose compulsive need to tell macabre tales is his way of masking the shame of being impotent.

The Broom's multilayered narrative structure and excessively antiminimalist style bring to mind the metafictional playground of Thomas Pynchon and Robert Coover. The book, joyously alive, is certainly not an easy or quick read. The challenge to the reader is wading through densely written passages that touch upon metaphysical conundrums, language games, theories of the self and tantalizing antinomies such as "the barber who shaves all and only those who do not shave themselves." But balancing his heady philosophizing is a playfulness of intent rooted in pop culture. Where else in fiction do we find a Gilligan's Isle theme bar replete with palm trees and cloddish bartenders in sailor hats who are paid to bumble about and spill drinks?

"My great horror for the last year has been that Viking is going to take a bath on me," says Wallace. He lights the first of a seemingly endless succession of cigarettes. "They picked up *The Broom of the System* at an auction for

$20,000. I thought it was going to be the *Heaven's Gate* of the publishing industry." He corrects himself. "Well, at the time it seemed like a lot of money to me."

Twenty grand for a first novel, plus a spate of favorable reviews, including one from the literary doyenne of the *New York Times*, Michiko Kakutani, well, that doesn't strike one as too shabby for a graduate student still grinding out short stories in Arizona's prestigious MFA program. "I wrote 'Lyndon' here," he says, "but I admit it didn't go over too well in workshop. There is a lopsided emphasis in writing programs on hermetic fiction, the mechanicalness of craft, technique, and point of view, as opposed to the more occult or spiritual side of writing—taking joys in the process of creation.

"I'm not interested in fiction that's only worried about capturing reality in an artful way. What pisses me off about so much fiction these days is that it's just boring, especially the young fiction coming out of the East Coast that's designed to appeal to the stereotypical yuppies, with an emphasis on fashion, celebrities, and materialism."

He pauses, realizing he's been lecturing. "Uh," he adds with a self-deprecating shrug, "what do I know?" After all, these are just the opinions of a twenty-five-year-old. "I don't claim to have any special insights into anything that's going on." I'm looking for a trace of sham, of disingenuousness, in his voice but it's nowhere to be found.

He grew up as an academic brat. His father is a philosophy professor at the University of Illinois at Champaign/Urbana and his mother teaches rhetoric at a local community college. "It was an intellectual household. I remember my parents reading *Ulysses* out loud to each other when they went to bed. My father read *Moby Dick* to my younger sister and me when we were six and eight. There was a near rebellion halfway through the novel. Here we were—still picking our noses—and learning the etymology of whale names.

"Later, in high school, competitive tennis and lusting after girls were pretty much my entire existence. Though college changed all that around." He graduated in 1985 from Amherst with a double major in English and philosophy—and with the highest GPA in his class. His senior philosophy thesis, he claims, had nothing to do with writing. "It offered a solution in how to deal with semantics and physical modalities concerning Aristotle's sea battle. If it is now true that there will be a sea battle tomorrow, is a sea battle necessary tomorrow? If it is now false, is a sea battle impossible tomorrow? It's a way to deal with propositions in the future tense in modal logic, since what is physically possible at a certain time is weird because one has to distinguish the time of the possibility of the event from the possibility of the time of the event."

Huh?

After graduation, he turned down an opportunity to study philosophy at Harvard and was lured west by a fellowship in the writing program at the University of Arizona, which he selected over Iowa and Johns Hopkins. "Writing fiction takes me out of time," he explains. "I sit down and the clock will not exist for me for a few hours. That's probably as close to immortal as we'll ever get. I'm scared of sounding pretentious because anyone who writes fiction is saying, 'Look at this thing I've written.'"

All that is left of his pie is the graham cracker crust which he mashes against the plate with his fork. Before he gets up from the table he decides to make another stab at explaining what he hopes to accomplish as a writer. "I spent a lot of time as a volunteer in a nursing home in Amherst last summer. I was reading Dante's *Divine Comedy* to an old man, Mr. Shulman. One day, I asked him where he was from. He said, 'Just east of here, the Rockies.' I said, 'Mr. Shulman, the Rockies are west of here.' He did a *voilà* with his hands, and then said, 'I move mountains.' That stuck with me. Fiction either moves mountains or it's boring; it moves mountains or it sits on its ass."

A Whiz Kid and
His Wacky First Novel

Helen Dudar/1987

Form *Wall Street Journal*, 24 April 1987. © 1987 by the Estate of Helen Dudar Goldman.
Reprinted by permission.

In his final year at Amherst College, David Foster Wallace faced a difficult career decision. He had to decide whether his future lay with graduate studies in philosophy or in what academia labels "creative writing." Few of us could have solved the problem as neatly: Mr. Wallace produced two senior honors theses that brought him a double summa cum laude. The philosophy paper, a highly technical mathematical affair, was, he reports, the more successful effort. But the fiction—which turned out to be a wild, funny, somewhat disheveled novel—really blissed him out.

He would sit down around lunch time to invent a few scenes, Mr. Wallace remembered the other day, and when he looked up, dinner time would have come and gone. "I don't know where I had been but I hadn't been on earth for a few hours. I have approached nothing like that in any kind of emotional and intellectual endeavor before."

Mr. Wallace's writing honors thesis, *The Broom of the System* (Viking/Penguin), completed in 1985 when he was twenty-three and revised during his summer vacation, was published this year to a good deal of critical attention, a lot of it favorable.

By the time it appeared, Mr. Wallace was in his final year in the graduate writers' program at the University of Arizona in Tucson. You would think that a brilliant young man who had produced his first novel before commencement would forgo more classes, but this one is not only well-educated, he is smart.

As he said on a recent trip east from Tucson, Mr. Wallace knew he was still "very raw" and needed to develop his powers of self-criticism. He had only begun working in fiction in his junior year, responding in part to professorial observations that his papers, while unscholarly, were certainly imaginative.

Through a friend, Mr. Wallace acquired an agent, Fred Hill of San Francisco. When the novel came on the market in late 1985, at least five houses wanted it. Gerald Howard, who runs Penguin's Contemporary American Fiction line, says he took care of the competition by "reading it very quickly and going nuts for it." His $20,000 floor, a nice figure for a first effort by an unknown, won the day. Mr. Wallace, shaggy-haired, slender, boyish, quietly droll and wonderfully vague about business matters, mutters there has been movie interest in an outline. Mr. Howard reports that Alliance Entertainment has paid a $10,000 option toward a $200,000 purchase if it likes the script treatment.

The CAF line is the eight-year-old reprint house for such sturdy modern masters as Donald Barthelme, William Kennedy, and Laurie Colwin. *The Broom* is the first novel it has published as an original and the first to appear simultaneously with the Viking hardcover, a nervous experiment, according to Mr. Howard. "If it hadn't worked, we would have fouled the marketplace for another effort of this sort."

Mr. Howard's apprehension is a reminder of how vital to writers and readers trade paperback editions have become. In the economics of modern mass-market paperback publishing, a serious literary novel that sells steadily but modestly is nearly impossible to keep in print. Nowadays, it is an outfit like CAF, as well as Random House's Vintage line and a clutch of small presses, that offers the possibility of a long life for much serious fiction.

It could be said that the Wallace novel is a seriously funny book about a collection of off-the-wall characters. It is—well, sort of—the 463-page odyssey of young Lenore Stonecipher Beadsman, who works on a deranged switchboard and owns a talkative cockatiel that becomes a star of television evangelical broadcasting and is searching for her missing great-grandmother, a Wittgenstein authority. It is about Lenore's boss, Rick Vigorous, who makes up for sexual incapacity by telling wonderfully sick stories. It is also Amherst as Animal House. Mr. Wallace, who was not happy there, has taken this revenge.

But then you can't be sure. In several of the book's psychiatric sessions, Mr. Wallace seems to impale modern psychotherapy. When you ask him about that, he confides, "I tend only to be able to have people say stuff that

I think is serious if I'm simultaneously making fun of the character. I think that's a weakness. It comes from being really self-conscious." The novel's main setting is Cleveland, which, of course, Mr. Wallace has never seen. A middle-westerner—he grew up in Champaign, Illinois, where his father is a philosophy professor at the University of Illinois—he wanted a heartland city that he could imagine instead of describe.

The book is also, sort of, about the way in which language sustains us and fails us. His title would seem to come from a Wittgensteinian model that proposes that what is fundamental to the broom—bristles or stick—depends on whether you want to sweep the floor or break windows. But the author wants you to know that *The Broom of the System* is also what his mother, a community-college teacher, calls roughage or dietary fiber.

Because of the crazy names and the absurdist comic edge to his narratives, reviewers often mention him in the same sentence with Thomas Pynchon and Don DeLillo. Mr. Wallace wishes they wouldn't: "These are writers I admire but the five-year-old in me pushes out its lower lip and says, 'Well, no, I'm a person, too. I do my own work.'" Besides, one of his heaviest influences has gone totally unnoticed. *The Broom* has entire virtuoso chapters of uninterrupted dialogue that, its author says, are indebted to Manuel Puig.

In his work habits, Mr. Wallace turns out to be nearly as eccentric as his characters. He seems to be able to write early drafts only in busy public places.

Museums and restaurants are preferred; when he reaches a late stage of composition, he will settle for a heavily trafficked library. Maybe, he speculates, he needs to be engaged in writing as a "secret" activity. Conceivably, his imagination is even fueled by a vaguely "illicit" setting. "It's totally neurotic," he says good-naturedly.

This summer, Mr. Wallace gets to spend half the season at Yaddo, an upstate New York writer's colony, where he plans to complete his first collection of short stories. It's not too early to worry about how he's going to do that in a woodland setting known and sought for the absolute isolation and privacy with which it succors the average creative spirit.

Looking for a Garde of Which to Be Avant: An Interview with David Foster Wallace

Hugh Kennedy and Geoffrey Polk/1993

From *Whiskey Island*, Spring 1993. © 1993 by Whiskey Island Magazine. Reprinted by permission.

At thirty, David Foster Wallace has been called the best of his generation of American writers. His novel, *The Broom of the System*, and his collection of short stories and novella, *Girl with Curious Hair*, have earned him wide critical acclaim, a prestigious Whiting Writers' Award, and an intensely devoted readership. Wallace, a mathematics and philosophy major at Amherst College, did not begin writing creatively until the age of twenty-one. His first novel was published while he was still an M.F.A. student at the University of Arizona at Tucson. His writing benefits from a mathematical and philosophical grasp of symbolic systems and large, overarching concepts, drawing out every implication to its fullest and often most hilarious extent. He is inventive in a way that recalls Pynchon, and culturally omnivorous in a way that recalls everyone from Don DeLillo to David Letterman, who is the subject of one of his stories. At Cleveland State University, Wallace read from his second novel to a large, appreciative audience. He hopes to complete this novel within a year of moving to his new home in Syracuse, New York.

We met with David Wallace in his hotel suite in downtown Cleveland, the day after his reading. He wore a striped mock turtleneck, gray chinos, and tan work boots. During the first half of the interview, Wallace spat Kodiak tobacco juice into a small white bucket, with one leg up on the gold and violet couch, then smoked and drank diet cola for the second half. He wore

11

his brown hair parted in the center, which often necessitated brushing it out of his eyes, and had a habit of lightly striking the back of his head with an open palm, a habit which, Wallace noted, descends in a direct line from his father, a philosopher at the University of Illinois Champagne/Urbana; through his father's teacher, Norman Malcolm, Wittgenstein's last student; back to Wittgenstein himself. Wallace spoke in a smooth, subdued Midwestern voice. His natural shyness in combination with his striking intelligence can make him appear off-putting, and he confessed that his family communicates primarily via jokes and wisecracks. He also noted that "two years ago, there was no way I would have done this. I would not have sat with two people I did not know well and talk. I couldn't have done it. I would have sat in the bathroom and called out answers to you." Once relaxed, however, he became generous, honest and articulate—even passionate—in his judgments and ideas about fiction.

H.K.

HK: I was interested in the way you made philosophy an element of your first novel, *Broom of the System*, and I wondered if you had to make a decision at any point whether you were going to write about philosophy the way philosophers do, and maybe if you then saw fiction as a way, culturally, to bracket concepts like philosophy, God, America, and so on.

WALLACE: I don't know about you guys, but I didn't start writing fiction until I was twenty-one, and at the beginning we all have to write our requisite amounts of shit, and my shit was basically disguised essays. They were like really bad Ayn Rand or something. I was a math and philosophy major at college. I wasn't a writer, so a lot of it had to do with the fact that *The Broom of the System* the first draft of that, was one of my honors theses as an undergraduate. The other one was a really hardcore math and semantics thing that used a lot of Wittgenstein. And the two kept bleeding into each other, for instance, the math thesis was written in conversational voice, which you're not supposed to do. So the two went back and forth.

The other thing is that my father is a professional philosopher, he was a student of Wittgenstein's last student, Norman Malcolm, who wrote his biography. A lot of *The Broom of the System* is weirdly autobiographical in ways that no one else knows. Like the title comes from my mother's pet name for roughage. She calls roughage and fiber "the broom of the system." I think there's a throwaway reference to that in the book.

HK: I wondered if your family, like Lenore Beadsman's [*The Broom of the*

System's protagonist], is "very verbal" and sees life as "more or less a verbal phenomenon."

WALLACE: The first draft of *Broom* had a lot of stuff about the family, and a lot of that stuff got cut because it wasn't very effective. But, yeah, my family works that way a lot. My family communicates almost entirely in terms of jokes. Basically all we do is tell jokes, which gets kind of weird. I think it's a lot of fun when you're growing up, but when you're a grownup and you try to talk about something serious, you realize it's a kind of slimy way to approach things.

The stuff that I'm working on now has a lot to do with the family, and . . . it's hard, it's hard to try to capture anything that's real, it's hard to try to figure out which family experiences are universal and which are idiosyncratic.

HK: I love the character of Lenore Beadsman, and I think she's quite memorable, particularly the way you convey her voice. How did you arrive at it?

WALLACE: I had a lot of trouble with her because I fell in love with her by the time the book was done. That's one reason why I haven't done anything along those lines since then. I was really upset when it was over. She's sort of a pastiche of a lot of people I know. She's probably got more of the way my brain works in her, and the way I speak, than anyone else. I think at the beginning I had two voices I could do well; one was hers and the other was this hypersensitive, really intellectual voice. One of the weaknesses in the book is that a lot of the characters seem to have the same voice: Rick Vigorous sort of sounds like David Bloemker who sort of sounds like Norman Bombardini and even Lenore's father. A lot of that is a parody of intellectual prose.

HK: I had the same reaction to Lenore. I was so sad that I had to leave her.

WALLACE: She was a real sweetheart.

HK: A question about Rick Vigorous. I've been thinking a lot about that scene where he goes back to Amherst after twenty years and he walks around the campus, still dividing insiders from outsiders. I wondered if you thought that all writers were somehow societal outsiders.

WALLACE: I don't know. I was very lonely in college. The stuff in the book that I like and that rings true is that stuff, which was true to me. It was how I felt. The writers I know, there's a certain self-consciousness about them, and a critical awareness of themselves and other people that helps their work. But that sort of sensibility makes it very hard to be with people, and not sort of be hovering near the ceiling, watching what's going on. One of the things you two will discover, in the years after you get out of school, is that managing to really be an alive human being, and also to do good work and be as obsessive as you have to be, is really tricky. It's not an accident when you see writers either become obsessed with the whole pop stardom thing or get into drugs and alcohol, or have terrible marriages. Or they simply disappear from the whole scene in their thirties or forties. It's very tricky.

GP: I think you have to sacrifice a lot.

WALLACE: I don't know if it's that voluntary or a conscious decision. In most of the writers I know, there's a self-centeredness, not in terms of preening in front of the mirror, but a tendency not only toward introspection but toward a terrible self-consciousness. Writing, you're having to worry about your effect on an audience all the time. Are you being too subtle or not subtle enough? You're always trying to communicate in a unique way, and so it makes it very hard, at least for me, to communicate in a way that I see ordinary, apple-cheeked Clevelanders communicating with each other in street corners.

My answer for myself would be no; it's not a sacrifice; it's simply the way that I am, and I don't think I'd be happy doing anything else. I think people who are congenitally drawn to this sort of profession are savants in certain ways and sort of retarded in certain other ways. Go to a writers' conference sometime and you'll see. People go to meet people who on paper are just gorgeous, and they're absolute geeks in person. They have no idea what to say or what to do. Everything they say is edited and undercut by some sort of editor in themselves. That's been true of my experience. I've spent a lot more of my energy in teaching the last two years, really sort of working on how to be a human being.

HK: We read an article for our fiction workshop by Ben Satterfeld, and it contains the by-now routine group of potshots at M.F.A. programs and how they create a cycle of mediocrity. Satterfeld goes through this piece lambasting insiders, people who've done graduate programs in writing, and argues that you've got to get out in the world and find your way on your own, not with all of these editors buzzing around you and all of these insiders in publishing getting you into print. Yet one of the only writers Satterfeld mentions specifically as doing really excellent, creative things right now is you, and yet you're a product of a B.A. and an M.F.A. I not only want to get your reaction to Satterfeld, but to the usual argument; what was the efficacy of an M.F.A. for you?

WALLACE: I wish I'd seen the article. [Laughs] Well, I didn't have a very happy experience in graduate school, but it seems there are different ways to learn from it. You can either learn by aligning yourself with the sort of company line at a program or you can play James Dean and align yourself against it. Sometimes it's not until you have professors—you know, authority figures—kicking your ass, and you still find yourself resisting what they're saying that you find out what you believe. It was interesting being here [at CSU]. I had a long talk with Neal Chandler about your program, and I decided that you guys are really lucky.

It seems to me that there are two kinds of graduate writing programs. There's a kind that it seems Cleveland State has and that for instance Syracuse University has, a Master's with a concentration in creative writing, where there are actual academic requirements. You are required to learn to be a writer as part of a broader education in the humanities. About those programs, I know that I wasn't in one, but from the outside it looks wonderful to me. One of my big complaints about Arizona was that though I liked a lot of the students, and I liked a lot of the regular faculty, I didn't much like the creative writing faculty. They really disparaged the idea of learning how to write as part of learning how to take part in the tradition of Western letters. At Arizona I took a lot of outside classes—I took a lot of theory, I took some math, I took some foreign languages, I took some history of the language—and people in the M.F.A. program thought I was nuts. Places like Arizona or Iowa or Stanford, it seems to me, only pretend to be schools. I'm not about to blast them, but I think you've got to distinguish between them and schools like Cleveland State and Syracuse, which are grad schools, where you end up with a Master's. The M.F.A. factories are really covert forms of patronage. For the faculty, they afford the comfort and security, usually, of lifetime employment. Teaching workshops, while it has its demands, is nothing like having to prepare lectures on the history of mathematics three times a week. It's nothing like it. And since writers are congenitally lazy about most things other than their writing, that's conducive, too.

But these programs are also forms of patronage for students, because it used to be that you got out of college and worked a shit job and lived in a loft in Soho and tried to be a writer. And Mr. Satterfeld may attach a certain romance to that. I know some people who've gone that route, and it's absolutely crushing, it's horrible. For instance, I've flirted with that kind of life since I've gotten out of an M.F.A. program, and I've been lucky because I've had a couple of books out. I get stuff taken easier than somebody who's going through slush piles, and it's still awful. It's no fun. But if you go to these programs, you can answer to your parents and to people who ask "What are you doing?" "Well, I'm in graduate school." People are off your back. Very often you get forms of financial aid. You can either get outright fellowships, like the one I had at Arizona, or you can get opportunities to teach, and support yourself that way. Sure, graduate teaching assistants get exploited a bit, but it's a lot better than asking people whether they want fries with that. It's a hell of a lot better.

HK: What would you like your writing to do?
WALLACE: You want an honest answer, right?

HK: Reasonably.
WALLACE: It's *very* hard to separate what you want the writing to do from your own desires about how you will be regarded because of the work. At three o'clock in the morning, when it's just me, I have the fantasies of ticker tape parades and Poet Laureate of the Western World and MacArthur Grants and Nobel Prizes, readings like the one last night except with 15,000 people, you know, that type of stuff. So no feelings about desired effect are pure, free of selfish ends.

But there are a few books I have read that I've never been the same after, and I think all good writing somehow addresses the concern of and acts as an anodyne against loneliness. We're all terribly, terribly lonely. And there's a way, at least in prose fiction, that can allow you to be intimate with the world and with a mind and with characters that you just can't be in the real world. I don't know what you're thinking. I don't know that much about you as I don't know that much about my parents or my lover or my sister, but a piece of fiction that's really true allows you to be intimate with . . . I don't want to say people, but it allows you to be intimate with a world that resembles our own in enough emotional particulars so that the way different things must feel is carried out with us into the real world. I think what I would like my stuff to do is make people less lonely. Or really to affect people. I think sometimes what I'm doing, if I try to be particularly offensive or outrageous or whatever, is just being really hungry for some kind of effect. I think you can see Bret Ellis doing that in *American Psycho*. You can't make sure that everybody's going to like you, but damn it, if you've got some skill you can make sure that people don't ignore you. A lot of writers hunger to have their work out there more and to have good book sales, which I used to think was crass materialism, that they wanted the money, but it turns out that what you want is to have some sort of effect. Maybe you've snapped to this already. It took me years to figure that out.

GP: In *Girl with Curious Hair*, a lot of the stories go beyond personal stories and into generational issues. For example, in "Lyndon," a lot of it seems to be looking at the differences between generations; for example, Lyndon Johnson's ideas about responsibility and what it means, versus the Sixties generation. In "Westward the Course of Empire Takes Its Way," there's the same kind of conflict between J. D. Steelritter and the kids about the idea of honor, which Mark Nechtr finally cops to, yet it's really an old-fashioned virtue. In "Girl with Curious Hair," I saw it as a take not only on conservative Reaganism, and the effects of his policies, which is a kind of sadism, but also on the Eighties punk generation, which has no politics at all. I keep getting to these generational issues in your stories. Do you agree with that?

WALLACE: It's getting kind of hard to remember. I finished that book in '88, and then there was a year of legal battles when it wasn't published, so it seems like a long time ago. I might have touched on this last night, but I went to grad school with a lot of people, a lot of poets especially, who were older, real Sixties worshipers, who thought that our problem was that we lost a lot of the rebellious, earnest integrity of the Sixties. I see our generation as inheritors of the Sixties. I'm talking particularly about the art of the Sixties, which abandoned a lot of conventional techniques in favor of black humor and a new emphasis on irony. You hadn't seen irony like that, really, since the pre-Romantics. It performs a really useful function by getting rid of a lot of platitudes and myths in America which were no longer serviceable, but it also hasn't left anything to rebuild with besides this ethos of jaded irony and self-aware nihilism and acquisitivism. One of the reasons this book was so much about TV is that we see so much of the rebellious Sixties ethos in television art now: stuff that used to be the art gesture, the self-consciousness, the metatechnique of that period. Now you've got season episodes of *Moonlighting* ending with the set breaking down. The original urge toward irony and self-consciousness that in the Sixties was young people's way of insulating themselves against the sort of ravening hypocrisy of institutions like the government or advertising has become insinuated in popular culture, and as it's been insinuated in popular culture, popular culture itself has become vastly more efficient and pervasive in American life. I mean, TV is so *good* now. MTV is just hypnotic. So you've got us kids, twenty to thirty-five, right on the edge, and all the kids coming after us really getting sucked into that stuff, but learning it in a way that doesn't allow any sort of incredulity at all. But anyway, one of the things I was doing in *Girl with Curious Hair* was to write a very traditionally moral book. This is a generation that has an inheritance of absolutely nothing as far as meaningful moral values, and it's our job to make them up, and we're not doing it. And we're being told, by the very systems that the Sixties were so right to fear, that we needn't worry about making up moral systems: you know, that there isn't more to being alive than being pretty, having intercourse a lot, and having a lot of possessions. But the darkly delicious thing is that these systems that are telling us this are using the techniques that the Sixties guys had used—by that I mean postmodern techniques like black irony, metafictional involutions, the whole sort of literature of self-consciousness. We are heirs to it.

I guess I still feel this way. I'm still writing about younger people trying to find themselves in the face not only of conform-or-die parents, but also this bright seductive electromagnetic system all around them that tells them that they don't have to. Does that make any sense?

GP: Do you buy John Gardner's answer, to be life-affirming? Last night (at your reading), you seemed to have a sympathy for your characters that takes you beyond being a satirist.

WALLACE: Well, Gardner isn't saying anything that Tolstoy didn't say, except Tolstoy said it in this wacko, fundamentalist Russian Orthodox Christian way. Tolstoy said that the purpose of art was to communicate the idea of Christian brotherhood from man to man and to pass along some sort of message. I think Gardner translates that into some sort of moral didacticism. I believe that Gardner underestimates what the possibilities of art are. But both of them are right: what fiction and poetry are doing is what they've been trying to do for two thousand years: affect somebody, make somebody feel a certain way, allow them to enter into relationships with ideas and with characters that are not permitted within the cinctures of the ordinary verbal intercourse we're having here, you know: you don't see me, I don't see you. But every two or three generations the world gets vastly different, and the context in which you have to learn how to be a human being, or to have good relationships, or decide whether or not there is a God, or decide whether there's such a thing as love, and whether it's redemptive, become vastly different. And the structures with which you can communicate those dilemmas or have characters struggle with them seem to become appropriate and then inappropriate again and so on. Nothing that's changed right now seems to me to be fundamentally important, and yet a whole lot of stuff is very, very different. So yeah, I'd agree with Gardner to the extent that he has the sense to be parroting Tolstoy—if you edit out the heavenly Christian stuff. I'm the only "postmodernist" you'll ever meet who absolutely worships Leo Tolstoy.

GP: In your stories, you often play with the boundaries between history and fiction. Does it feel odd appropriating historical figures?

WALLACE: It's got legal repercussions. The first draft of the Letterman story ("My Appearance") was due to come out in *Playboy*, and it was very different. It had actual transcripts of an interview between Letterman and Susan St. James. I fucked up and didn't tell the editors, and about two weeks before the story was due to come out they reran that interview and a couple of people from *Playboy* saw it, and I got a new asshole drilled. And all the other magazines that ran my stories, their lawyers were running around screaming, and the book almost didn't come out. So there are problems that way.

In terms of a lot of the pop culture stuff, one of the ways that things have changed is that fiction used to be a kind of travelogue. It used to be a way to take people to foreign lands and exotic cultures, or to important people, and give readers access to worlds they didn't have access to. The world that we live in is very different. I can get up and watch satellite footage of a riot in Peking while I eat a Tex-Mex breakfast while I listen to Third World music on my CD player. Fiction's job used to be to make the strange familiar, to take you somewhere and let you feel that this was familiar to you. It seems that one of the things about living now is that *everything* presents itself as familiar, so one of the things the artist has to do now is take a lot of this familiarity and remind people that it's strange. So to take the most banal, low-art images from television and from politics and from advertising, and to transfigure them—OK, it's sort of a heavy art gesture—but I think it's got some validity. I think if you can estrange this stuff, and you can make people look at, say, *Jeopardy!* or an advertisement and view it not as a message from God, but as a piece of art, a product of human imagination and human effort with a human agenda, that there's a way in which you distance a reader from phenomena that I think he needs to be distanced from. It's not that all this stuff is in your mind as you're doing it. This is just one of the defenses I've made up for the questions that come up about it, and I think it's valid.

GP: Are there any writers now living that really knock you out?

WALLACE: I'm a huge Don DeLillo fan, although I think his latest book is one of his worst. The DeLillo of *Americana* and *End Zone* and *Great Jones Street, The Names,* and *Libra* I love. Maybe *Gravity's Rainbow* is a better book, but I can't think of anybody in this tradition since Nabokov who's put out a better corpus of work than DeLillo. I like Bellow, and I really like the early John Updike—*The Poorhouse Fair, Of the Farm, The Centaur,* just in terms of sheer fucking beautiful writing. There are a lot of the Latinists too: Julio Cortázar, Manuel Puig, both recently dead. There are young writers now I was telling you about, like Mark Leyner; William T. Vollman, who's got four books coming out this year; Jon Franzen, Susan Daitch, Amy Homes. The best book I've read recently is by Paul Auster's wife, who's named Siri Hustvedt. She's a Norwegian from Minnesota, who wrote this book called *The Blindfold.* It's not a lot of fun, but God is it smart. It's the best piece of feminist postmodernism I've ever read. It makes Kathy Acker look sick because it's so well crafted. I'm not sure there are any really towering giants. I think some Pynchon, some Bellow, some Ozick will be read a hundred years from now; I think DeLillo, maybe.

GP: Do you have any advice for young writers?
WALLACE: Send me at least 50 percent of everything that you make.

GP: That won't even cover the postage!
WALLACE: This is a long haul. Writing is a long haul. I'm hoping that none of the stuff that I've done so far is anywhere close to the best stuff I can do. Let's hope we're not fifty-five and doing the same thing. I'd say avoid burning out. You can burn out by struggling in privation and neglect for many years, but you can also burn out if you're given a little bit of attention. People come to your hotel room and think you have interesting things to say. You can allow that to make you start to think that you can't say anything unless it's interesting. For me, 50 percent of the stuff I do is bad, and that's just going to be the way it is, and if I can't accept that then I'm not cut out for this. The trick is to know what's bad and not let other people see it.

An Expanded Interview
with David Foster Wallace

Larry McCaffery/1993

From the *Review of Contemporary Fiction*, Summer 1993. © 1993 by the Review of Contemporary Fiction and Larry McCaffery. Reprinted by permission.

LARRY McCAFFERY: Your essay following this interview is going to be seen by some people as being basically an apology for television. What's your response to the familiar criticism that television fosters relationships with illusions or simulations of real people (Reagan being a kind of quintessential example)?

DAVID FOSTER WALLACE: It's a try at a comprehensive diagnosis, not an apology. U.S. viewers' relationship with TV is essentially puerile and dependent, as are all relationships based on seduction. This is hardly news. But what's seldom acknowledged is how complex and ingenious TV's seductions are. It's seldom acknowledged that viewers' relationship with TV is, albeit debased, intricate and profound. It's easy for older writers just to bitch about TV's hegemony over the U.S. art market, to say the world's gone to hell in a basket and shrug and have done with it. But I think younger writers owe themselves a richer account of just why TV's become such a dominating force on people's consciousness, if only because we under like forty have spent our whole conscious lives being *part* of TV's audience.

LM: Television may be more complex than what most people realize, but it seems rarely to attempt to *challenge* or *disturb* its audience, as you've written me you wish to. Is it that sense of challenge and pain that makes your work more "serious" than most television shows?

DFW: I had a teacher I liked who used to say good fiction's job was to comfort the disturbed and disturb the comfortable. I guess a big part of serious fiction's purpose is to give the reader, who like all of us is sort of marooned in her own skull, to give her imaginative access to other selves. Since an ineluctable part of being a human self is suffering, part of what we humans come to art for is an experience of suffering, necessarily a vicarious experience, more like a sort of *generalization* of suffering. Does this make sense? We all suffer alone in the real world; true empathy's impossible. But if a piece of fiction can allow us imaginatively to identify with characters' pain, we might then also more easily conceive of others identifying with our own. This is nourishing, redemptive; we become less alone inside. It might be just that simple. But now realize that TV and popular film and most kinds of "low" art—which just means art whose primary aim is to make money—is lucrative precisely because it recognizes that audiences prefer 100 percent pleasure to the reality that tends to be 49 percent pleasure and 51 percent pain. Whereas "serious" art, which is not primarily about getting money out of you, is more apt to make you uncomfortable, or to force you to work hard to access its pleasures, the same way that in real life true pleasure is usually a by-product of hard work and discomfort. So it's hard for an art audience, especially a young one that's been raised to expect art to be 100 percent pleasurable and to make that pleasure effortless, to read and appreciate serious fiction. That's not good. The problem isn't that today's readership is *dumb*, I don't think. Just that TV and the commercial-art culture's trained it to be sort of lazy and childish in its expectations. But it makes trying to engage today's readers both imaginatively and intellectually unprecedentedly hard.

LM: Who do you imagine your readership to be?
DFW: I suppose it's people more or less like me, in their twenties and thirties, maybe, with enough experience or good education to have realized that the hard work serious fiction requires of a reader sometimes has a payoff. People who've been raised with U.S. commercial culture and are engaged with it and informed by it and fascinated with it but still hungry for something commercial art can't provide. Yuppies, I guess, and younger intellectuals, whatever. These are the people pretty much all the younger writers I admire—Leyner and Vollmann and Daitch, Amy Homes, Jon Franzen, Lorrie Moore, Rick Powers, even McInerney and Leavitt and those guys—are writing for, I think. But, again, the last twenty years have seen big changes in how writers engage their readers, what readers need to expect from any kind of art.

LM: The media seems to me to be one thing that has drastically changed this relationship. It's provided people with this television-processed culture for so long that audiences have forgotten what a relationship to serious art is all about.

DFW: Well, it's too simple to just wring your hands and claim TV's ruined readers. Because the U.S's television culture didn't come out of a vacuum. What TV is extremely good at—and realize that this is *all it does*—is discerning what large numbers of people think they want, and supplying it. And since there's always been a strong and distinctive American distaste for frustration and suffering, TV's going to avoid these like the plague in favor of something anesthetic and easy.

LM: You really think this distaste is distinctly American?

DFW: It seems distinctly Western-industrial, anyway. In most other cultures, if you hurt, if you have a symptom that's causing you to suffer, they view this as basically healthy and natural, a sign that your nervous system knows something's wrong. For these cultures, getting rid of the pain without addressing the deeper cause would be like shutting off a fire alarm while the fire's still going. But if you just look at the number of ways that we try like hell to alleviate mere symptoms in this country—from fast-fast-fast-relief antacids to the popularity of lighthearted musicals during the Depression—you can see an almost compulsive tendency to regard pain itself as the problem. And so pleasure becomes a value, a teleological end in itself. It's probably more Western than U.S. per se. Look at utilitarianism—that most English of contributions to ethics—and you see a whole teleology predicated on the idea that the best human life is one that maximizes the pleasure-to-pain ratio. God, I know this sounds priggish of me. All I'm saying is that it's shortsighted to blame TV. It's simply another symptom. TV didn't invent our aesthetic childishness here any more than the Manhattan Project invented aggression. Nuclear weapons and TV have simply intensified the consequences of our tendencies, upped the stakes.

LM: Near the end of "Westward the Course of Empire Takes Its Way," there's a line about Mark that "It would take an architect who could hate enough to feel enough to love enough to perpetrate the kind of special cruelty only real lovers can inflict." Is that the kind of cruelty you feel is missing in the work of somebody like Mark Leyner?

DFW: I guess I'd need to ask you what kind of cruelty you thought the narrator meant there.

LM: It seems to involve the idea that if writers care enough about their audience—if they love them enough and love their art enough—they've got to be cruel in their writing practices. "Cruel" the way an army drill sergeant is when he decides to put a bunch of raw recruits through hell, knowing that the trauma you're inflicting on these guys, emotionally, physically, psychically, is just part of a process that's going to strengthen them in the end, prepare them for things they can't even imagine yet.

DFW: Well, besides the question of where the fuck do "artists" get off deciding for readers what stuff the readers need to be prepared for, your idea sounds pretty Aristotelian, doesn't it? I mean, what's the purpose of creating fiction, for you? Is it essentially mimetic, to capture and order a protean reality? Or is it really supposed to be therapeutic in an Aristotelian sense?

LM: I agree with what you said in "Westward" about serious art having to engage a range of experiences; it can't be merely "metafictional," for example, it has to deal with the world outside the page and variously so. How would you contrast your efforts in this regard versus those involved in most television or most popular fiction?

DFW: This might be one way to start talking about differences between the early postmodern writers of the fifties and sixties and their contemporary descendants. When you read that quotation from "Westward" just now, it sounded to me like a covert digest of my biggest weaknesses as a writer. One is that I have a grossly sentimental affection for gags, for stuff that's nothing but funny, and which I sometimes stick in for no other reason than funniness. Another's that I have a problem sometimes with concision, communicating only what needs to be said in a brisk efficient way that doesn't call attention to itself. It'd be pathetic for me to blame the exterior for my own deficiencies, but it still seems to me that both of these problems are traceable to this schizogenic experience I had growing up, being bookish and reading a lot, on the one hand, watching grotesque amounts of TV, on the other. Because I liked to read, I probably didn't watch quite as much TV as my friends, but I still got my daily megadose, believe me. And I think it's impossible to spend that many slack-jawed, spittle-chinned, formative hours in front of commercial art without internalizing the idea that one of the main goals of art is simply to *entertain*, give people sheer pleasure. Except to what end, this pleasure-giving? Because, of course, TV's *real* agenda is to be *liked*, because if you like what you're seeing, you'll stay tuned. TV is completely unabashed about this; it's its sole *raison*. And sometimes when I look at my own stuff I feel like I absorbed too much of this *raison*. I'll catch myself thinking up gags or trying formal stunt-pilotry and see that none of this stuff is really in the service of the story itself; it's serving the rather darker purpose of communicating to the reader "Hey! Look at me! Have a look at what a good writer I am! *Like* me!"

Now, to an extent there's no way to escape this altogether, because an author needs to demonstrate some sort of skill or merit so that the reader will trust her. There's some weird, delicate, I-trust-you-not-to-fuck-upon-me relationship between the reader and writer, and both have to sustain it. But there's an unignorable line between demonstrating skill and charm to gain trust for the story vs. simple showing off. It can become an exercise in trying to get the reader to like and admire you instead of an exercise in creative art. I think TV promulgates the idea that good art is just that art which makes people like and depend on the vehicle that brings them the art. This seems like a poisonous lesson for a would-be artist to grow up with. And one consequence is that if the artist is excessively dependent on simply being *liked*, so that her true end isn't in the work but in a certain audience's good opinion, she is going to develop a terrific hostility to that audience, simply because she has given all her power away to them. It's the familiar love-hate syndrome of seduction: "I don't really care what it is I say, I care only that you like it. But since your good opinion is the sole arbiter of my success and worth, you have tremendous power over me, and I fear you and hate you for it." This dynamic isn't exclusive to art. But I often think I can see it in myself and in other young writers, this desperate desire to please coupled with a kind of hostility to the reader.

LM: In your own case, how does this hostility manifest itself?

DFW: Oh, not always, but sometimes in the form of sentences that are syntactically not incorrect but still a real bitch to read. Or bludgeoning the reader with data. Or devoting a lot of energy to creating expectations and then taking pleasure in disappointing them. You can see this clearly in something like Ellis's *American Psycho*: it panders shamelessly to the audience's sadism for a while, but by the end it's clear that the sadism's real object is the reader herself.

LM: But at least in the case of *American Psycho* I felt there was something more than just this desire to inflict pain—or that Ellis was being cruel the way you said serious artists need to be willing to be.

DFW: You're just displaying the sort of cynicism that lets readers be manipulated by bad writing. I think it's a kind of black cynicism about today's world that Ellis and certain others depend on for their readership. Look, if the contemporary condition is hopelessly shitty, insipid, materialistic, emotionally retarded, sadomasochistic and stupid, then I (or any writer) can get away with slapping together stories with characters who are stupid, vapid, emotionally retarded, which is easy, because these sorts of characters require no development. With descriptions that are simply lists of brand-name consumer products. Where stupid people say insipid stuff to each other. If what's always distinguished bad writing—flat characters, a narrative world that's clichéd and not recognizably human, etc.—is also a description of today's world, then bad writing becomes an ingenious mimesis of a bad world. If readers simply believe the world is stupid and shallow and mean, then Ellis can write a mean shallow stupid novel that becomes a mordant deadpan commentary on the badness of everything. Look man, we'd probably most of us agree that these are dark times, and stupid ones, but do we need fiction that does nothing but dramatize how dark and stupid everything is? In dark times, the definition of good art would seem to be art that locates and applies CPR to those elements of what's human and magical that still live and glow despite the times' darkness. Really good fiction could have as dark a worldview as it wished, but it'd find a way both to depict this dark world *and* to illuminate the possibilities for being alive and human in it. You can defend *Psycho* as being a sort of performative digest of late-eighties social problems, but it's no more than that.

LM: Are you saying that writers of your generation have an obligation not only to depict our condition but also to provide the *solutions* to these things?
DFW: I don't think I'm talking about conventionally political or social-action-type solutions. That's not what fiction's about. Fiction's about what it is to be a fucking *human being*. If you operate, which most of us do, from the premise that there are things about the contemporary U.S. that make it distinctively hard to be a real human being, then maybe half of fiction's job is to dramatize what it is that makes it tough. The other half is to dramatize the fact that we still *are* human beings, now. Or can be. This isn't that it's fiction's duty to edify or teach, or to make us good little Christians or Republicans; I'm not trying to line up behind Tolstoy or Gardner. I just think that fiction that isn't exploring what it means to be human today isn't good art. We've got all this "literary" fiction that simply monotones that we're all becoming less and less human, that presents characters without souls or love, characters who really are exhaustively describable in terms of what brands of stuff they wear, and we all buy the books and go like "Golly, what a mordantly ef-

fective commentary on contemporary materialism!" But we already all *know* U.S. culture is materialistic. This diagnosis can be done in about two lines. It doesn't engage anybody. What's engaging and artistically real is, taking it as axiomatic that the present is grotesquely materialistic, how is it that we as human beings still have the capacity for joy, charity, genuine connections, for stuff that doesn't have a price? And can these capacities be made to thrive? And if so, how, and if not, why not?

LM: Not everyone in your generation is taking the Ellis route. Both the other writers in this issue of *RCF* seem to be doing exactly what you're talking about. So, for example, even though Vollmann's *Rainbow Stories* is a book that is in its own way as sensationalized as *American Psycho*, the effort there is to depict those people not as flattened, dehumanized stereotypes but as human beings. I'd agree, though, that a lot of contemporary writers today adopt this sort of flat, neutral transformation of people and events into fiction without bothering to make the effort of refocusing their imaginations on the people who still exist underneath these transformations. But Vollmann seems to be someone fighting that tendency in interesting ways.

This brings us back to the issue of whether this isn't a dilemma serious writers have always faced. Other than lowered (or changed) audience expectations, what's changed to make the task of the serious writer today more difficult than it was thirty or sixty or a hundred or a thousand years ago? You might argue that the task of the serious writer is *easier* today because what took place in the sixties had the effect of finally demolishing the authority that mimesis had assumed. Since you guys don't have to fight that battle anymore, you're liberated to move on to other areas.

DFW: This is a double-edged sword, our bequest from the early postmodernists and the poststructuralist critics. On the one hand, there's sort of an embarrassment of riches for young writers now. Most of the old cinctures and constraints that used to exist—censorship of content is a blatant example—have been driven off the field. Writers today can do more or less whatever we want. But on the other hand, since everybody can do pretty much whatever they want, without boundaries to define them or constraints to struggle against, you get this continual avant-garde rush forward without anyone bothering to speculate on the destination, the *goal* of the forward rush. The modernists and early postmodernists—all the way from Mallarmé to Coover, I guess—broke most of the rules for us, but we tend to forget what they were forced to remember: the rule-breaking has got to be for the *sake* of something. When rule-breaking, the mere *form* of renegade avant-gardism, becomes an end in itself, you end up with bad language poetry and *American Psycho*'s nipple-shocks and Alice Cooper eating shit on stage. Shock stops being a byproduct of progress and becomes an end in itself. And it's bullshit. Here's an analogy. The invention of calculus was shocking because for a long time it had simply been presumed that you couldn't divide by zero. The integrity of math itself seemed to depend on the presumption. Then some genuine titans came along and said, "Yeah, maybe you can't divide by zero, but what would happen if you *could*? We're going to come as close to doing it as we can, to see what happens."

LM: So you get the infinitesimal calculus—the "philosophy of as if."
DFW: And this purely theoretical construct wound up yielding incredible practical results. Suddenly you could plot the area under curves and do rate-change calculations. Just about every material convenience we now enjoy is a consequence of this "as if." But what if Leibniz and Newton had wanted to divide by zero only to show jaded audiences how cool and rebellious they were? It'd never have happened, because that kind of motivation doesn't yield results. It's hollow. Dividing-as-if-by-zero was titanic and ingenious because it was in the service of something. The math world's shock was a price they had to pay, not a payoff in itself.

LM: Of course, you also have examples like Lobochevsky and Riemann, who are breaking rules with no practical application at the time—but then later on somebody like Einstein comes along and decides that this worthless mathematical mind game that Riemann developed actually described the universe more effectively than the Euclidean game. Not that those guys were breaking the rules just to break the rules, but part of that was just that: what happens if everybody has to move *counter-clockwise* in Monopoly. And at first it just seemed like this game, without applications.
DFW: Well, the analogy breaks down because math and hard science are pyramidical. They're like building a cathedral: each generation works off the last one, both its advances and its errors. Ideally, each piece of art's its own unique object, and its evaluation's always present-tense. You could justify the worst piece of experimental horseshit by saying "The fools may hate my stuff, but generations later I will be appreciated for my groundbreaking rebellion." All the beret-wearing *artistes* I went to school with who believed that line are now writing ad copy someplace.

LM: The European avant-garde believed in the transforming ability of innovative art to directly affect people's consciousness and break them out of their cocoon of habituation, etc. You'd put a urinal in a Paris museum, call it a "fountain," and wait for the riots next day. That's an area I'd say has changed things for writers (or any artist)—you can have very aesthetically radical works today using the same features of formal innovation that you'd find in the Russian Futurists or Duchamp and so forth, only now these things are on MTV or TV ads. Formal innovation as trendy image. So it loses its ability to shock or transform.

DFW: These are exploitations. They're not trying to break us free of anything. They're trying to lock us tighter into certain conventions, in this case habits of consumption. So the *form* of artistic rebellion now becomes . . .

LM: . . . yeah, another commodity. I agree with Fredric Jameson and others who argue that modernism and postmodernism can be seen as expressing the cultural logic of late capitalism. Lots of features of contemporary art are directly influenced by this massive acceleration of capitalist expansion into all these new realms that were previously just not accessible. You sell people a memory, reify their nostalgia, and use this as a hook to sell deodorant. Hasn't this recent huge expansion of the technologies of reproduction, the integration of commodity reproduction and aesthetic reproduction, and the rise of media culture lessened the impact that aesthetic innovation can have on people's sensibilities? What's your response to this as an artist?

DFW: You've got a gift for the lit-speak, LM. Who wouldn't love this jargon we dress common sense in: "formal innovation is no longer transformative, having been co-opted by the forces of stabilization and postindustrial inertia," blah blah. But this co-optation might actually be a good thing if it helps keep younger writers from being able to treat mere formal ingenuity as an end in itself. MTV-type co-optation could end up a great prophylactic against cleveritis—you know, the dreaded grad-school syndrome of like "Watch me use seventeen different points of view in this scene of a guy eating a Saltine." The only real point of that shit is "Like me, because I'm clever"—which of course is itself derived from commercial art's axiom about audience-affection determining art's value.

What's precious about somebody like Bill Vollmann is that, even though there's a great deal of formal innovation in his fictions, it rarely seems to exist for just its own sake. It's almost always deployed to make some point (Vollmann's the most editorial young novelist going right now, and he's great at using formal ingenuity to make the editorializing a component of his narrative instead of an interruption) or to create an effect that's internal to the text. His narrator's always weirdly effaced, the writing unself-conscious, despite all the "By-the-way-Dear-Reader" intrusions. In a way it's sad that Vollmann's integrity is so remarkable. Its remarkability means it's rare. I guess I don't know what to think about these explosions in the sixties you're so crazy about. It's almost like postmodernism is fiction's fall from biblical grace. Fiction became *conscious* of itself in a way it never had been. Here's a really pretentious bit of pop analysis for you: I think you can see Cameron's *Terminator* movies as a metaphor for all literary art after Roland Barthes, viz., the movies' premise that the Cyberdyne NORAD computer becomes conscious of itself as *conscious*, as having interests and an agenda; the Cyberdyne becomes literally self-referential, and it's no accident that the result of this is nuclear war, Armageddon.

LM: Isn't Armageddon the course you set sail for in "Westward"?

DFW: Metafiction's real end has always been Armageddon. Art's reflection on itself is terminal, is one big reason why the art world saw Duchamp as an Antichrist. But I still believe the move to involution had value: it helped writers break free of some long-standing flat-earth-type taboos. It was standing in line to happen. And for a little while, stuff like *Pale Fire* and *The Universal Baseball Association* was valuable as a meta-aesthetic breakthrough the same way Duchamp's urinal had been valuable.

LM: I've always felt that the best of the metafictionists—Coover, for example, Nabokov, Borges, even Barth—were criticized too much for being only interested in narcissistic, self-reflexive games, whereas these devices had very real political and historical applications.

DFW: But when you talk about Nabokov and Coover, you're talking about real geniuses, the writers who weathered real shock and invented this stuff in contemporary fiction. But after the pioneers always come the crank-turners, the little gray people who take the machines others have built and just turn the crank, and little pellets of metafiction come out the other end. The crank-turners capitalize for a while on sheer fashion, and they get their plaudits and grants and buy their IRAs and retire to the Hamptons well out of range of the eventual blast radius. There are some interesting parallels between postmodern crank-turners and what's happened since poststructural theory took off here in the U.S., why there's such a big backlash against poststructuralism going on now. It's the crank-turners' fault. I think the crank-turner's replaced the critic as the real angel of death as far as literary movements are concerned, now. You get some bona fide artists who come along and really divide by zero and weather some serious shit-storms of shock and ridicule in order to promulgate some really important ideas. Once they triumph, though, and their ideas become legitimate and accepted, the crank-turners and wannabes come running to the machine, and out pour the gray pellets, and now the whole thing's become a hollow form, just another institution of fashion. Take a look at some of the critical-theory Ph.D. dissertations being written now. They're like de Man and Foucault in the mouth of a dull child. Academia and commercial culture have somehow become these gigantic mechanisms of commodification that drain the weight and color out of even the most radical new advances. It's a surreal inversion of the death-by-neglect that used to kill off prescient art. Now prescient art suffers death-by-acceptance. We love things to death, now. Then we retire to the Hamptons.

LM: This is also tied to that expansion of capitalism blah blah blah into realms previously thought to be uncommodifiable. Hyperconsumption. I mean, whoever thought rebellion could be tamed so easily? You just record it, turn the crank, and out comes another pellet of "dangerous" art.
DFW: And this accelerates the metastasis from genuine envelope-puncturing to just another fifteen-minute form that gets cranked out and cranked out and cranked out. Which creates a bitch of a problem for any artist who views her task as continual envelope-puncturing, because then she falls into this insatiable hunger for the appearance of novelty: "What can I do that hasn't been done yet?" Once the first-person pronoun creeps into your agenda you're dead, art-wise. That's why fiction-writing's lonely in a way most people misunderstand. It's yourself you have to be estranged from, really, to work.

LM: A phrase in one of your recent letters really struck me: "The magic of fiction is that it addresses and antagonizes the loneliness that dominates people." It's that suggestion of antagonizing the reader that seems to link your goals up with the avant-garde program—whose goals were never completely hermetic. And "Westward the Course of Empire Takes Its Way" seems to be your own meta-metafictional attempt to deal with these large areas in ways that are not merely metafiction.
DFW: "Aggravate" might be better than "antagonize," in the sense of aggravation as intensification. But the truth is it's hard for me to know what I really think about any of the stuff I've written. It's always tempting to sit back and make finger-steeples and invent impressive-sounding theoretical

justifications for what one does, but in my case most of it'd be horseshit. As time passes I get less and less nuts about anything I've published, and it gets harder to know for sure when its antagonistic elements are in there because they serve a useful purpose and when they're just covert manifestations of this "look-at-me-please-love-me-I-hate-you" syndrome I still sometimes catch myself falling into. Anyway, but what I think I meant by "antagonize" or "aggravate" has to do with the stuff in the TV essay about the younger writer trying to struggle against the cultural hegemony of TV. One thing TV does is help us deny that we're lonely. With televised images, we can have the facsimile of a relationship without the work of a real relationship. It's an anesthesia of *form*. The interesting thing is why we're so desperate for this anesthetic against loneliness. You don't have to think very hard to realize that our dread of both relationships and loneliness, both of which are like sub-dreads of our dread of being trapped inside a self (a psychic self, not just a physical self), has to do with angst about death, the recognition that I'm going to die, and die very much alone, and the rest of the world is going to go merrily on without me. I'm not sure I could give you a steeple-fingered theoretical justification, but I strongly suspect a big part of real art-fiction's job is to aggravate this sense of entrapment and loneliness and death in people, to move people to countenance it, since any possible human redemption requires us first to face what's dreadful, what we want to deny.

LM: It's this inside/outside motif you developed throughout *The Broom of the System*.

DFW: I guess maybe, though there it's developed in an awful clunky way. The popularity of *Broom* mystifies me. I can't say it's not nice to have people like it, but there's a lot of stuff in that novel I'd like to reel back in and do better. I was like twenty-two when I wrote the first draft of that thing. And I mean a *young* twenty-two. I still thought in terms of distinct problems and univocal solutions. But if you're going to try not just to depict the way a culture's bound and defined by mediated gratification and image, but somehow to redeem it, or at least fight a rearguard against it, then what you're going to be doing is paradoxical. You're at once allowing the reader to sort of escape self by achieving some sort of identification with another human psyche—the writer's, or some character's, etc.—and you're *also* trying to antagonize the reader's intuition that she is a self, that she is alone and going to die alone. You're trying somehow both to deny and affirm that the writer is over here with his agenda while the reader's over there with her agenda, distinct. This paradox is what makes good fiction sort of magical, I think. The paradox can't be resolved, but it can somehow be mediated—"re-mediated," since this is probably where poststructuralism rears its head for me—by the fact that language and linguistic intercourse is, in and of itself, redeeming, remedy-ing.

This makes serious fiction a rough and bumpy affair for everyone involved. Commercial entertainment, on the other hand, smooths everything over. Even the *Terminator* movies (which I revere), or something really nasty and sicko like the film version of *A Clockwork Orange*, is basically an anesthetic (and think for a second about the etymology of "anesthetic"; break the word up and think about it). Sure, *A Clockwork Orange* is a self-consciously sick, nasty film about the sickness and nastiness of the postindustrial condition, but if you look at it structurally, slo-mo and fast-mo and arty cinematography aside, it does what all commercial entertainment does: it proceeds more or less chronologically, and if its transitions are less cause-and-effect-based than most movies', it still kind of eases you from scene to scene in a way that drops you into certain kinds of easy cerebral rhythms. It admits of passive spectation. Encourages it. TV-type art's biggest hook is that it's figured out ways to *reward* passive spectation. A certain amount of the form-conscious stuff I write is trying—with whatever success—to do the opposite. It's supposed to be uneasy. For instance, using a lot of flash-cuts between scenes so that some of the narrative arrangement has got to be done by the reader, or interrupting flow with digressions and interpolations that the reader has to do the work of connecting to each other and to the narrative. It's nothing terribly sophisticated, and there has to be an accessible payoff for the reader if I don't want the reader to throw the book at the wall. But if it works right, the reader has to fight *through* the mediated voice presenting the material to you. The complete suppression of a narrative consciousness, with its own agenda, is why TV is such a powerful selling tool. This is McLuhan, right? "The medium is the message" and all that? But notice that TV's mediated message is *never* that the medium's the message.

LM: How is this insistence on mediation different from the kind of meta-strategies you yourself have attacked as preventing authors from being anything other than narcissistic or overly abstract or intellectual?

DFW: I guess I'd judge what I do by the same criterion I apply to the self-conscious elements you find in Vollmann's fiction: do they serve a purpose beyond themselves? Whether I can provide a payoff and communicate a function rather than just seem jumbled and prolix is the issue that'll decide whether the thing I'm working on now succeeds or not. But I think right now it's important for art-fiction to antagonize the reader's sense that what she's experiencing as she reads is mediated through a human consciousness, one with an agenda not necessarily coincident with her own. For some reason I probably couldn't even explain, I've been convinced of this for years, that one distinctive thing about truly "low" or commercial art is this apparent suppression of a mediating consciousness and agenda. The example I think of first is the novella "Little Expressionless Animals" in *Girl with Curious Hair*. Readers I know sometimes remark on all the flash-cuts and the distortion of linearity in it and usually want to see it as mimicking TV's own pace and phosphenic flutter. But what it's really trying to do is just the *opposite* of TV—it's trying to prohibit the reader from forgetting that she's receiving heavily mediated data, that this process is a relationship between the writer's consciousness and her own, and that in order for it to be anything like a real full human relationship, she's going to have to put in her share of the linguistic work.

This might be my best response to your claim that my stuff's not "realistic." I'm not much interested in trying for classical, big-R Realism, not because there hasn't been great U.S. Realist fiction that'll be read and enjoyed forever, but because the big R's form has now been absorbed and suborned by commercial entertainment. The classical Realist form is soothing, familiar, and anesthetic; it drops us right into spectation. It doesn't set up the sort of expectations serious 1990s fiction ought to be setting up in readers.

LM: *The Broom of the System* already displays some of the formal tendencies found in the stories in *Girl with Curious Hair* and in your new work—that play with temporal structure and flash-cuts, for instance, for heightened rhetorical effects of various sorts, for defamiliarizing things. Would you say your approach to form/content issues has undergone any radical changes since you were a "young twenty-two"?
DFW: Assuming I understand what you mean by "form/content," the only way I can answer you is to talk about my own background. Oh boy, I get to make myself sound all fascinating and artistic and you'll have no way to check up. Return with us now to Deare Olde Amherst. For most of my college career I was a hard-core syntax wienie, a philosophy major with a specialization in math and logic. I was, to put it modestly, quite good at the stuff, mostly because I spent all my free time doing it. Wienieish or not, I was actually chasing a special sort of buzz, a special moment that comes sometimes. One teacher called these moments "mathematical experiences." What I didn't know then was that a mathematical experience was aesthetic

in nature, an epiphany in Joyce's original sense. These moments appeared in proof-completions, or maybe algorithms. Or like a gorgeously simple solution to a problem you suddenly see after filling half a notebook with gnarly attempted solutions. It was really an experience of what I think Yeats called "the click of a well-made box." Something like that. The word I always think of it as is "click."

Anyway, I was just awfully good at technical philosophy, and it was the first thing I'd ever been really good at, and so everybody, including me, anticipated I'd make it a career. But it sort of emptied out for me somewhere around age twenty. I just got tired of it, and panicked because I was suddenly not getting joy from the one thing I was clearly supposed to do because I was good at it and people liked me for being good at it. Not a fun time. I think I had kind of a mid-life crisis at twenty, which probably doesn't augur real well for my longevity.

So what I did, I went back home for a term, planning to play solitaire and stare out the window, whatever you do in a crisis. And all of a sudden I found myself writing fiction. My only real experience with fun writing had been on a campus magazine with Mark Costello, the guy I later wrote *Signifying Rappers* with. But I had had experience with chasing the click, from all the time spent with proofs. At some point in my reading and writing that fall I discovered the click existed in literature, too. It was real lucky that just when I stopped being able to get the click from math logic I started to be able to get it from fiction. The first fictional clicks I encountered were in Donald Barthelme's "The Balloon" and in parts of the first story I ever wrote, which has been in my trunk since I finished it. I don't know whether I have much natural talent going for me fiction-wise, but I know I can hear the click, when there's a click. In Don DeLillo's stuff, for example, almost line by line I can hear the click. It's maybe the only way to describe writers I love. I hear the click in most Nabokov. In Donne, Hopkins, Larkin. In Puig and Cortázar. Puig clicks like a fucking Geiger counter. And none of these people write prose as pretty as Updike, and yet I don't much hear the click in Updike.

But so here I am at like twenty-one and I don't know what to do. Do I go into math logic, which I'm good at and pretty much guaranteed an approved career in? Or do I try to keep on with this writing thing, this *artiste* thing? The idea of trying to be a "writer" repelled me, mostly because of all the foppish aesthetes I knew at school who went around in berets stroking their chins calling themselves writers. I have a terror of seeming like those guys, still. Even today, when people I don't know ask me what I do for a living, I usually tell them I'm "in English" or I "work free-lance." I don't seem to be able to call myself a writer. And terms like "postmodernist" or "surrealist" send me straight to the bathroom, I've got to tell you.

LM: I spend time in toilet stalls myself. But I noticed you didn't take off down the hall when I said earlier that your work didn't seem "realistic." Do you really agree with that?

DFW: Well, it depends whether you're talking little-r realistic or big-R. If you mean is my stuff in the Howells/Wharton/Updike school of U.S. Realism, clearly not. But to me the whole binary of realistic vs. unrealistic fiction is a canonical distinction set up by people with a vested interest in the big-R tradition. A way to marginalize stuff that isn't soothing and conservative. Even the goofiest avant-garde agenda, if it's got integrity, is never, "Let's eschew all realism," but more, "Let's try to countenance and render real aspects of real experiences that have previously been excluded from art." The result often seems "unrealistic" to the big-R devotees because it's not a recognizable part of the "ordinary experience" they're used to countenancing. I guess my point is that "realistic" doesn't have a univocal definition. By the way, what did you mean a minute ago when you were talking about a writer "defamiliarizing" something?

LM: Placing something familiar in an unfamiliar context—say, setting it in the past or within some other structure that will re-expose it, allow readers to see the real essence of the thing that's usually taken for granted because it's buried underneath all the usual sludge that accompanies it.

DFW: I guess that's supposed to be deconstruction's original program, right? People have been under some sort of metaphysical anesthesia, so you dismantle the metaphysics' axioms and prejudices, show it in cross section and reveal the advantages of its abandonment. It's literally aggravating: you awaken them to the fact that they've been unconsciously imbibing some narcotic pharmakon since they were old enough to say Momma. There's many different ways to think about what I'm doing, but if I follow what you mean by "defamiliarization," I guess it's part of what getting the click right is for me. It might also be part of why I end up doing anywhere from five to eight total rewrites to finish something, which is why I'm never going to be a Vollmann or an Oates.

LM: Were your teachers strongly committed to the big-R tradition?

DFW: I took this workshop from Alan Lelchuk. He was a minor light in the

Jewish-American intellectual *Commentary* type thing, a disciple of Roth, I think. And Lelchuk thought that I was insane. Lelchuk thought that the stuff I was doing was pretentious, and wordy, and unnecessarily abstract. Nine times out of ten he was right, but every once in a while I would feel a click. But when I did the stuff that he wanted me to, I never heard the click (I'd do it the way I wanted, and because I wanted at least an A-, I would then transform it into the way he wanted it, which was straight, standard Updikean metaphor, Freytag's pyramid if you want). From undergraduates, that's okay. Anyway, this experience of beating my head against the wall has followed me all along.

LM: How do you mean?
DFW: I seem to like to put myself in positions where I get to be the rebel. So after going through this terrible experience in my undergrad workshop, I chose to repeat it by going a grad school where I would once again be the misunderstood eccentric blah blah blah blah surrounded by these guys who essentially want to write *New Yorker* stories. That's not exactly true—Ronnie Hansen was cool, and he was there, but only for my last semester. But most of these guys were real middle-of-the-roaders that I just wasn't going to fit in with. And yet I *chose* to go there. That place did help improve the integrity of my loyalty to the click. For instance, the first draft of "Little Expressionless Animals" was done like as a straight realistic story, except the hook was that it was set on *Jeopardy* . . . but it seemed lame. I didn't have the click when I got started and it never went anywhere. I remember an interviewer asking Thomas Flanagan, who writes only historical novels (*The Tenants of Time* and *The Year of the French*, etc.) why he only writes about the past, and Flanagan said because whenever he starts to write something set in the present, it just feels wrong to him. I could immediately understand what he meant; writing about the present didn't have the click for him. Particularly with short stories, before I actually get going with something, I'll try a couple of different ways until I start to get an idea that I'm going to be able to tell that it's going to have some sort of fidelity to the way it tastes in my mouth. I want to hear that click.

LM: You've mentioned the recent change about what writers can assume about their readers in terms of expectations and so on. Are there other ways the postmodern world has influenced or changed the role of serious writing today?
DFW: If you mean a postindustrial, mediated world, it's inverted one of

fiction's big historical functions, that of providing data on distant cultures and persons. The first real generalization of human experience that novels tried to accomplish. If you lived in Bumfuck, Iowa, a hundred years ago and had no idea what life was like in India, good old Kipling goes over and presents it to you. And of course the poststructural critics now have a field day on all the colonialist and phallocratic prejudices inherent in the idea that writers were *presenting* alien cultures instead of *"re-presenting"* them— jabbering natives and randy concubines and white man's burden, etc. Well, but fiction's presenting function for today's reader has *been* reversed: since the whole global village is now presented as familiar, electronically imme-diate—satellites, microwaves, intrepid PBS anthropologists, Paul Simon's Zulu back-ups—it's almost like we need fiction writers to restore strange things' ineluctable *strangeness*, to defamiliarize stuff, I guess you'd say.

LM: David Lynch's take on suburbia. Or Mark Leyner's take on his own daily life—
DFW: And Leyner's real good at it. For our generation, the entire world seems to present itself as "familiar," but since that's of course an illusion in terms of anything really important about people, maybe any "realistic" fic-tion's job is opposite what it used to be—no longer making the strange fa-miliar but making the familiar *strange* again. It seems important to find ways of reminding ourselves that most "familiarity" is mediated and delusive.

LM: What you're describing strikes me as being basically different from the motivations underlying, say, the temporal dislocations you find in Faulkner or Joyce.
DFW: Faulkner and Joyce were attempting somehow to be mimetic and doing that meant they had to create these dislocations. Their idea was, well, *experience* is vastly more dislocated and fragmentary, scrambled, jumbled, you pick 'em, than most people think—certainly more so than novelists usu-ally let on—and so they'll *show* you this. But I'd say that a whole lot of what I'm trying to do in my writing—and I don't know whether this is good or bad—is my desire to make something pretty. And for me, a lot of prettiness in written art has to do with sound and tempo—which is why I read a lot more poetry than I do fiction. I'm just very interested in rhythms—not just sentence rhythms but narrative rhythms that occur with certain repetitions or when you stop and go back. I know I'm not subtle at all about repeating things in certain works.

LM: Have you tried your hand at poetry?

DFW: I've written prose poems and some short pieces that are probably close to poetry, but none of them succeed very much and I don't feel much inclination to do poetry. To be honest with you, I don't think I'm talented enough to be a poet. You need such a clear mind to be a poet, an ability to compress and distill, to make the abstract concrete. The best I can do is try to make the concrete concrete. When I'm writing something and I get lost in my own thoughts and my own moods, I'm at sea. I do rip poetry off a lot, although a lot of times the way I'm doing this isn't obvious. This is one reason why dealing with copy editors is usually such a nightmare for me; they make these changes or suggestions and I go stet stet stet stet stet because a lot of times I'm trying to do with punctuation what poets are trying to do with line breaks. One of my few strengths as a writer is that I think I have a good ear for rhythm and for speech and speech rhythms. I can't render as well as somebody like Updike—I just don't *see* that well, with enough precision and accuracy—but I do hear real well and I can translate that.

LM: "Postmodernism" usually implies "an integration of pop and 'serious' culture." But a lot of the pop culture in the works of the younger writers I most admire these days—you, Leyner, Gibson, Vollmann, Eurudice, Daitch, et al.—seems to be introduced less to integrate high and low culture, or to valorize pop culture, than to place this stuff in a new context so we can be *liberated* from it. Wasn't that, for example, one of the things you were doing with *Jeopardy* in "Little Expressionless Animals"?

DFW: One new context is to take something almost narcotizingly banal— it's hard to think of anything more banal than a U.S. game show; in fact the banality's one of TV's great hooks, as the TV essay discusses—and try to reconfigure it in a way that reveals what a tense, strange, convoluted set of human interactions the final banal product is. The scrambled, flash-cut form I ended up using for the novella was probably unsubtle and clumsy, but the form clicked for me in a way it just hadn't when I'd done it straight.

LM: A lot of your works (including *Broom*) have to do with this breakdown of the boundaries between the real and "games," or the characters playing the game begin to confuse the game structure with reality's structure. Again, I suppose you can see this in "Little Expressionless Animals," where the real world outside *Jeopardy* is interacting with what's going on inside the game show—the boundaries between inner and outer are blurred.

DFW: And, too, in the novella what's going on on the show has repercussions for everybody's lives outside it. The valence is always distributive. It's interesting that most serious art, even avant-garde stuff that's in collusion with literary theory, still refuses to acknowledge this, while serious *science* butters its bread with the fact that the separation of subject/observer and object/experiment is impossible. Observing a quantum phenomenon's been proven to alter the phenomenon. Fiction likes to ignore this fact's implications. We still think in terms of a story "changing" the reader's emotions, cerebrations, maybe even her life. We're not keen on the idea of the story sharing its valence with the reader. But the reader's own life "outside" the story changes the story. You could argue that it affects only "her reaction to the story" or "her take on the story." But these things *are* the story. This is the way Barthian and Derridean poststructuralism's helped me the most as a fiction writer: once I'm done with the thing, I'm basically dead, and probably the text's dead; it becomes simply language, and language lives not just in but *through* the reader. The reader becomes God, for all textual purposes. I see your eyes glazing over, so I'll hush.

LM: Let's go back for just a moment to your sense of the limits of metafiction: in both your current *RCF* essay and in the novella "Westward" in *Girl with Curious Hair*, you imply that metafiction is a game that only reveals itself, or that can't share its valence with anything outside itself—like the daily world.

DFW: Well, but metafiction is more valuable than that. It helps reveal fiction as a mediated experience. Plus it reminds us that there's always a recursive component to utterance. This was important, because language's self-consciousness had always been there, but neither writers nor critics nor readers wanted to be reminded of it. But we ended up seeing why recursion's dangerous, and maybe why everybody wanted to keep linguistic self-consciousness out of the show. It gets empty and solipsistic real fast. It spirals in on itself. By the mid-seventies, I think, everything useful about the mode had been exhausted, and the crank-turners had descended. By the eighties it'd become a godawful trap. In "Westward" I got trapped one time just trying to expose the illusions of metafiction the same way metafiction had tried to expose the illusions of the pseudo-unmediated realist fiction that came before it. It was a horror show. The stuff's a permanent migraine.

LM: Why is meta-metafiction a trap? Isn't that what you were doing in "Westward"?

DFW: That's a Rog. And maybe "Westward"'s only real value'll be show-ing the kind of pretentious loops you fall into now if you fuck around with recursion. My idea in "Westward" was to do with metafiction what Moore's poetry or like DeLillo's *Libra* had done with other mediated myths. I wanted to get the Armageddon-explosion, the goal metafiction's always been about, I wanted to get it over with, and then out of the rubble reaffirm the idea of art being a living transaction between humans, whether the transaction was erotic or altruistic or sadistic. God, even talking about it makes me want to puke. The *pretension.* Twenty-five-year-olds should be locked away and denied ink and paper. Everything I wanted to do came out in the story, but it came out as just what it was: crude and naive and pretentious.

LM: Of course, even *The Broom of the System* can be seen as a metafiction, as a book about language and about the relationship between words and reality.

DFW: Think of *The Broom of the System* as the sensitive tale of a sensitive young WASP who's just had this mid-life crisis that's moved him from coldly cerebral analytic math to a coldly cerebral take on fiction and Austin-Witt-genstein-Derridean literary theory, which also shifted his existential dread from a fear that he was just a 98.6° calculating machine to a fear that he was nothing but a linguistic construct. This WASP's written a lot of straight humor, and loves gags, so he decides to write a coded autobio that's also a funny little poststructural gag: so you get Lenore, a character in a story who's terribly afraid that she's really nothing more than a character in a sto-ry. And, sufficiently hidden under the sex-change and the gags and theoreti-cal allusions, I got to write my sensitive little self-obsessed bildungsroman. The biggest cackle I got when the book came out was the way all the reviews, whether they stomped up and down on the overall book or not, all praised the fact that at least here was a first novel that wasn't yet another sensitive little self-obsessed bildungsroman.

LM: Had you considered writing a more direct autobiographical novel? Why go to such lengths to hide yourself?
DFW: Because that's how hidden I was then.

LM: You wrote in one of your letters to me that you felt that the stuff that you're doing now is more obviously autobiographical. Could you talk a bit about how you meant that? Do you mean more autobiographical in a semi-literal way—that you're depicting events or people or situations in your new writing that are based on actual ones in your own life? Or do you mean this more generally—that you're writing closer to your own emotions or personality rather than projecting some other kind of perspective? I'm interested in how this might apply to something like "Forever Overhead," whose emotional impact moved me more than the earlier stories in *Girl with Curious Hair*. Is "Overhead" an example of your writing more directly out of personal (or "autobiographical") materials?

DFW: What was it about that story that moved you?

LM: There was something very convincing about the terror of this boy poised up there on the diving board, the people watching—something very primal in the way that Kafka is. Surreal but not abstract at all.

DFW: That incident really happened to me. I went up on a diving board, and I changed my mind at the top, but there were all these people behind me so there I was. I've always felt it's a failed story, maybe because that memory, that moment of great fear, is intensely shameful to me. Talking about it like this is interesting, because I may be wrong when I think it's a failed story. I wrote this essay for Houghton-Mifflin about how much I hate the story; I said it was a story about my going up on a diving board, a shameful incident and an incident involving public shame and two different kinds of terror. The problem I have with the story is that when I was writing it, the emotion I felt most keenly was shame—shame that this past shame was still so shameful for me, and that such a little incident would still be such a big deal. So the way I perceived the story was as an attempt to take a real incident and pump it up. I was going to exploit the classic idea of the double bind, make the kid going through puberty, have the diving board covered with skin so that the diving board becomes very heavily a symbol for initiation into adulthood. Welcome to the machine, you've got to dive off, all this kind of stuff.

LM: It also seemed like a metaphor about your own writing—finding yourself so exposed out there, everybody expecting something from you, that double bind . . .

DFW: Nah, that would be too self-pitying. It's a weird story alright. I did the first draft of that story in college and it's been through about twenty drafts over the course of about eight years, which is not usually how I do stuff. This is weird, you know—I want to redo this essay for Houghton-Mifflin because the way I perceive it is: here was a regular incident that originally had a real emotional quality about it but that now as an adult I wasn't really able to own up to. I'm ashamed of the fact that the shame is still so important to me, so what do I do? I perform certain standard literary moves. I pile in a lot of metaphors, I try to make the writing as pretty as I can, swinging for the fence on every single one. I load it with standard Hamlet-esque constructions of double binds. I do all this initiation-into-adulthood stuff. Basically, I try to frost it with so much literary meaning that what's *really* going on, which is the sham, of it gets buried. Since you responded the way you did, it might be that there's something plangent about the way all this frosting is ladled onto it so that the shame comes through anyway.

LM: Maybe your frosting didn't cover up the taste of the cake as much as you thought it would? That feeling certainly came through for me.
DFW: If there's a pathos about the story, it may be that the story's trying so hard to do something with an incident that is really so common, mundane. When I was writing it, there was this sense that nobody else had ever gone through this; then it occurred to me that when you think how many swimming pools there are. . . . Anyway, so here you've got a story that proceeds from an exactly opposite assumption from what I think a story ought to. Instead of writing a story that's seeking somehow to bind human beings and their experience—you know, my shame is your shame is our shame and thus we are redeemed, right?—I wound up writing something that wound up being, this is my shame and only mine, nobody else has it, and it's inherently repulsive; and so while I've got to get it out, I'm going to disguise it to make it as gratifying for you a literary exercise as I can. It sounds like what happened, though, was that maybe I failed to disguise it—but that this failure may be becomes its success. This is probably a good example of how and why authors are so often stupid about their own work. There's no way you can avoid the intentional fallacy about your own work. In terms of "Forever Overhead," I know, of course, that much of that story is an effort to hide, to distract you from this shameful event, and knowing this, I assume the story is a failure because it's really an evasion; but, of course, the way the reader sees it becomes entirely different. And if that's the case, asking a writer about what his program is, what his motivations and intentions are when he's writing, seems at best something like pulling the wings off a fly. I guess what gives me hope about this discussion we're having is realizing that it was my failure to hide what I wanted to hide that made the story succeed. God, what a ghastly enterprise to be in, though—and what an odd way to achieve success. I'm an exhibitionist who wants to hide, but is unsuccessful at hiding; therefore, somehow I succeed.

LM: Wittgenstein's work, especially the *Tractatus*, permeates *The Broom of the System* in all sorts of ways, both as content and in terms of the metaphors you employ. But in the later stages of his career, Wittgenstein concluded that language was unable to refer in the direct, referential way he'd argued it could in the *Tractatus*. Doesn't that mean language is a closed loop—there's no permeable membrane to allow the inside from getting through to the outside? And if that's the case, then isn't a book *only* a game? Or does the fact that it's a language game make it somehow different?

DFW: There's a kind of tragic fall Wittgenstein's obsessed with all the way from the *Tractatus Logico-Philosophicus* in 1922 to the *Philosophical Investigations* in his last years. I mean a real Book-of-Genesis-type tragic fall. The loss of the whole external world. The *Tractatus*'s picture theory of meaning presumes that the only possible relation between language and the world is denotative, referential. In order for language both to be meaningful and to have some connection to reality, words like *tree* and *house* have to be like little pictures, representations of real trees and houses. Mimesis. But nothing more. Which means we can know and speak of nothing more than little mimetic pictures. Which divides us, metaphysically and forever, from the external world. If you buy such a metaphysical schism, you're left with only two options. One is that the individual person with her language is trapped in here, with the world out there, and never the twain shall meet. Which, even if you think language's pictures really are mimetic, is an awful lonely proposition. And there's no iron guarantee the pictures truly *are* mimetic, which means you're looking at solipsism. One of the things that makes Wittgenstein a real artist to me is that he realized that no conclusion could be more horrible than solipsism. And so he trashed everything he'd been lauded for in the *Tractatus* and wrote the *Investigations*, which is the single most comprehensive and beautiful argument against solipsism that's ever been made. Wittgenstein argues that for language even to be possible, it must always be a function of relationships between persons (that's why he spends so much time arguing against the possibility of a "private language"). So he makes language dependent on human community, but unfortunately we're still stuck with the idea that there is this world of referents out there that we can never really join or know because we're stuck in here, in language, even if we're at least all in here together. Oh yeah, the other original option. The other option is to expand the linguistic subject. Expand the self.

LM: Like Norman Bombardini in *Broom of the System*.

DFW: Yeah, Norman's gag is that he literalizes the option. He's going to forget the diet and keep eating until he grows to "infinite size" and eliminates loneliness that way. This was Wittgenstein's double bind: you can either treat language as an infinitely small dense dot, or you let it become the world—the exterior and everything in it. The former banishes you from the Garden. The latter seems more promising. If the world is itself a linguistic construct, there's nothing "outside" language for language to have to picture or refer to. This lets you avoid solipsism, but it leads right to the postmodern, poststructural dilemma of having to deny yourself an existence independent of language. Heidegger's the guy most people think got us into this bind, but when I was working on *Broom of the System* I saw Wittgenstein as the real architect of the postmodern trap. He died right on the edge of explicitly treating reality as linguistic instead of ontological. This eliminated solipsism, but not the horror. Because we're still stuck. The *Investigation*'s line is that the fundamental problem of language is, quote, "I don't know my way about." If I were separate from language, if I could somehow detach from it and climb up and look down on it, get the lay of the land so to speak, I could study it "objectively," take it apart, deconstruct it, know its operations and boundaries and deficiencies. But that's not how things are. I'm *in* it. We're *in* language. Wittgenstein's not Heidegger, it's not that language *is* us, but we're still *in* it, inescapably, the same way we're in like Kant's space-time. Wittgenstein's conclusions seem completely sound to me, always have. And if there's one thing that consistently bugs me writing-wise, it's that I don't feel I really *do* know my way around inside language—I never seem to get the kind of clarity and concision I want.

LM: Ray Carver comes immediately to mind in terms of compression and clarity, and he's obviously someone who wound up having a huge influence on your generation.

DFW: Minimalism's just the other side of metafictional recursion. The basic problem's still the one of the mediating narrative consciousness. Both minimalism and metafiction try to resolve the problem in radical ways. Opposed, but both so extreme they end up empty. Recursive metafiction worships the narrative consciousness, makes *it* the subject of the text. Minimalism's even worse, emptier, because it's a fraud: it eschews not only self-reference but any narrative personality at all, tries to pretend there *is* no narrative consciousness in its text. This is so fucking American, man: either make something your God and cosmos and then worship it, or else kill it.

LM: But did Carver really do that? I'd say his narrative voice is nearly always insistently *there*, like Hemingway's was. You're never allowed to forget.

DFW: I was talking about minimalists, not Carver. Carver was an artist, not a minimalist. Even though he's supposedly the inventor of modern U.S. minimalism. "Schools" of fiction are for crank-turners. The founder of a movement is never part of the movement. Carver uses all the techniques and anti-styles that critics call "minimalist," but his case is like Joyce, or Nabokov, or early Barth and Coover—he's using formal innovation in the service of an original vision. Carver invented—or resurrected, if you want to cite Hemingway—the techniques of minimalism in the service of rendering a world he saw that nobody'd seen before. It's a grim world, exhausted and empty and full of mute, beaten people, but the minimalist techniques Carver employed were perfect for it; they created it. And minimalism for Carver wasn't some rigid aesthetic program he adhered to for its own sake. Carver's commitment was to his stories, each of them. And when minimalism didn't serve them, he blew it off. If he realized a story would be best served by expansion, not ablation, he'd expand, like he did to "The Bath," which he later turned into a vastly superior story. He just chased the click. But at some point his "minimalist" style caught on. A movement was born, proclaimed, promulgated by the critics. Now here come the crank-turners. What's especially dangerous about Carver's techniques is that they seem so easy to imitate. It doesn't seem like each word and line and draft has been bled over. That's part of his genius. It looks like you can write a minimalist piece without much bleeding. And you can. But not a good one.

LM: For various reasons, the sixties postmodernists were heavily influenced by other art forms—television, for instance, or the cinema or painting—but in particular their notions of form and structure were often influenced by jazz. Do you think that your generation of writers has been similarly influenced by rock music? For instance, you and Mark Costello collaborated on the first book-length study of rap (*Signifying Rappers*); would you say that your interest in rap has anything to do with your writerly concerns? There's a way in which I can relate your writing with rap's "postmodern" features, its approach to structure and social issues. Sampling. Recontextualizing.

DFW: About the only way music informs my work is in terms of rhythm; sometimes I associate certain narrators' and characters' voices with certain pieces of music. Rock music itself bores me, usually. The phenomenon of rock interests me, though, because its birth was part of the rise of mass popular media, which completely changed the ways the U.S. was unified and split. The mass media unified the country geographically for pretty much the first time. Rock helped change the fundamental splits in the U.S. from geographical splits to generational ones. Very few people I talk to understand what "generation gap"'s implications really were. Kids loved rock partly because their parents didn't, and obversely. In a mass-mediated nation, it's no longer North vs. South. It's under-thirty vs. over-thirty. I don't think you can understand the sixties and Vietnam and love-ins and LSD and the whole era of patricidal rebellion that helped inspire early postmodern fiction's whole "We're-going-to-trash-your-BeaverCleaver-plasticized-GOP-image-of-life-in-America" attitude without understanding rock 'n' roll. Because rock was and is all about busting loose, exceeding limits, and limits are usually set by parents, ancestors, older authorities.

LM: But so far there aren't many others who have written anything interesting about rock—Richard Meltzer, Peter Guralnik . . .
DFW: There's some others. Lester Bangs. Todd Gitlin, who also does great TV essays. The thing that especially interested Mark and me about rap was the nasty spin it puts on the whole historical us-vs.-them aspect of postmodern pop. Anyway, what rock 'n' roll did for the multicolored young back in the fifties and sixties, rap seems to be doing for the young black urban community. It's another attempt to break free of precedent and constraint. But there are contradictions in rap that seem perversely to show how, in an era where rebellion itself is a commodity used to sell other commodities, the whole idea of rebelling against white corporate culture is not only impossible but incoherent. Today you've got black rappers who make their reputation rapping about Kill the White Corporate Tools, and are then promptly signed by white-owned record corporations, and not only feel no shame about "selling out" but then release platinum albums about not only Killing White Tools but also about how wealthy the rappers now are after signing their record deal! You've got music here that both hates the white GOP values of the Reaganoid eighties and extols a gold-and-BMW materialism that makes Reagan look like a fucking Puritan. Violently racist and anti-Semitic black artists being co-opted by white-owned, often Jewish-owned record labels, and celebrating that fact in their art. The tensions are delicious. I can feel the spittle starting again just thinking about it.

LM: This is another example of the dilemma facing avant-garde wannabes today—the appropriation (and ensuing "taming") of rebellion by the system people like Jameson are talking about.

DFW: I don't know much about Jameson. To me rap's the ultimate distillate of the U.S. eighties, but if you really step back and think not just about rap's politics but about white enthusiasm for it, things get grim. Rap's conscious response to the poverty and oppression of U.S. blacks is like some hideous parody of sixties black pride. We seem to be in an era when oppression and exploitation no longer bring a people together and solidify loyalties and help everyone rise above his individual concerns. Now the rap response is more like "You've always exploited us to get rich, so now goddamn it we're going to exploit ourselves and get rich." The irony, self-pity, self-hatred are now conscious, celebrated. This has to do with what we were talking about regarding "Westward" and postmodern recursion. If I have a real enemy, a patriarch for my patricide, it's probably Barth and Coover and Burroughs, even Nabokov and Pynchon. Because, even though their self-consciousness and irony and anarchism served valuable purposes, were indispensable for their times, their aesthetic's absorption by U.S. commercial culture has had appalling consequences for writers and everyone else. The TV essay's really about how poisonous postmodern irony's become. You see it in David Letterman and Gary Shandling and rap. But you also see it in fucking Rush Limbaugh, who may well be the Antichrist. You see it in T. C. Boyle and Bill Vollmann and Lorrie Moore. It's pretty much all there is to see in your pal Mark Leyner. Leyner and Limbaugh are the nineties' twin towers of postmodern irony, hip cynicism, a hatred that winks and nudges you and pretends it's just kidding.

Irony and cynicism were just what the U.S. hypocrisy of the fifties and sixties called for. That's what made the early postmodernists great artists. The great thing about irony is that it splits things apart, gets us up above them so we can see the flaws and hypocrisies and duplicities. The virtuous always triumph? Ward Cleaver is the prototypical fifties father? *Sure.* Sarcasm, parody, absurdism, and irony are great ways to strip off stuff's mask and show' the unpleasant reality behind it. The problem is that once the rules for art are debunked, and once the unpleasant realities the irony diagnoses are revealed and diagnosed, *then* what do we do? Irony's useful for debunking illusions, but most of the illusion-debunking in the U.S. has now been done and redone. Once everybody knows that equality of opportunity is bunk and Mike Brady's bunk and Just Say No is bunk, now what do we do? All we seem to want to do is keep ridiculing the stuff. Postmodern irony and cynicism's become an end in itself, a measure of hip sophistication and literary savvy. Few artists dare to try to talk about ways of working toward redeeming what's wrong, because they'll look sentimental and naive to all the weary ironists. Irony's gone from liberating to enslaving. There's some great essay somewhere that has a line about irony being the song of the prisoner who's come to love his cage.

LM: Humbert Humbert, the rutting gorilla, painting the bars of his own cage with such elegance. In fact, Nabokov's example raises the issue of whether cynicism and irony are really a given. In *Pale Fire* and *Lolita*, there's an irony about these structures and inventions and so forth, but this reaction is deeply humanistic rather than being merely ironic. This seems true in Barthelme, for instance, or Stanley Elkin, Barth. Or Robert Coover. The other aspect has to do with the presentation of themselves or their consciousness. The beauty and the magnificence of human artistry isn't merely ironic.

DFW: But you're talking about the click, which is something that can't just be bequeathed from our postmodern ancestors to their descendants. No question that some of the early postmodernists and ironists and anarchists and absurdists did magnificent work, but you can't pass the click from one generation to another like a baton. The click's idiosyncratic, personal. The only stuff a writer can get from an artistic ancestor is a certain set of aesthetic values and beliefs, and maybe a set of formal techniques that might—just might—help the writer to chase his own click. The problem is that, however misprised it's been, what's been passed down from the postmodern heyday is sarcasm, cynicism, a manic ennui, suspicion of all authority, suspicion of all constraints on conduct, and a terrible penchant for ironic diagnosis of unpleasantness instead of an ambition not just to diagnose and ridicule but to redeem. You've got to understand that this stuff has permeated the culture. It's become our language; we're so in it we don't even see that it's one perspective, one among many possible ways of seeing. Postmodern irony's become our environment.

LM: Mass culture is another very "real" part of that environment—rock music or television or sports, talk shows, game shows, whatever; that's the milieu you and I live in, I mean that's the world . . .

DFW: I'm always stumped when critics regard references to popular culture in serious fiction as some sort of avant-garde stratagem. In terms of the world I live in and try to write about, it's inescapable. Avoiding any reference to the pop would mean either being retrograde about what's "permissible" in serious art or else writing about some other world.

LM: You mentioned earlier that writing parts of *Broom of the System* felt like recreation for you—a relief from doing technical philosophy. Are you ever able to shift into that "recreational mode" of writing today? Is it still "play" for you?

DFW: It's not play anymore in the sense of laughs and yucks and nonstop thrills. The stuff in *Broom* that's informed by that sense of play ended up pretty forgettable, I think. And it doesn't sustain the enterprise for very long. And I've found the really tricky discipline to writing is trying to play without getting overcome by insecurity or vanity or ego. Showing the reader that you're smart or funny or talented or whatever, trying to be liked, integrity issues aside, this stuff just doesn't have enough motivational calories in it to carry you over the long haul. You've got to discipline yourself to talk out of the part of you that loves the thing, loves what you're working on. Maybe that just plain loves. (I think we might need woodwinds for this part, LM.) But sappy or no, it's true. The last couple years have been pretty arid for me good-work-wise, but the one way I've progressed I think is I've gotten convinced that there's something kind of timelessly vital and sacred about good writing. This thing doesn't have that much to do with talent, even glittering talent like Leyner's or serious talent like Daitch's. Talent's just an instrument. It's like having a pen that works instead of one that doesn't. I'm not saying I'm able to work consistently out of the premise, but it seems like the big distinction between good art and so-so art lies somewhere in the art's heart's purpose, the agenda of the consciousness behind the text. It's got something to do with love. With having the discipline to talk out of the part of yourself that can love instead of the part that just wants to be loved. I know this doesn't sound hip at all. I don't know. But it seems like one of the things really great fiction-writers do—from Carver to Chekhov to Flannery O'Connor, or like the Tolstoy of "The Death of Ivan Ilych" or the Pynchon of *Gravity's Rainbow*—is *give* the reader something. The reader walks away from real art heavier than she came to it. Fuller. All the attention and engagement and work you need to get from the reader can't be for your benefit; it's got to be for hers. What's poisonous about the cultural environment today is that it makes this so scary to try to carry out. Really good work probably comes out of a willingness to disclose yourself, open yourself up in spiritual and emotional ways that risk making you look banal or melodramatic or naive or unhip or sappy, and to ask the reader really to feel something. To be willing to sort of die in order to move the reader, somehow. Even now I'm scared about how sappy this'll look in print, saying this. And the effort actually to do it, not just talk about it, requires a kind

of courage I don't seem to have yet. I don't see that kind of courage in Mark
Leyner or Emily Prager or Brett Ellis. I sometimes see flickers of it in Vollmann and Daitch and Nicholson Baker and Amy Homes and Jon Franzen.
It's weird—it has to do with quality but not that much with sheer writing
talent. It has to do with the click. I used to think the click came from, "Holy
shit, have I ever just done something good." Now it seems more like the real
click's more like, "Here's something good, and on one side I don't much matter, and on the other side the individual reader maybe doesn't much matter,
but the thing's good because there's extractable value here for both me and
the reader." Maybe it's as simple as trying to make the writing more generous
and less ego-driven.

LM: Music genres like the blues or jazz or even rock seem to have their ebb
and flow in terms of experimentalism, but in the end they all have to come
back to the basic elements that comprise the genre, even if these are very
simple (like the blues). The trajectory of Bruce Springsteen's career comes
to mind. What interests fans of any genre is that they really know the formulas and the elements, so they also can respond to the constant, built-in
metagames and intertextualities going on in all genre forms. In a way the
responses are aesthetically sophisticated in the sense that it's the infinite
variations-on-a-theme that interests them. I mean, how else can they read
a million of these things (real genre fans are not stupid people necessarily)?
My point is that people who really care about the forms—the serious writers
and readers in fiction—don't want all the forms *broken*, they want variation
that allows the essence to emerge in new ways. Blues fans could love Hen-
drix because he was still playing the blues. I think you're seeing a greater
appreciation for fiction's rules and limits among postmodern writers of all
generations. It's almost a relief to realize that all babies were *not* tossed out
with the bathwater back in the sixties.
DFW: You're probably right about appreciating limits. The sixties' movement in poetry to radical free verse, in fiction to radically experimental recursive forms—their legacy to my generation of would-be artists is at least
an incentive to ask very seriously where literary art's true relation to limits
should be. We've seen that you can break any or all of the rules without
getting laughed out of town, but we've also seen the toxicity that anarchy
for its own sake can yield. It's often useful to dispense with standard formulas, of course, but it's just as often valuable and brave to see what can
be done within a set of rules—which is why formal poetry's so much more
interesting to me than free verse. Maybe our touchstone now should be

G. M. Hopkins, who made up his *own* set of formal constraints and then blew everyone's footwear off from inside them. There's something about free play within an ordered and disciplined structure that resonates for readers. And there's something about complete caprice and flux that's deadening.

LM: I suspect this is why so many of the older generation of postmodernists—Federman, Sukenick, Steve Katz, and others (maybe even Pynchon fits in here)—have recently written books that rely on more traditional forms. That's why it seems important right now for your generation to go back to traditional forms and reexamine and rework those structures and formulas. This is already happening with some of the best younger writers in Japan. You recognize that if you just say, "Fuck it, let's throw everything out!" there's nothing in the bathtub to make the effort worthwhile.

DFW: For me, the last few years of the postmodern era have seemed a bit like the way you feel when you're in high school and your parents go on a trip, and you throw a party. You get all your friends over and throw this wild disgusting fabulous party. For a while it's great, free and freeing, parental authority gone and overthrown, a cat's-away-let's-play Dionysian revel. But then time passes, and the party gets louder and louder, and you run out of drugs, and nobody's got any money for more drugs, and things get broken and spilled, and there's a cigarette burn on the couch, and you're the host and it's your house too, and you gradually start wishing your parents would come back and restore some fucking order in your house. It's not a perfect analogy, but the sense I get of my generation of writers and intellectuals or whatever is that it's 3:00 a.m. and the couch has several burn-holes and somebody's thrown up in the umbrella stand and we're wishing the revel would end. The postmodern founders' patricidal work was great, but patricide produces orphans, and no amount of revelry can make up for the fact that writers my age have been literary orphans throughout our formative years. We're kind of wishing some parents would come back. And of course we're uneasy about the fact that we wish they'd come back—I mean, what's wrong with us? Are we total pussies? Is there something about authority and limits we actually *need*? And then the uneasiest feeling of all, as we start gradually to realize that parents in fact aren't ever coming back—which means *we're* going to have to be the parents.

The Next Big Thing: Can a Downstate Author Withstand the Sensation over His 1,079-Page Novel?

Mark Caro/1996

From *Chicago Tribune*, 23 February 1996. Reprinted with permission of the Chicago Tribune; copyright © Chicago Tribune; all rights reserved.

David Foster Wallace's new novel, *Infinite Jest*, weighs about four pounds and runs 1,079 pages, almost 100 of which are endnotes in teeny-tiny type.

It's not the sort of book, in other words, that you're likely to see on the beach, unless it's a really windy day and a pair of sandals and a tote bag prove inadequate in holding down the towel.

Yet the novel has become what the hypesters like to call the literary sensation of this young year. It has attracted attention across the nation's mainstream print media—*Time, Newsweek, Spin, Esquire, Elle, GQ* . . . —and the reviews have been the type that authors compose in their heads as fantasy-fulfillment exercises.

Details writer David Streitfeld: "*Infinite Jest* is bigger, more ambitious and better than anything else being published in the U.S. right now."

New York magazine's Walter Kirn: "Next year's book awards have been decided. The plaques and citations can now be put in escrow. With *Infinite Jest*, by David Foster Wallace . . . the competition has been obliterated. It's as though Paul Bunyan had joined the NFL or Wittgenstein had gone on *Jeopardy!* The novel is that colossally disruptive. And that spectacularly good."

Wallace—sitting in his Spartan three-walls-and-a-door office at Illinois State University, where he teaches English literature and creative writing—said last Friday he hadn't read the *New York* magazine review (immediate response: "Wow") or many others. He chooses to squint at the figurative spotlight.

"Part of me is extremely pleased and gratified, and part of me suspects a trap—that somehow there's been a great deal of excitement but that nobody's actually read it and that people are going to find out that this thing's actually pretty hard," said the novelist, who turned thirty-four on Wednesday. "So all this fuss will have been based on a misunderstanding."

Nevertheless, Wallace was reluctantly gearing up to join the machinery. On Sunday, he left his Bloomington ranch house and two black Labrador-mix dogs to embark on a two-week coast-to-coast publicity tour.

He'll read excerpts of *Infinite Jest* (including next Thursday at 7 p.m. at Barbara's Bookstore, 3130 N. Broadway) and participate in interviews where he hoped—quixotically—to deflect any attention from himself.

His self-conscious embarrassment about the trip is reflected in a note on his office door: "D. F. Wallace is out of town on weird personal authorized emergencyish leave from 2/17/96 to 3/3/96 and from 3/5/96 to 3/10/96."

Sharing the hype

Good friend Jonathan Franzen, the New York-based author of *The Twenty-Seventh City* and *Strong Motion*, sympathized with the inherent tension in promoting *Infinite Jest*. Franzen, who calls the book a critique of "the culture of passive entertainment," noted, "The prospect of this book being hyped by Dave's personality has multiple ironies."

"The irony is not lost on me," conceded Wallace.

(The author, by the way, was wearing a yellow bandanna around his head and a white T-shirt, and he abided the university building's no-smoking rule and his own nicotine addiction by stashing a clump of smokeless tobacco inside his lower lip and occasionally leaning behind his desk to spit the juice into a waste basket.)

"For me the nicest of all possible worlds is if some of this hype could kind of spread itself out a little bit, because there's a lot of really good, fairly serious stuff coming out every year that for some reason or another doesn't catch the eye of the great beast," he said, citing such fellow youngish as writers Franzen, Richard Powers, William T. Vollmann, A. M. Homes, Jeffrey Eugenides, and George Saunders.

Written over three years during which Wallace lived in Syracuse, New York, and Bloomington (he began teaching at ISU in the fall of 1993), *Infi-*

nite Jest is a grandly conceived, dizzyingly executed, darkly comic vision of America's not-so-distant future.

The U.S., having turned much of New England into a toxic waste dump and ceded it to Canada, has evolved into the Organization of North American Nations (O.N.A.N., with any lewd implications being intentional). The action hopscotches among several corporate-sponsored postmillennium years, which are identified not with numbers but labels such as the Year of the Depend Adult Undergarment, the Year of the Tucks Medicated Pad and the Year of Dairy Products from the American Heartland.

The plot defies a nifty summary that'll let you fake your way through a cocktail party. Let's just say it throws a wide net around a pot-smoking high-school tennis phenom who compulsively reads the *Oxford English Dictionary* (characteristics shared with Wallace), substance-abuse treatment programs and the ex-burglar/ex-junkie head of a halfway house, a physician's desk reference's worth of pharmaceutical information, terrorist activities by Quebecois separatists and their secret weapon: a film (on a cartridge) that shares the novel's name and is so entertaining that it either kills or lobotomizes those who watch it.

The novel's ample humor runs from sly and obscure to broad slapstick: a bricklayer's insurance claim letter over an accident involving a bucket of bricks and a pulley is a gleefully low high point. Yet alienation, loneliness, obsessive secret-keeping, addiction, and despair hang in the air like dark clouds on a windless November day.

Wallace said that when he began writing *Infinite Jest*, he didn't realize how large its scope would be. "I wanted to do a book that was sad," he said. "That was really the only idea that was in my head."

His look at life

The novel's melancholy tone grew out of observations Wallace was making as he looked outward and inward. "It seemed to me that there was something sort of sad about the country . . . that at a time when our lives are more comfortable and more full probably of pleasure, sheer pleasure, than any other time in history, that people were essentially miserable," he said.

He included himself near the top of the list. Born and raised in Urbana, where his father remains a philosophy professor at the University of Illinois, the Amherst College graduate attracted the Hot Young Writer buzz (and facile Thomas Pynchon comparisons) when he had two books—the novel

The Broom of the System (1987) and short-story collection *Girl with Curious Hair* (1989)—published while he was in his mid-twenties.

He may not have been a star along the lines of the more commercial Jay McInerney and Brett Easton Ellis, but he received enough attention to "mess up my wiring."

"I went through a real bad three years," he said of the late '80s/early '90s, when he lived in Boston (enrolling briefly in Harvard University's Ph.D. program in philosophy) and Syracuse. He even once checked himself into a hospital to be put on a suicide watch.

"In a weird way it seemed like there was something very American about what was going on, that things were getting better and better for me in terms of all the stuff I thought I wanted, and I was getting unhappier and unhappier," he said.

After a few years of not writing, Wallace plunged himself into *Infinite Jest*. He observed open Alcoholics Anonymous meetings in Boston and made himself an expert on the histories of art films, various international alliances, recovery movements, and pharmacology.

The research reaped personal as well as professional dividends. "If I hadn't gone to a bunch of AA meetings, I wouldn't have gotten rid of my TV, because I started to realize the TV didn't make me happy, but I couldn't stop watching it," he said.

The theme of addiction carried over to the writing itself, with some friends thinking he had vanished or weirded out. "It made it difficult to be a good friend and to get really immersed in other people's problems because I was trying to remember whether somebody was left-handed from 350 pages ago or something like that," he said.

Wallace sold the book to Little, Brown and Co. based on the first 250 pages, which he'd projected to represent a fifth of the final product. So although he knew—and was grateful—that the publisher was prepared for a lengthy work, he did have pause that readers might resist the presumed arrogance of his expecting them to traverse almost 1,100 dense pages.

"When I was in my twenties, I thought I was really smart and really clever and that anybody would be privileged to read whatever I'd written," he said. "It's not that I'm entirely over that problem, but I think as one gets older, you begin to realize there needs to be some sort of payoff."

Wallace tried to bridge the gap between avant-garde fiction—too much of which he considers "hellaciously unfun to read"—and commercial escapism. So he'll be frustrated if *Infinite Jest* succeeds Salman Rushdie's *The Sa-*

tanic Verses and Stephen Hawking's *A Brief History of Time* as books that decorate many a shelf without being read.

"I wanted to do something that was really hard but was also really fun and made it worthwhile to spend the effort and the attention to read the thing," he said.

"What it's like to be alive"

Still, he's been fascinated by some reader reactions so far, including some who liken its jump-cut style and information bombardment to cruising the Internet. "I've never been on the Internet," he said. "This is sort of what it's like to be alive. You don't have to be on the Internet for life to feel this way. . . .

"The image in my mind—and I actually had dreams about it all the time—was that this book was really a very pretty pane of glass that had been dropped off the twentieth story of a building."

Life, incidentally, feels better for Wallace now than several years ago. The teaching takes the pressure off the writing—financially and emotionally—and he has enjoyed being back in Illinois despite the flat, dull landscape.

"I thought it would be very boring here, and I'd only stay here a couple of years, but I like this much better than the East Coast," he said.

Victoria Harris, a fellow English professor at ISU, said the students and faculty are grateful to have Wallace there. "He's personally the funniest person I've ever met," she said. "I think he's a treasure. The local fame is something we all like, I think, even more than David."

As for how he'll react to this latest wave of adulation and publicity, Wallace said, "I'd be an idiot if I weren't concerned about it. I'm going to do two weeks of this tour and then it's over, and then I'm back to my life. And I've gotten a lot better at saying 'no.'"

The stuff to which Wallace is saying "no" includes TV interviews (though he's considering an appearance on an unnamed PBS show) and the "What's David really like?" kind of features.

"If you're trying to be a writer in a culture where one of our big religions is celebrity—and there's all kinds of very weird emotional and spiritual and philosophical stuff going on about watching and being watched and celebrity and image—then you really need to be outside it a bit.

"To the extent that you are watched, I think you're compromised. You now have access to that world in a way that the ordinary reader doesn't. You can't speak for that reader anymore."

The Salon Interview:
David Foster Wallace

Laura Miller/1996

From *Salon*, 8 March 1996. © 1996 by the Salon Media Group. Reprinted by permission.

David Foster Wallace's low-key, bookish appearance flatly contradicts the unshaven, bandanna-capped image advanced by his publicity photos. But then, even a hipster novelist would have to be a serious, disciplined writer to produce a 1,079-page book in three years. *Infinite Jest*, Wallace's mammoth second novel, juxtaposes life in an elite tennis academy with the struggles of the residents of a nearby halfway house, all against a near-future background in which the U.S., Canada, and Mexico have merged, Northern New England has become a vast toxic waste dump, and everything from private automobiles to the very years themselves are sponsored by corporate advertisers. Slangy, ambitious, and occasionally over-enamored with the prodigious intellect of its author, *Infinite Jest* nevertheless has enough solid emotional ballast to keep it from capsizing. And there's something rare and exhilarating about a contemporary author who aims to capture the spirit of his age.

The thirty-four-year-old Wallace, who teaches at Illinois State University in Bloomington-Normal and exhibits the careful modesty of a recovering smart aleck, discussed American life on the verge of the millennium, the pervasive influence of pop culture, the role of fiction writers in an entertainment-saturated society, teaching literature to freshmen, and his own maddening, inspired creation during a recent reading tour for *Infinite Jest*.

MILLER: What were you intending to do when you started this book?
WALLACE: I wanted to do something sad. I'd done some funny stuff and some heavy, intellectual stuff, but I'd never done anything sad. And I wanted

58

it not to have a single main character. The other banality would be: I wanted to do something real American, about what it's like to live in America around the millennium.

MILLER: And what is that like?

WALLACE: There's something particularly sad about it, something that doesn't have very much to do with physical circumstances, or the economy, or any of the stuff that gets talked about in the news. It's more like a stomach-level sadness. I see it in myself and my friends in different ways. It manifests itself as a kind of lostness. Whether it's unique to our generation I really don't know.

MILLER: Not much of the press about *Infinite Jest* addresses the role that Alcoholics Anonymous plays in the story. How does that connect with your overall theme?

WALLACE: The sadness that the book is about, and that I was going through, was a real American type of sadness. I was white, upper-middle-class, obscenely well-educated, had had way more career success than I could have legitimately hoped for, and was sort of adrift. A lot of my friends were the same way. Some of them were deeply into drugs, others were unbelievable workaholics. Some were going to singles bars every night. You could see it played out in twenty different ways, but it's the same thing.

Some of my friends got into AA. I didn't start out wanting to write a lot of AA stuff, but I knew I wanted to do drug addicts and I knew I wanted to have a halfway house. I went to a couple of meetings with these guys and thought that it was tremendously powerful. That part of the book is supposed to be living enough to be realistic, but it's also supposed to stand for a response to lostness and what you do when the things you thought were going to make you OK, don't. The bottoming out with drugs and the AA response to that was the starkest thing that I could find to talk about that.

I get the feeling that a lot of us, privileged Americans, as we enter our early thirties, have to find a way to put away childish things and confront stuff about spirituality and values. Probably the AA model isn't the only way to do it, but it seems to me to be one of the more vigorous.

MILLER: The characters have to struggle with the fact that the AA system is teaching them fairly deep things through these seemingly simplistic clichés.

WALLACE: It's hard for the ones with some education, which, to be mercenary, is who this book is targeted at. I mean this is caviar for the general literary fiction reader. For me there was a real repulsion at the beginning. "One Day at a Time," right? I'm thinking 1977, Norman Lear, starring Bonnie Franklin. Show me the needlepointed sampler this is written on. But apparently part of addiction is that you need the substance so bad that when they take it away from you, you want to die. And it's so awful that the only way to deal with it is to build a wall at midnight and not look over it. Something as banal and reductive as "One Day at a Time" enabled these people to walk through hell, which from what I could see the first six months of detox is. That struck me.

It seems to me that the intellectualization and aestheticizing of principles and values in this country is one of the things that's gutted our generation. All the things that my parents said to me, like "It's really important not to lie." OK, check, got it. I nod at that but I really don't feel it. Until I get to be about thirty and I realize that if I lie to you, I also can't trust you. I feel that I'm in pain, I'm nervous, I'm lonely, and I can't figure out why. Then I realize, "Oh, perhaps the way to deal with this is really not to lie." The idea that something so simple and, really, so aesthetically uninteresting—which for me meant you pass over it for the interesting, complex stuff—can actually be nourishing in a way that arch, meta, ironic, pomo stuff can't, that seems to me to be important. That seems to me like something our generation needs to feel.

MILLER: Are you trying to find similar meanings in the pop culture material you use? That sort of thing can be seen as merely clever, or shallow.
WALLACE: I've always thought of myself as a realist. I can remember fighting with my professors about it in grad school. The world that I live in consists of 250 advertisements a day and any number of unbelievably entertaining options, most of which are subsidized by corporations that want to sell me things. The whole way that the world acts on my nerve endings is bound up with stuff that the guys with leather patches on their elbows would consider pop or trivial or ephemeral. I use a fair amount of pop stuff in my fiction, but what I mean by it is nothing different than what other people mean in writing about trees and parks and having to walk to the river to get water a hundred years ago. It's just the texture of the world I live in.

MILLER: What's it like to be a young fiction writer today, in terms of getting started, building a career and so on?
WALLACE: Personally, I think it's a really neat time. I've got friends who disagree. Literary fiction and poetry are real marginalized right now. There's

a fallacy that some of my friends sometimes fall into, the ol' "The audience is stupid. The audience only wants to go this deep. Poor us, we're marginalized because of TV, the great hypnotic blah, blah." You can sit around and have these pity parties for yourself. Of course this is bullshit. If an art form is marginalized it's because it's not speaking to people. One possible reason is that the people it's speaking to have become too stupid to appreciate it. That seems a little easy to me.

If you, the writer, succumb to the idea that the audience is too stupid, then there are two pitfalls. Number one is the avant-garde pitfall, where you have the idea that you're writing for other writers, so you don't worry about making yourself accessible or relevant. You worry about making it structurally and technically cutting edge: involuted in the right ways, making the appropriate intertextual references, making it look smart. Not really caring about whether you're communicating with a reader who cares something about that feeling in the stomach which is why we read. Then, the other end of it is very crass, cynical, commercial pieces of fiction that are done in a formulaic way—essentially television on the page—that manipulate the reader, that set out grotesquely simplified stuff in a childishly riveting way.

What's weird is that I see these two sides fight with each other and really they both come out of the same thing, which is a contempt for the reader, an idea that literature's current marginalization is the reader's fault. The project that's worth trying is to do stuff that has some of the richness and challenge and emotional and intellectual difficulty of avant-garde literary stuff, stuff that makes the reader confront things rather than ignore them, but to do that in such a way that it's also pleasurable to read. The reader feels like someone is talking to him rather than striking a number of poses.

Part of it has to do with living in an era when there's so much entertainment available, genuine entertainment, and figuring out how fiction is going to stake out its territory in that sort of era. You can try to confront what it is that makes fiction magical in a way that other kinds of art and entertainment aren't. And to figure out how fiction can engage a reader, much of whose sensibility has been formed by pop culture, without simply becoming more shit in the pop culture machine. It's unbelievably difficult and confusing and scary, but it's neat. There's so much mass commercial entertainment that's so good and so slick, this is something that I don't think any other generation has confronted. That's what it's like to be a writer now. I think it's the best time to be alive ever and it's probably the best time to be a writer. I'm not sure it's the easiest time.

MILLER: What do you think is uniquely magical about fiction?

WALLACE: Oh, Lordy, that could take a whole day! Well, the first line of attack for that question is that there is this existential loneliness in the real world. I don't know what you're thinking or what it's like inside you and you don't know what it's like inside me. In fiction I think we can leap over that wall itself in a certain way. But that's just the first level, because the idea of mental or emotional intimacy with a character is a delusion or a contrivance that's set up through art by the writer. There's another level that a piece of fiction is a conversation. There's a relationship set up between the reader and the writer that's very strange and very complicated and hard to talk about. A really great piece of fiction for me may or may not take me away and make me forget that I'm sitting in a chair. There's real commercial stuff can do that, and a riveting plot can do that, but it doesn't make me feel less lonely.

There's a kind of Ah-ha! Somebody at least for a moment feels about something or sees something the way that I do. It doesn't happen all the time. It's these brief flashes or flames, but I get that sometimes. I feel unalone—intellectually, emotionally, spiritually. I feel human and unalone and that I'm in a deep, significant conversation with another consciousness in fiction and poetry in a way that I don't with other art.

MILLER: Who are the writers who do this for you?

WALLACE: Here's the hard thing about talking about that: I don't mean to say my work is as good as theirs. I'm talking about stars you steer by.

MILLER: Understood.

WALLACE: OK. Historically the stuff that's sort of rung my cherries: Socrates's funeral oration, the poetry of John Donne, the poetry of Richard Crashaw, every once in a while Shakespeare, although not all that often, Keats' shorter stuff, Schopenhauer, Descartes's *Meditations on First Philosophy* and *Discourse on Method*, Kant's *Prolegomena to Any Future Metaphysic*, although the translations are all terrible, William James's *The Varieties of Religious Experience*, Wittgenstein's *Tractatus*, Joyce's *Portrait of the Artist as a Young Man*, Hemingway—particularly the ital stuff in *In Our Time*, where you just go oomph!, Flannery O'Connor, Cormac McCarthy, Don De-Lillo, A. S. Byatt, Cynthia Ozick—the stories, especially one called "Levitations," about 25 percent of the time Pynchon. Donald Barthelme, especially a story called "The Balloon," which is the first story I ever read that made me want to be a writer, Tobias Wolff, Raymond Carver's best stuff—the really famous stuff. Steinbeck when he's not beating his drum, 35 percent of Stephen Crane, *Moby-Dick*, *The Great Gatsby*.

And, my God, there's poetry. Probably Phillip Larkin more than anyone else, Louise Glück, Auden.

MILLER: What about colleagues?

WALLACE: There's the whole "great white male" deal. I think there are about five of us under forty who are white and over six feet and wear glasses. There's Richard Powers who lives only about forty-five minutes away from me and who I've met all of once. William Vollmann, Jonathan Franzen, Donald Antrim, Jeffrey Eugenides, Rick Moody. The person I'm highest on right now is George Saunders, whose book *Civilwarland in Bad Decline* just came out, and is well worth a great deal of attention. A. M. Homes: her longer stuff I don't think is perfect, but every few pages there's something that just doubles you over. Kathryn Harrison, Mary Karr, who's best known for *The Liar's Club* but is also a poet and I think the best female poet under fifty. A woman named Cris Mazza. Rikki Ducornet, Carole Maso. Carole Maso's *Ava* is just—a friend of mine read it and said it gave him an erection of the heart.

MILLER: Tell me about your teaching.

WALLACE: I was hired to teach creative writing, which I don't like to teach.

There's two weeks of stuff you can teach someone who hasn't written fifty things yet and is still kind of learning. Then it becomes more a matter of managing various people's subjective impressions about how to tell the truth vs. obliterating someone's ego.

I like to teach freshman lit because ISU gets a lot of rural students who aren't very well educated and don't like to read. They've grown up thinking that literature means dry, irrelevant, unfun stuff, like cod liver oil. Getting to show them some more contemporary stuff—the one we always do the second week is a story called "A Real Doll," by A. M. Homes, from *The Safety of Objects*, about a boy's affair with a Barbie doll. It's very smart, but on the surface, it's very twisted and sick and riveting and real relevant to people who are eighteen and five or six years ago were either playing with dolls or being sadistic to their sisters. To watch these kids realize that reading literary stuff is sometimes hard work, but it's sometimes worth it and that reading literary stuff can give you things that you can't get otherwise, to see them wake up to that is extremely cool.

MILLER: How do you feel about the reaction to the length of your book? Did it just sort of wind up being that long, or do you feel that you're aiming for a particular effect or statement?

WALLACE: I know it's risky because it's part of this equation of making demands on the reader—which start out financial. The other side of it is publishing houses hate it because they make less money. Paper is so expensive. If the length seems gratuitous, as it did to a very charming Japanese lady from the *New York Times*, then one arouses ire. And I'm aware of that. The manuscript that I delivered was 1700 manuscript pages, of which close to 500 were cut. So this editor didn't just buy the book and shepherd it. He line-edited it twice. I flew to New York, and all that. If it looks chaotic, good, but everything that's in there is in there on purpose. I'm in a good emotional position to take shit for the length because the length strikes people as gratuitous, then the book just fails. It's not gratuitous because I didn't feel like working on it or making the cuts.

It's a weird book. It doesn't move the way normal books do. It's got a whole bunch of characters. I think it makes at least an in-good-faith attempt to be fun and riveting enough on a page-by-page level so I don't feel like I'm hitting the reader with a mallet, you know, "Hey, here's this really hard impossibly smart thing. Fuck you. See if you can read it." I know books like that and they piss me off.

MILLER: What made you choose a tennis academy, which mirrors the halfway house in the book?

WALLACE: I wanted to do something with sport and the idea of dedication to a pursuit being kind of like an addiction.

MILLER: Some of the characters wonder if it's worth it, the competitive obsession.

WALLACE: It's probably like this in anything. I see my students do this with me. You're a young writer. You admire an older writer, and you want to get to where that older writer is. You imagine that all the energy that your envy is putting into it has somehow been transferred to him, that there's a flipside to it, a feeling of being envied that's a good feeling the way that envy is a hard feeling. You can see it as the idea of being in things for some kind of imaginary goal involving prestige rather than for the pursuit itself. It's a very American illness, the idea of giving yourself away entirely to the idea of working in order to achieve some sort of brass ring that usually involves people feeling some way about you—I mean, people wonder why we walk around feeling alienated and lonely and stressed out?

Tennis is the one sport I know enough about for it to be beautiful to me, for me to think that it means something. The nice thing about it is that I've got *Tennis* magazine wanting to do something about me. For me personally it's been great. I may get to hit with the pros some day. It has that advantage.

The Wasted Land

David Streitfeld/1996

From *Details*, March 1996. © by David Streitfeld. Reprinted by permission.

America: home of the brave, land of the freaked. In Infinite Jest, *David Foster Wallace examines the United States of depression, addiction, and obsession.*

The city of Normal, Illinois, has taken its name as its destiny. It boasts a two-block downtown so low-key that no one ever goes there, a strip containing every fast-food outlet known to man, and 19,000 Illinois State students who would probably rather be at the University of Illinois. The landscape is featureless, the weather extreme, the thrills obscure.

David Foster Wallace likes it here. He's bought a house just outside of town, teaches at the university, has acquired two huge hounds, and likes the idea of having children. One of Wallace's deepest desires is to be normal in Normal.

It'll never happen. The thirty-four-year-old writer has just published *Infinite Jest*, a thousand-page marvel about a disparate group of people trying to shed their various addictions and become productive members of society, able to stand living in places like Normal. Little, Brown is issuing the novel with the usual flurry of hype, which for once is justified: *Infinite Jest* is bigger, more ambitious, and better than anything else being published in the U.S. right now.

The principal setting is Boston, about a dozen years in the future. The United States, Canada, and Mexico are ruled by the Organization of North American Nations, a union that's violently opposed by Quebecois terrorists. Commercialization has gotten to the point where years no longer have numbers but names supplied by corporate sponsors, like the Year of the Depend Adult Undergarment.

One plot thread unspools at a halfway house for drug addicts; another revolves around three brothers and their father, who runs a tennis academy until he kills himself by putting his head in a microwave oven. For readers who go the distance, there are dozens of richly drawn characters and marvelous subplots, but even the most casual browser will quickly realize this is a writer intimately familiar with three subjects: addiction, depression, and tennis.

The latter topic, at least, is easy to explain. When Wallace, who grew up in nearby Champaign-Urbana, first picked up a tennis racket at the relatively late age of twelve, he discovered a natural affinity for the game. In fact, he used to come and compete on the same indoor tennis courts we're at now. "I can still see dried bits of tears on the floor," he jokes. Tonight's opponent is John, a twenty-five-year-old friend seeking to unwind before his GREs. In *Infinite Jest*, a tennis master advises a neophyte to "learn to do nothing, with your whole head and body, and everything will be done by what's around you," but Wallace doesn't quite play this way. He hustles up and down the court, sweats buckets. John, meanwhile, never ruffles the part in his hair.

Fiction is an easier game for Wallace. At Amherst College, he was a self-described "math weenie," but his professors would often comment that his math papers read more like stories. Then a friend wrote a novel for his senior thesis, so Wallace did too. After graduation, he signed up with the creative writing program at the University of Arizona. By the end of his first year he had a contract for a novel. The kid was a natural.

During the mid-'80s, it was hip to be a writer just out of puberty. The Brat Pack, led by Jay McInerney and Bret Easton Ellis, was in full flower. The publicity surrounding a writer was often more important than his work. Dozens of wannabes published their first novels to a brief flurry of attention, and were never heard from again.

But it turned out that Wallace's *Broom of the System*, an exuberant tale of a switchboard operator's search for love, was actually pretty good. Reviewers used words like "hilarious" and "wonderful," and made the usual comparisons to Thomas Pynchon, the reigning god of hilarious metafiction. A follow-up volume of short stories, *Girl with Curious Hair*, drew equally admiring nods.

It was all so quick, so easy, that Wallace began to flounder. "I didn't have a big draft of the celebrity thing, but I had a little sip," he says. "I did a lot of drugs, slept around, did all the things I'd never gotten to do, all the things I thought all the cool people did."

Before long, Wallace had dropped out of his philosophy Ph.D. program at Harvard and stopped trying to publish fiction. Living in a series of crummy apartments around Boston, he began to degenerate. "I was haunted by the idea that I was a sham and a whore and a fraud."

He doesn't want *Infinite Jest* to be seen as autobiography, which it's not. On the other hand, if Wallace hadn't been hospitalized in 1988 and put on a suicide watch, he might not have written so accurately about Kate, a character in *Infinite Jest* who keeps trying to die: "It's like something horrible is about to happen," she explains to her doctor, "there's the feeling that there's something you have to do right away to stop it but you don't know what it is you have to do, and then it's happening, too, the whole horrible time, it's about to happen and also it's happening all at the same time."

Kate traces some of her problems back to an extreme fondness for marijuana, with which her creator also seems very familiar.

"In this country," he says, "we're unprecedentedly safe, comfortable, and well fed, with more and better venues for stimulation. And yet if you were asked, 'Is this a happy or unhappy country?' you'd check the 'unhappy' box. We're living in an era of emotional poverty, which is something that serious drug addicts feel most keenly."

The writer argues that "drug addiction is really a form of religion, albeit a bent one. An addict gives himself away to his substance utterly. He believes in it and trusts it, and his love for it is more important than his place in the community, his job, or his friends."

Unlike some of his characters, Wallace managed to extricate himself from the downward spiral before the damage became permanent—these days, he won't even drink beer. Moreover, he got the raw impetus for a new book. By this point, Wallace was living in upstate New York, in an apartment so small that he had to move everything onto the bed when he wanted to write. "It was," he says, "like spending two years in a submarine."

Mary Karr, who last year became something of a famous writer herself with the publication of her grim childhood memoir *The Liar's Club*, was Wallace's snorkel to the atmosphere. They didn't last, despite the heart-shaped tattoo on Wallace's upper arm inscribed MARY. It's a gesture he now regrets, noting, "A tattoo-based relationship probably has fundamental problems."

If Wallace were inclined to get a matching tattoo for his other arm, it would probably say JEEVES AND DRONE, after his beloved hounds, whom he calls his "kids." "I'm worried I'm going to become one of those lonely thirty-year-olds who's really into dogs," he confides, describing exactly what he is already.

Despite the holiday season, his modest ranch house, just downwind of the slaughterhouse, didn't boast a single colored light until I shamed him into picking some up at Walmart. "It's kind of sad," he confesses. "I'm not good at the little domestic things." His refrigerator displays coupons for every pizza parlor within a thirty-mile radius.

It's a circumscribed life, but it is, after all, normal—and Wallace plans to remain faithful to it even if 1996 turns out to be the Year of *Infinite Jest*. Which it might. Reading the novel may require a huge commitment of time, but *Infinite Jest* unerringly pinpoints how Americans have turned the pursuit of pleasure into an addiction, and it does so in an entertaining, even moving way. Count on the literary world to bow down before him.

Unfortunately, he doesn't want to be part of the scene. "Not that there's anything wrong with it. I just can't handle it." Much easier to be the only writer in Normal. "No one's as tolerant of you as someone who has no fucking idea what you're doing."

He'll blend in even more after he starts attending church. Brought up an atheist, he has twice failed to pass through the Rite of Christian Initiation for Adults, the first step toward becoming a Catholic. The last time, he made the mistake of referring to "the cult of personality surrounding Jesus." That didn't go over big with the priest, who correctly suspected Wallace might have a bit too much skepticism to make a fully obedient Catholic. "I'm a typical American," says Wallace. "Half of me is dying to give myself away, and the other half is continually rebelling."

Recently he found a Mennonite house of worship, which he finds sympathetic even if the hymns are impossible to sing. "The more I believe in something, and the more I take something other than me seriously, the less bored I am, the less self-hating. I get less scared. When I was going through that hard time a few years ago, I was scared all the time." It's not a trip he ever plans to take again.

David Foster Wallace Winces at the Suggestion That His Book Is Sloppy in Any Sense

Anne Marie Donahue/1996

From *Boston Phoenix*, 21–28 March 1996. © 1996 by the Phoenix Media/Communications Group. Reprinted by permission.

"It may be a mess, but it's a very careful mess," he says. "A lot of work went into making it look like that. That might sound like a pathetic lie, but it's not. Now, as you can see, my dander's getting up."

Wallace's dander, however, isn't perceptibly on the rise. Seated in his hotel room at the Copley Plaza, shortly after doing Christopher Lydon's radio show and before heading out for a reading, Wallace looks tired but entirely calm. And he remains that way except when he thinks he might be coming off as pretentious or self-promoting, when he's forced to face a photographer, and when he's asked to talk about himself. "The less I'm being watched, the more I can watch, and the better it is for me and for my work," he explains. "If people really want to know what I ate for lunch, I guess that's okay. But it's kind of toxic."

Whatever the cost of celebrity, Wallace, at thirty-four, is about as famous as serious writers get in this country before they've been dead for quite a while. Although he's glad that *Infinite Jest* has attracted attention, he seems genuinely baffled by all the fuss about him. "I'm somebody who spends much of his life in libraries," he says. "I'm just not that interesting."

Asked why he chose to be a writer, Wallace dodges, saying, "There isn't much else I want to do," and talks instead about writers in general: "Most of the writers I know are weird hybrids. There's a strong streak of egomania coupled with extreme shyness. Writing's kind of like exhibitionism in private. And there's also a strange loneliness, and a desire to have some kind of conversation with people, but not a real great ability to do it in person.

"When I was younger," he goes on, "I saw my relationship with the reader as sort of a sexual one. But now it seems more like a late-night conversation with really good friends, when the bullshit stops and the masks come off."

Why the conversation took the form and direction it did in *Infinite Jest* isn't something Wallace is anxious to explain. "You do what you do, and then afterwards you think up why you did it, so there's an element of bullshit about any explanation," he says. "I'm not going to run some lit crit thing on you," says Wallace, who teaches English at Illinois State University. "But the book doesn't work the way novels normally work." He inhales deeply and then pushes the air back out through his teeth in spurts, making a noise like a kid's imitation of a chugging locomotive. "It's really designed more like a piece of music than like a book, so a lot of it consists of leitmotifs and things that curve back. And there's all this stuff about movement within limits and whether you can puncture the limits or not."

When Wallace's erudition starts to show, he seems to feel obliged to explain it, as if it were a broken leg. "I come from a weird background. My parents are academics, and they read a lot. And I read a lot," he says, neglecting to mention that he also studied philosophy at Harvard. "So I come to writing from a pretty hard-core, abstract place. It comes out of technical philosophy and continental European theory, and extreme avant-garde shit. I'm not just talking Pynchon and Gaddis. That's commercial avant-garde. I'm talking like Beckett, and Fiction Collective 2, and Dalkey Archive." Suddenly, he slaps his forehead, swears, and makes the train noise again.

"On the other hand," he continues, "I'm somebody who can't even own a TV anymore, because I'll just sit there slack-jawed and consume enormous amounts of what is, in terms of art, absolute shit. But it's very pleasurable shit.

"If you're torn in these two different directions," he says, "it's very odd. The project, at least with this book, was to do something long and difficult that was also fun. I'm not saying it succeeds. I wanted to write something that would make somebody say, 'Holy, shit, I've got to read this,' and then seduce them into doing a certain amount of work. And that—if I can be pretentious for a second—is what art ought to do."

One task he requires of his readers "keeping track of enormous amounts of information." Others include "being required to pay attention to some of the strategies that regular entertainment uses" and "having certain formu-laic expectations that go along with reading commercial stuff fucked with. Not just disdained. Fucked with."

Case in point: the ending. "I think that some of that commercial stuff evidences a real contempt for the reader, by having such a reductive idea of what the reader wants. Like they're children and have to have their fantasies enabled and have a happy ending," says Wallace. "Plot-wise, the book doesn't come to a resolution. But if the readers perceive it as me giving them the finger, then I haven't done my job. On the surface, it might seem like it just stops. But it's supposed to stop and then kind of hum and project. Musically and emotionally, it's a pitch that seemed right."

Young Writers and the TV Reality

Donn Fry/1997

From *Seattle Times*, 6 March 1997. © 1997 by The Seattle Times Co. Reprinted by Permission.

There's just no getting around it, as far as David Foster Wallace is concerned: Reality ain't what it used to be.

After all, fiction writers of his generation—Wallace is thirty-five—were raised in an environment in which the average American family spends six hours a day in front of the television. He sees that reflected in myriad ways: young people's diffident, inarticulate conversations—or lack of them; their preference for visual imagery over the printed page; their acceptance of fractured, bite-size storytelling techniques in place of the leisurely narratives of an earlier generation of writers.

"I was born in 1962, and the first serious disciplinary run-in I had with my parents was over the amount of television I was watching," said Wallace, picking through a room-service breakfast in his Seattle hotel as he contemplated the state of American fiction.

He had arrived frazzled at 3 a.m. and, he admitted, watched a little TV "to unwind."

"We are surrounded by narrative: every television show, every movie, every commercial," Wallace said. "They all have a very clear agenda—not one that's mine—but I've absorbed literally hundreds of thousands of hours of very skillful manipulation.

"As a result, I'm far less trusting of standard narrative techniques."

He means that the "backyard-barbecue and three-martini" mother lode of American realism mined by an earlier generation of writers—writers from Updike Country—simply fails to connect with him, either as writer or reader.

Rather, Wallace is a descendant of that subversive, anarchic branch of American literature ("Nabokov's children," he calls them) that began veering

73

off the main stem in the 1960s: novelists such as Thomas Pynchon (*Gravity's Rainbow*), John Barth (*The Sot-Weed Factor*), Robert Coover (*The Public Burning*), William Gaddis (*J R*, *The Recognitions*) and—Wallace's favorite— Don DeLillo (*White Noise, Libra*).

Wallace's own techno-media-savvy approach to fiction is best exemplified by his massive (1,079-page), grandly chaotic-comedic tour de force, *Infinite Jest*, which was published last year to lavish critical praise and has just been released in paperback (Back Bay/Little, Brown, $14.95). It's also a subject he addresses in his new collection of essays, *A Supposedly Fun Thing I'll Never Do Again* (Little, Brown, $23.95).

"For younger writers (today), TV's as much a part of reality as Toyotas and gridlock. We literally cannot imagine life without it," declares Wallace in one essay. While acknowledging the downside of America's fixation with television, he declines to join in disdainful pummeling of the medium:

> Though I'm convinced that television today lies . . . behind a genuine crisis for U.S. culture and literature," he writes in the lively, irreverent style that characterizes both his fiction and criticism, "I do not agree with reactionaries who regard TV as some malignancy visited on an innocent populace, sapping IQs and compromising SAT scores while we all sit there on ever fatter bottoms with little mesmerized spirals revolving in our eyes.

Yet, ironically, he would seem to see evidence every day that supports the "anti-TV paranoia" he bemoans. When not writing fiction and essays, Wallace teaches literature and creative writing at Illinois State University—and tries to fathom an even younger generation that often appears to have abandoned the written word altogether.

"My students don't like to read," acknowledged Wallace, who himself projects the air of a brainy, intense but good-humored grad student, in his rumpled jeans, wire-rimmed specs and uncooperative long hair. "They'll say it's boring, but what they really mean is that it's too hard, the ratio of work to pleasure is too high."

Students who don't like to read also don't like to write. One fears for the next generation of American fiction writers—and Wallace is not reassuring, detecting "an inherent hostility" to well-crafted composition.

"The bigger problem with college students is that in high school they have been taught something called 'expressive writing'—where any thought you have is considered good and valid—and you have to convince them that just because it's their opinion doesn't necessarily mean it's interesting or that anyone wants to read it.

"The biggest problem I have is converting them from 'expressive writing' to communicative writing."

Despite Wallace's intimate understanding of the "genuine crisis for U.S. culture and literature" created by television's seductive power—one plot strand in *Infinite Jest* involves a video so pleasurably mesmerizing that it immobilizes anyone who watches it—the young novelist has come to prefer the company of his two dogs and the solitude of his "little brick house out in the country," in the central Illinois farmland.

"I don't own a television anymore," said Wallace, who gave it up about five years ago, when *Infinite Jest* was beginning to take shape. "The reason is fairly simple: I'm too busy; I've got too much other stuff to do."

The "Infinite Story" Cult Hero behind 1,079-Page Novel Rides the Hype He Skewered

Matthew Gilbert/1997

From *Boston Globe*, 9 April 1997. © 1997 by The New York Times Co. Reprinted by permission.

There is The Thing, plunked down in the coliseum of our consciousness. There is The Viewer of this Thing, sitting in the stands, hand on chin. And there is The Viewer of The Viewer of The Thing—the postmodernist metaphysician hovering in the helicopter above, discussing the way people watch.

And then, somewhere out in the cosmos, watching the watcher watch himself watching, talking about talking about talking, there is David Foster Wallace, novelist, essayist, recovering ironist, and wizard of giddy self-consciousness.

Wallace is the writer best known for a multitiered novel called *Infinite Jest* that weighs in at 1,079 pages, 96 of which are footnotes in a section at the end. When *Infinite Jest* was released last year, the critics dubbed it a Pynchonesque work of genius and "The Grunge American Novel," and trend writers called Wallace the post-Brat-Pack-premillennial Jay McInerney and the voice of Generation X, despite his age, which is thirty-five. He became the hero of grad students and alternative readers everywhere, including the Internet, where there are websites devoted to him.

Now, the more affordable paperback of *Infinite Jest* has arrived in bookstores, along with an exhilarating new collection of essays, *A Supposedly Fun Thing I'll Never Do Again*, and the press-phobic Wallace is doing the promotional circuit once again, exposing himself to more media generalization and imprecision and hype out of loyalty to his publisher, Little, Brown.

Wallace is a strapping Illinoisan whose brown hair leaks out from a loose ponytail. Like his prose, his interviewee style is maximalist and filled with sub-commentary, with Wallace repeatedly qualifying his statements and simultaneously conducting a review of his interviewer's interviewing style, which he calls "psychiatric." Nothing is simple to Wallace, and a question on his feelings about his year in the American hype machine yields first a pre-response and then a gaggle of responses. "Do you want a univocal answer?" he asks. "Because I can pretend as if I feel one way about it. But, of course, the reality is that at last count I feel about fifty-three different ways." For the sake of the concision of daily journalism, he is granted four feelings about becoming famous.

— Feeling No. 1, edited down: "I think the book is the best thing I've ever done, and I'm proud of it, and it was an extremely pleasant surprise to have it get a lot of attention, and some of that is absolutely great."

— Feeling No. 2: "I'm also someone who has problems with self-consciousness. There's part of me that craves attention, but it's an increasingly small part. I've seen attention [mess up] writers I admire. I'm leery of it, and a great deal of the hype occurred at the time when rudimentary arithmetic yields the result that most people haven't read the book. So it's hard to take it seriously at the same time that it's gratifying."

— Feeling No. 3: "I had never been interviewed before. In the first interview I did, I was talking about old girlfriends and who I didn't like. And this guy shut off the tape recorder halfway through and said, 'I need to explain a few things to you.' He put a couple of embarrassing things in his story, but 90 percent of the horrible stuff he didn't put in out of his own decency. So big feeling number three: This"—his finger points back and forth between us—"is hard."

— Feeling No. 4: "Exquisite irony, because a lot of the book is about hype and spin and position. So it's really an enormous cosmic joke. It's like, OK kid, you want to learn a little bit about hype? Have a taste from the big boys' drinking fountain. And not a big gulp, because I'm well aware of where books exist in the consciousness of the culture. I thought I was very sophisticated and had learned a lot about hype from TV. But it's entirely different. The cliché that getting a lot of attention is not the same as getting a lot of affection takes on new dimensions when you learn it through experience."

One of the miracles of *Infinite Jest* is the marketing campaign, which has turned the book's enormity into a plus—the "are-you-reader-enough?" approach. "They've been able to take length and difficulty, which are not particularly sexy features, and spin it such that they look sexy," he says. "Questions about the length are very boring to me—'How did you write such a long book?' 'I used a really long pen, next question'—but it has become a hook, like 'Oh, it's the big book.'"

But the novel, with its dazzling comic despair, would undoubtedly have found a passionate readership on its own merits. It's set in the next decade, when the United States has taken over most of Canada, forming the Organization of North American Nations (ONAN), and when the years are sponsored by companies and named after them—Year of the Whopper, for instance, or Year of the Tucks Medicated Pad. Located in what used to be Boston, the plot takes many roads, most of them connected to the characters at the Enfield Tennis Academy and an addiction treatment center next door, Ennet House. The pages are filled with obsessive specificity—a dozen-page memory of the disassembly of a bed, anyone?—and broad satire, including a movie, called *Infinite Jest*, that's so entertaining it fatally immobilizes its viewers.

Wallace's writing style, particularly with its astounding number of footnotes, has inspired many comparisons to computer hypertext. It's as if you have the option to click on a sentence, and it links you to another relevant spot, from which you later return to the original text. "Straight narrative feels contrived to me, both as a reader and as a writer," Wallace says. "With something set a little bit in the future, that has surreal elements, I'm especially looking for a way to fracture the narrative. . . . You decide: Do you want to read the footnotes? All at the end? Do you want to flip back and forth? Do you use two bookmarks? There are ways to [play] with the reader that are benign, and a certain amount of [playing] with the reader seems to be extremely useful." He likens footnotes to vaudevillian call-and-response, and says they are a good vehicle for humor.

But footnotes have become an addiction of sorts for David Foster Wallace, a fact brought home to him when a magazine approached him about writing a regular column called "Footnotes," in which he would be required to do That David Foster Wallace Thing and use notes. "I got to the point where I couldn't quit using them," he says. "It got worse and worse." After writing a much-footnoted piece for *Premiere* magazine on filmmaker David Lynch, which is reprinted in *A Supposedly Fun Thing*, he went through footnote detox. "I'm just not allowed to use them anymore," he says with conviction.

Addiction is a topic that wends its way into most Wallace profiles. The selling of *Infinite Jest* has involved much talk of its author's personal struggles with drugs and alcohol, presenting Wallace as a grungy but fragile wunderkind in recovery from some hard-living years. (One journalist even took a sneaky tour through the medicine cabinet in Wallace's Normal, Illinois, home.) The media-ized story goes like this:

At Amherst College in the early 1980s, young David turned away from a future as a philosopher to write fiction. His senior thesis became a draft of his first novel, *The Broom of the System*, which was published in 1987. Living in Brighton, success gone to his head, Wallace fell into bad habits, including alcohol, drugs, and a suicide-watch visit to a local hospital. He changed his lifestyle, wrote *Infinite Jest*, and moved back to Illinois, where he grew up, to teach at Illinois State University. He dabbled in religion. He lived happily ever after.

Presented with this condensation, Wallace laughs. "The new American myth, yes? . . . I'll tell you what the truth is."

—"I have done some drugs, I did a lot of them in my teenage years and there was a kind of resurgence of it after my first book got taken. And the biggest reason was that suddenly I got to go to parties with big writers, and some of these big writers ride their lives hard. I was twenty-three and I had the idea that this was like wearing a coat and tie if you're a banker, that if you're a writer you're supposed to live this way. I just wasn't cut out for it neurologically."

—"A whole lot of it was not sleeping very much, a tendency to think in these loops as if stoned while not being stoned. I don't know if it could be called a breakdown. I was in a lucky position of having something like a midlife crisis in my late twenties. When you're starting out writing fiction, the ego is a tremendous force, and a big part of you dreams of a certain level of success, and I got some of that, and it didn't make me happy."

—"I went into Newton-Wellesley [Hospital]. I was feeling so miserable and so angry at myself that I was afraid I was going to hurt myself, so I put myself in there so that I would stop worrying about it. I would not be talking with you about it if it hadn't slipped to the press last year. It's not really anyone's business. . . . It was embarrassing for me, but it was also a time when I gave up a lot of ideas about why I became a writer and what I wanted."

—"I'm interested in religion, only because certain churches seem to be a place where things can be talked about. What does your life mean? Do you believe in something bigger than you? Is there something about gratifying every single desire you have that is harmful? . . . I haven't been successful in completing initiation in any church, though, and I don't know that I'd call myself a religious person."

—"One place where I discovered stuff was being talked about was AA meetings. I'm not in AA, but I went to open meetings. . . . There's a certain amount of goo, and there's a certain amount of serious [stuff]. Like the fact that it takes enormous courage to appear weak. Hadn't heard that anywhere else. I was just starting to entertain the fact that that might be true."

As Wallace speaks, he holds before him a glass that slowly fills with a brown, foamy, beerlike liquid. He is chewing tobacco, first distorting his top lip with a mound of the stuff, then moving the hidden activity to a rear cavity, all the while spitting into the glass. This process goes on without much drama throughout the interview, in contrast to Wallace's conversation, which is impassioned and gentlemanly, as befits a former philosophy student. "Allow me to be defensive for a moment," he says at one point, talking about his use of irony.

Irony. It's the style of the 1990s, and many readers of *Infinite Jest* have used the word in describing Wallace's sensibility. Wallace has done an enormous amount of thinking on the subject, much of which he includes in "E Unibus Pluram," an essay about TV and fiction in *A Supposedly Fun Thing*. Irony and ridicule, he writes, "are agents of a great despair and stasis in US culture," and irony, once a rebel's weapon, has been co-opted and disempowered by pop culture. "Irony tyrannizes us," he writes. "All US irony is based on an implicit 'I don't really mean what I'm saying.'"

The centerpiece of our interview is Wallace's forty-five-minute light show on the dangers of irony in America. His fascinating theories extend from Socrates to David Letterman, whom Wallace calls "the archangel" of contemporary irony. "The particular kind of irony I'm talking about," he says, "when Letterman comes out and says, 'What a fine crowd,' and everybody roars with laughter, came about in the '60s." At that time, with writers like Ken Kesey, he says, irony was an appropriate response to a *Leave It to Beaver* world in need of being punctured.

But today's irony simply masks "terror of appearing sentimental or melodramatic or manipulative in all those old-fashioned ways," Wallace says, "while pretending that in itself the irony is not manipulative." It is rigorously used to sell products, and Wallace says he even finds himself "selling" himself with irony to his students at Illinois State. "All I have to do on the first day to get them to like me is I will call attendance and, in the middle, I will go, 'Bueller? Bueller?'" The reference to the 1986 movie *Ferris Bueller's Day Off*, he says, "shows that I'm conscious of the fact that as the teacher I am the dull-voiced authority figure and I am poking fun of it.

"It's OK, it's hip and it's cool and it's the language we speak. And yet it's also terrifying to me that my students have no idea the extent to which they are tyrannized by corporate culture. They're so tyrannized they're not aware that they're tyrannized. It's like being subjects of fascism and believing that you're in a democracy."

Wallace says he hates the thought of *Infinite Jest* being yoked in with the culture of cool irony and hip detachment. "I wanted to do something sad. . . . There are, I hope, ways in which the irony in the book is at least conscious enough of itself and its close relation to despair that it's not just another Isuzu commercial. You know, 'It's all just a joke, don't take me seriously,' which is so unbelievably easy and sells like sex."

With its wide acclaim, *Infinite Jest* appeared to be a shoo-in for the 1996 National Book Awards. That it was not even nominated became the focus of a controversy last year, and writers and critics used the snub of *Infinite Jest* to publicly air their concern about the awards and fiction in America.

"I'm going to tell you the truth, and it's going to sound like a Nixonian evasion," Wallace says. "I would have loved to have gotten nominated for the National Book Award. I would also love to win the Illinois State Lottery." He says that all the hype might have caused a backlash, and that the nominating committee may have been composed of people who don't like "avant-garde" fiction. The controversy, he says, had more to do with that schism in American fiction than with *Infinite Jest*.

Surprisingly, movie rights for *Infinite Jest* have been sold, he says. "I'm in the odd position of having taken the money and hoping that it doesn't get made. And I'm feeling confident it won't, since the chances for eighteen-hour movies are small, unless they wanted to dispense catheters upon entering the theater."

What is Wallace working on at the moment? "Right at this moment? Attempting to somehow be candid without exposing myself to ridicule." No, really, how does a writer follow up a novel like *Infinite Jest*? Wallace gives his most concise answer of the day: "That's one thing that I absolutely cannot talk about," he says.

David Foster Wallace

Tom Scocca/1998

From *Boston Phoenix*, 23 February 1998. © 1988 by the Phoenix Media/Communications Group. Reprinted by permission.

FEBRUARY 23, 1998: "I've never been considered Press before," writes David Foster Wallace at the beginning of his 1993 essay "Getting Away from Already Pretty Much Being Away from It All." That may be technically true; when *Harper's* sent Wallace to do the piece, for which he was issued press credentials and explored the Illinois State Fair, he went as a novelist on a lark. Still, reading that disclaimer now feels a bit like watching an ingénue fumble with a pool cue before running the table: the fifty-five-page piece, like most of the other six essays gathered in *A Supposedly Fun Thing I'll Never Do Again*, is a masterly example of nonfiction.

Wallace's reputation still rests mainly on his fiction, especially 1996's 1079-page *Infinite Jest* (Little, Brown). But the humor and intellectual deftness that made the thirty-five-year-old Wallace a hot young property in the world of literary novels—he won a MacArthur "genius" grant last year, and the words *virtuosity* and *brilliance* tend to tumble across his blurb pages— also make him a captivating reporter. The writing in *A Supposedly Fun Thing*, the 1997 collection of his magazine work now reissued in paperback, has the sort of conceptual and stylistic force that gets a writer talked about as a generational icon. The title essay, a ninety-six-page account (including 137 of Wallace's distinctive footnotes) of a seven-day Caribbean luxury cruise, has assumed epochal status; *Phoenix* book reviewer Jordan Ellenberg called another essay—the athlete profile "Tennis Player Michael Joyce's Professional Artistry as a Paradigm of Certain Stuff about Choice, Freedom, Discipline, Joy, Grotesquerie, and Human Completeness"—"the best piece of sports writing I have ever read."

In advance of the Boston reading on his *A Supposedly Fun Thing* paperback tour, he spoke to the *Phoenix* by phone from his home in Bloomington, Illinois.

Q: Okay, for basic reader orientation, are you doing this from Bloomington?
A: Yes, sir.

Q: Are you looking forward to seeing Boston?
A: Yeah. I was there last year, and I read at the Brattle Theatre. Last night I went and saw *Good Will Hunting*, which takes place not exactly where I used to live, in Boston, but pretty darn close, so I've been all flush with nostalgia for it. I was in Boston from summer of '89 until spring of '92.

Q: So what did you think of *Good Will Hunting*?
A: I think it's the ultimate nerd fantasy movie. It's a bit of a fairy tale, but I enjoyed it a lot. Minnie Driver is really to fall sideways for. And there's all kinds of cool stuff. It's actually a movie that's got calculus in it. It takes place in Boston.

One guy I talked to who saw it described it as a cross between *Ordinary People* and *The Computer Wore Tennis Shoes*. If you see it, you'll see that that's not un-germane. Do you remember *The Computer Wore Tennis Shoes*? It's got Kurt Russell. There's an electrical accident in the computer room when he's a student in some college. It's like the old sci-fi, toxic-accident-turns-him-into-Spiderman thing. These are great old computers, with like reel-to-reel tapes running back and forth, and it apparently injects him with every bit of data known to man, and he goes on College Bowl. You should check it out. Disney, I think '69, '70.

Q: How do the different kinds of writing differ for you, fiction versus nonfiction?
A: Golly. You know, I'm not a journalist and I don't pretend to be one, and most of the pieces in the book were assigned to me with these maddening instructions like, "Just go to a certain spot, and kind of turn 360 degrees a few times and tell us what you see."

I'll be honest: I think of myself as a fiction writer. Fiction's more important for me, so I'm more scared and tense about fiction, more worried about whether I'm any good or not. The weird thing is that when a couple of the nonfiction pieces got attention, then other magazines started to call. And then I start thinking of myself as doing that, too, and Mr. Ego gets in there and I begin worrying and sweating over that stuff.

Q: As you're getting more offers, are there things you don't want to write about?

A: Well, I've decided I'm not going to do any more nonfiction for a while, 'cause I'll use that as an excuse not to work on fiction. The funny thing is, I think magazines are all so desperate for stuff that—when was it? There was that really long piece about the cruise, and a version of it appeared in *Harper's*, and for I think about six days I was really hot with these editors. There was one offer to go to a nudist colony and write about being in a nudist colony, and there was one offer—Elizabeth Taylor was having the product launch of some new perfume, which bizarrely was being held at an Air Force base. There was an offer to interview David Bowie. I don't know anything about David Bowie. For a while there were all these offers and it was really neat. I took a couple that I thought were going to be kind of interesting to me, but most of them I just kind of laughed and said, Thanks anyway.

Q: There are several places around the book where you lay down a challenge to the editors—where you say that they probably won't like this, or they'll cut this. Were there some of those that didn't make it into the original magazine articles?

A: Well, the reason for doing the book—other than the fact that Little, Brown said they'd publish it, and I of course am a whore—is that this was the chance to do the long, original versions of these things that had gone through meat grinders in various magazines.

I'd worked really hard on these things, and then magazines sliced and diced them, and here was the chance to do kind of a director's cut. [Laughs.] You don't have to put in the thing about me being a whore—by which I simply meant it's just a big thrill to have a publishing company be willing to publish one of your books.

Q: How long was the initial version of the title essay [about the cruise], and how much writing time did that represent?

A: I always try to fool the magazine editors by sending stuff single-spaced, in eight-point font. Which of course insults them because they think, what, I think they're idiots? So then they call me up and get pissed and I send it back in twelve-point font, double-spaced. I think the cruise essay was about 110 pages, and it ended up getting cut just about in half. And every time I'd bitch and moan to *Harper's* they would say, Well, this is still going to be the longest thing we've ever put in *Harper's*. At which point I would have to shut up or look like an even bigger prima donna than I am.

But the cruise thing took almost three months to do, and then it took another two weeks—I had to go to New York and sit in a room with the editor. It was very exciting. Rewrote the ending like an hour before they had to wrap the magazine. It was like that moment in *Broadcast News* when Joan Cusack was having to run through the hallway to get the tape to Jack Nicholson in time to run it. Kind of like my peak moment in the magazine industry, and it was one I'll always remember.

Q: How do you handle being responsible for facts—after writing fiction, coming to a genre where the things you say have to be on some level verifiably true?
A: The thing is, really, between you and me and the *Boston Phoenix*'s understanding readers, you hire a fiction writer to do nonfiction, there's going to be the occasional bit of embellishment. Not to mention the fact that when people tell you stuff, very often it comes out real stilted, if you just write down exactly what they said. You sort of have to rewrite it so it sounds more out loud, which I think means putting in some *like*s or taking out punctuation that the person might originally have said. And I don't really make any apologies for that.

Q: Have you heard back from the people that you're writing about? Trudy [in "A Supposedly Fun Thing"] especially comes to mind—
A: [groan]

Q: —who you described as looking like—
A: That was a very, very bad scene, because they were really nice to me on the cruise and actually sent me a couple cards and were looking forward to the thing coming out, and then it came out, and I never heard from them again.
    The thing is, saying that somebody looks like Jackie Gleason in drag—it might not be very nice, but if you could have seen her, it was *true*. It was just absolutely true.
    One reason why I don't do a lot of these is that there's a real delicate balance between fucking somebody over and telling the truth to the reader. The Michael Joyce essay was really, really upsetting. It was originally commissioned by a different magazine, and I screwed up, because I really got to like this kid. There was some stuff that he told me and then asked me not to print, and I didn't. But I, dickhead that I am, made the mistake of telling the magazine this, and they ended up killing the piece.

One reason why I might have put in some not-particularly-kind stuff on the cruise is that I felt like I'd learned my lesson. I wasn't going to hurt anybody, but I was going to tell the truth. I couldn't worry so about Trudy's feelings that I couldn't say the truth, which was—you know, a terrific, really nice, and not unattractive lady who did happen to look just like Jackie Gleason in drag.

Q: Your footnotes have a way of making the reader break stride, or have to loop around and backtrack. How hard do you want the reader to have to work?
A: I don't really think that way, because I don't want to go down that path of trying to anticipate, like a chess player, every reader's reaction. The honest thing is, the footnotes were an intentional, programmatic part of *Infinite Jest*, and you get sort of addicted to them. A lot of these pieces were written around the time that I was typing and working on *Infinite Jest*. It's a kind of loopy way of thinking that it seems to me is in some ways mimetic.

I don't know about you, but certainly the way I think about things and experience things is not particularly linear, and it's not orderly, and it's not pyramidical, and there are a lot of loops.

Most of the nonfiction pieces are basically just: Look, I'm not a great journalist, and I can't interview anybody. But what I can do is slice open my head for you, and let you see a cross-section of an averagely bright person's head. And in a way, the footnotes I think are better representations of thought patterns and fact patterns.

The tricky thing with the footnotes is that they are an irritant, and they require a little extra work, and so they either have to be really germane or they have to be fun to read. It does get to be a problem, though, when every single gag that occurs to me, I think I can toss in as a footnote. The most heavily cut thing in the book was the David Lynch essay. The book editor had me cut like a third of it, and a lot of it was footnotes that were just gags. And I think he had a good point.

Q: How much gag writing do you do? To what extent do you try to be deliberately humorous?
A: [Sighs.] I'll tell you, I think another reason I'm not doing any more of these for a while is that by the end there really was kind of a schtick emerging: the somewhat neurotic, hyperconscious guy showing you how weird this thing is that not everybody thinks is weird. I think it's more trying to notice stuff that everybody else notices but they don't really notice that they notice. Which I think a fair number of good comedians do, too.

Q: I mean, when you have something like the oil rigs "bobbing fellatially" . . .
A: Yeah, except that's exactly how it looks.

Q: That is exactly how they look, but it's funny enough to . . .
A: But that was another big fight, 'cause I originally had *fellatically*, which I thought sounded better and had more of a kind of harsh, glottal, fellatiatory sound, and then the copyeditor goes, "There's no such word, we've got to say *fellatially*," and I think that sounds like *palatially*, and I don't like it, and so forty-eight hours is spent thumb-wrestling over this bullshit.

Q: You said there was a period of time, like six days, when you were really hot with magazine editors. How's the whole pendulum of fame swinging?
A: The degree of fame we're talking about here—getting hot as a writer for six days is equivalent to a fan base of, like, a local TV weatherman, right? Magazines are certainly not calling every day to ask me to do stuff anymore, which to be honest is something of a relief, 'cause there's other stuff I'm working on.

I've been doing this since the mid-'80s, and so, since the mid-'80s, I've watched I don't know how many writers get hot and then not get hot, and then get hot again, and then not get hot. A lot of it is just the peristalsis of the industry. The industry, I think, is so pressed, and so anxious to create heat and buzz around specific people. It's the same way movies are, the same way music is, although the amount of money at stake in books is vanishingly small. It's nice when the phone doesn't ring as much, and it's not very good for me when people treat me like a big shot, because then I get puffed up inside. But other than that, it doesn't really make much difference.

Q: How big does the big-shot treatment get?
A: I remember giving a reading at a bookstore in Harvard Square. It was December of '91, and *Harper's* had this whole idea that they were going to put on these readings. The *Harper's* PR person came to Boston, and I came and I gave a reading, and nobody showed up. There was a snowstorm, but the basic point is, nobody showed up. So me and the PR guy went out and ate, like, three pieces of cake each and apologized to each other for three hours.

So, being used to that kind of stuff, giving a reading in New York and having some people not be able to get in is weird, and it makes you feel like you're a big shot. Temporarily. The Sauron-like eye of the culture passes over you, like in *Lord of the Rings*. You're old enough to know *Lord of the Rings*. A bitchingly good read, I think.

Q: Are there any nonfiction writers who've inspired your work?

A: Ever since I was in college, I've been an enormous fan of both Joan Didion and Pauline Kael. And, I don't know . . . I think prosewise, Pauline Kael is unequaled. Maybe John McPhee, at his very best, is as good. I don't know what influence they have, but in terms of just being a slobbering fan of . . . Frank Conroy's first book, Tobias Wolff's *This Boy's Life*. Oh, God, there's a book by a mathematician named Hardy at Oxford called *A Mathematician's Apology*. Hardy gets mentioned in *Good Will Hunting*, by the way. Anyway. There are quite a few that are just really, really, really, really good. But I'd say Pauline Kael is the best. Annie Dillard's really good, but she's much more sort of restrained.

Q: There's one other thing that I wanted to ask you about, which was the relationship between footnotes and hypertext.

A: I've had people say that, and I would love them to think that there's some grand theory. I sometimes use a computer to type when I've got a lot of corrections to do, but I don't have a modem, I've never been on the Internet. There's a guy in my department who teaches hypertext, but I don't really know anything about it.

Q: You do your stuff by typewriter?

A: I mostly typewrite. Some of the magazine stuff I did on disk, because you learn that the magazines very often will ask for a disk. And there's this great term they use: they say, Well, we'll just take the disk and *massage* it. I still can't get them to be entirely clear what "massage" means. I guess it means, like, changing the formats or something. I think it's a terrific term to use for a disk.

But basically, I can type and I can save stuff onto disk, and that's just about it, in terms of computers. I feel like an old fogy.

Good luck on this. You're going to exceed whatever word limit, I'll bet.

Q: Yeah. Well, we're just going to take the whole tape and, you know, cut it down into something that—

A: Just massage the tape.

Q: We're going to massage the tape.

A: Cool.

David Foster Wallace: In the Company of Creeps

Lorin Stein/1999

From *Publishers Weekly*, 3 May 1999. © 1999 by PWxyz. Reprinted by permission.

"It wasn't till I saw the galleys that I noticed how horrific this stuff was." Sunday evening in Normal, Illinois, David Foster Wallace and *PW* are lost somewhere near the lingerie department of the local Kmart, on the lookout for audiocassettes, and Wallace is taking this unforeseen pre-interview delay to air a couple of last-minute reservations about the *PW* interview process. "Am I expected to have insight or opinions about the publishing industry?" Wallace freezes mid-aisle, for maybe the third time in two minutes, as if he might bolt for the check-out. "Because what I know about the publishing industry could be inscribed with a dry Magic Marker on the lip of a Coke bottle."

The author of *Infinite Jest* (Little, Brown, 1996)—the 1079-page, heavily annotated tome that has already done as much as any single book this decade to change the sound and aims of American fiction—is wearing calf-high duckboots (jeans tucked in), a nylon backpack, and a tortoiseshell hairband too small for his head. The combination of duckboots and hairband, not to mention stubble and granny glasses, and Wallace's all-around largeness (he stoops at about 6'2"), gives him a demeanor that's both endearingly little girlish and hard to synthesize. He has the look of a man who needs a bobby pin.

In person, Wallace doesn't resemble his author photos—and the skittish but basically cheerful—looking guy next to the Martha Stewart Home Furnishings display simply does not look anything like anyone who could have just written his latest collection, *Brief Interviews with Hideous Men*, just out from Little, Brown, a cycle of darkly comic stories, peopled by sexual predators and spiritual bankrupts, in which rape and masturbation make a mockery of romantic love; family attachments are measured by the damage they do; and even the story titles ("Adult World," "A Radically Condensed History of Postindustrial Life") dare readers to exempt themselves from the nightmarishness of Wallace's vision.

In the brief q&a pieces, scattered through the collection, that give the book its title, a female interviewer interrogates a series of creepy men about their relationships with women. Although we never hear her questions, only their answers, Wallace thinks of her as the book's protagonist. "Something bad happens to her over the course of the book," Wallace says, sitting over a post-Kmart burger in a nearby diner, "like something *really* bad."

Chewing to smithereens one toothpick after another (he quit smoking mid-February), Wallace is quick to agree that *Brief Interviews* is his most disturbing work. "I had no idea quite how upsetting the book was going to be, or that friends would see it as reflecting things that were going on with me—which, if that's true, then I'm the literary equivalent of the person who writes 'Help me' on the mirror without knowing it."

Wallace says he never planned to write the fictional interviews that lend the book its title and tone. He just sat down one week and "four or five came out." The challenge of writing in the q&a form amused him at first. It was a trick he had attempted but never mastered in *Infinite Jest*. Soon he found himself revisiting other unfinished business from the novel.

That business wasn't formal, but thematic. Set in and around a Boston of the near future, *Infinite Jest* unfolds mostly in an elite tennis academy and, a few blocks away, in a halfway house for recovering drug addicts. Over the course of the novel, as the kids and grownups cross each other's paths, Wallace paints the diorama of a country in which every form of pleasure or desire, from sports and TV to human relationships, threatens to turn into a need, where the pursuit of happiness masks a near-universal despair.

Wallace claims that the novel's "sadness-and-addiction stuff" came from his observations of the culture of AA when he lived in Boston during his late twenties. "Boston has open AA meetings and these things are fascinating. You see for the most part privileged people who, through their own inability to preserve autonomy in the face of available pleasure, have ruined their lives and look like Dachau survivors. That is what *Infinite Jest* is about, in one sense, but at the same time I only came up with this afterwards, in interviews, when I was trying to construct some kind of halfway truthful narrative about why I wrote what I wrote."

In retrospect, Wallace says, he was unsatisfied with the character of Orin

Incandenza, the novel's closest thing to a sex addict. Incandenza, a football hero, drifts through *Infinite Jest* seducing women who remind him of his mother. "Much was made of Orin's sexual behavior, but in the novel it never coalesced. I remember making this connection and beginning to write more of the 'interviews' with that in mind. But it wasn't till I saw the galleys [for the new book] that I noticed how horrific this stuff was. The scary thing is that these last few years have been for the most part very nice and very quiet, though discomfiting in certain ways." Wallace characterizes the public reception of both *Infinite Jest* and a followup essay collection, *A Supposedly Fun Thing I'll Never Do Again* (Little, Brown, 1997) as a "schizophrenia of attention." And although "schizophrenia" is a strong word, at thirty-seven years old Wallace clearly keeps his career as one of his generation's most revered literary experimenters separate from his private life teaching English at Illinois State, just down the highway from his parents' home in Urbana. Details of that private life are largely off the record, although he does acknowledge a "solid, monogamous, good relationship" with a "really cool person" and ownership of a dog who's "pretty close to clinically depressed." (Ever since the *New York Times Magazine* published the contents of Wallace's medicine cabinet, he has declared his house off-limits to the press.)

Wallace is especially reticent about his late twenties and early thirties when, following the publication of his first two books, he struggled with depression and substance abuse, years when nothing he wrote came to fruition, but during which time *Infinite Jest* ("a six-year novel that got written in three years") was taking shape. He claims not to understand the attention that reporters have paid to his postadolescent personal problems: "It's a miracle that Little, Brown found people who gave a shit about any of that stuff." At its funniest, Wallace's fiction satirizes misery and isolation as conditions that are, essentially, boring, unworthy of the self. In the same way, Wallace seems honestly to find his career as a writer not just easier to talk about, but more interesting than his demons.

The son of a grammarian mother and a father who studied with Wittgenstein's student and biographer Norman Malcolm, Wallace planned to follow in his father's footsteps as a philosopher. But in his junior year at Amherst College, he took time off "mostly to drive a schoolbus in Urbana"; when he returned to Amherst the next year, his best friends were already preparing to graduate. One of them had persuaded the administration to let him write a piece of fiction as part of his senior thesis. Friendless in his own senior year, Wallace followed suit.

The result was the first draft of *The Broom of the System*—a ribald, sophisticated novel about unrequited love, a corrupt psychiatrist and disappearing senior citizens, that incorporated Thomas Pynchon's sense of slapstick and big chunks of Wittgenstein's philosophy of language, and won Wallace a generous fellowship in the University of Arizona's graduate writing program. Wallace took the fellowship, but not without backward glances at logic and semantics. (In 1989 he enrolled as a Ph.D. candidate in Harvard's philosophy program, but dropped out after a semester.)

At Arizona Wallace almost got thrown out by hard-line realists who "aggressively disliked" his writing and combative classroom manner ("I was a prick"), but was taken up by San Francisco agent Bonnie Nadell. Today Nadell is one of four readers with whom Wallace shares new work. "Bonnie and I have very different tastes, but when something really sucks, she'll tell me so that it doesn't make me want to jump off a bridge."

Wallace credits Nadell with a "Phil Spector" instinct for pairing him with the right editors. The first of these was Gerry Howard, who acquired *Broom* for Viking in 1986 and "under whose stern tutelage (thank God) the novel was written again." According to Wallace, he hasn't always been easy to edit. "I learned some stuff from Gerry, but I didn't listen to him, and *Girl*"—Wallace's first story collection, *Girl with Curious Hair*—"was my comeuppance."

This comeuppance wasn't purely artistic (although Wallace says certain stories in that collection now strike him as "wildly narcissistic"); it was legal. Wallace based one of the collection's stories, about *The Letterman Show*, on an actual Letterman appearance by the actress Susan Saint James—and neglected to mention the fact to Howard or to the *New American Library* legal team. ("I don't know why. I was twenty-six, for God's sake, I should have known better. I just didn't think it mattered.") When NBC happened to rerun the Saint James spot, two weeks before *Playboy* closed the issue in which the story was due to run, *Playboy* panicked. Viking's lawyers then started looking at the collection and found even more cause for alarm in another story, involving real-life game show hosts Merv Griffin, Pat Sajak, and Alex Trebek. Already in galleys, *Girl* was dropped from Viking's list. Meanwhile, says Wallace, he was sending the lawyers "these involved philosophical letters. I was clueless, and I was scared because I thought this was the best work I was ever going to do. I'll owe Gerry for life for bringing it to Norton."

Which is what Howard (joining an exodus of Viking editors under NAL management) did. Wallace says he could have stayed with Howard at Norton, but "unfortunately, Norton did not authorize him to pay out advances sufficient to allow people to live," so when Wallace had written half of *Infinite Jest*, Nadell sold the book to Michael Pietsch, at Little, Brown.

Pietsch's work on *Infinite Jest* is already widely celebrated. Wallace praises not just the laser-surgical feat of cutting "two or three hundred pages" from a novel full of microscopic subplots and cross-references, but Pietsch's diplomacy as he shuttled between marketers, who worried over the novel's size, and Wallace, whose "big hope was that two or three thousand people would read the book.

"This wasn't a matter of liking my editor. We don't mix socially: I'm nervous around Michael; he's an authority figure for me. But I feel like I know him, and I trust him, and that's priceless."

Brief Interviews owes its own debt to Pietsch, who helped arrange the rest of the book's material to emphasize the arc of the "interviews" themselves, and to echo Q's descent into what Wallace—a child of atheists who has twice "flunked out" of Catholic instruction—only half-joking, calls "the spiritual emptiness of heterosexual interaction in postmodern America." But even though Wallace insists that *Brief Interviews* is more than just a collection, and admits that certain stories in it were difficult to write, he claims it was an easier book to walk away from than *Infinite Jest*.

"Novels are like marriages," Wallace says, taking another toothpick from the box he carries in his backpack. "You have to get into the mood to write them-not because of what writing them is going to be like, but because it's so sad to end them. When I finished my first book, I really felt like I'd fallen in love with my main character and that she'd died. You have to understand, writing a novel gets very weird and invisible-friend-from-childhood-ish, then you kill that thing, which was never really alive except in your imagination, and you're supposed to go buy groceries and talk to people at parties and stuff. Characters in stories are different. They come alive in the corners of your eyes.

"You don't have to live with them."

David Foster Wallace Warms Up

Patrick Arden/1999

From *Book*, July–August 1999. © 1999 by Patrick Arden. Reprinted by permission.

In which a (not too) brief interview with the author leads to his requesting a shrimp from a previously barred photographer.

After all the attention David Foster Wallace received following the surprising success of his 1996 novel, *Infinite Jest*, he's dedicated to protecting his privacy. Responses to the 1,079 -page social satire and human tragedy—which famously included 388 endnotes—were overwhelmingly positive. He was described as "brilliant" (*Kirkus Reviews*), "a genius" (*Chicago Tribune*), and "the funniest writer of his generation" (*Village Voice*). Wallace followed his celebrated epic with a 1997 collection of nonfiction "essays and arguments," *A Supposedly Fun Thing I'll Never Do Again*, and for the next two years he continued to show up regularly in magazines as mainstream as *Elle* and *Spin*. Journalists even waxed rhapsodic about his publicity photo, as if it were the very picture of his age—an unshaven young man lost in thought, a bandanna wrapped around his long hair like a bandage protecting a head wound.

Do Not Disturb

Now, the thirty-seven-year-old Wallace, a professor at Illinois State University in Bloomington-Normal, has warned me that his unlisted telephone number will be good for only another month, when he'll have it changed. "My number has a shelf life of one year," he says. "Then some weird thing happens where I end up getting calls from people that I don't want to get calls from. So you draw the circle in again." His girlfriend has just moved into his house, but they've made a pact not to discuss each other's work. He defends that bargain as a necessary measure to guard their intimacy.

When I first call, he picks up the phone as I'm leaving a message on his machine, and immediately starts laying down ground rules for the interview. First, no photos. "Little, Brown has like twelve different shots of me— can't you use one of those?" he pleads. "I'm tired of having my picture taken." And he doesn't want to meet at his house; instead he directs me to a Cracker Barrel restaurant just off the I-55 interchange in Bloomington. His instructions are painstakingly detailed.

Brief Interviews with Hideous Men, the book we're to discuss, is a collection of Wallace's short fiction. The title is taken from a series of one-sided conversations in which men discuss their problems with the opposite sex. The questions of the female interrogator are deleted.

The men's troubles range from the comic to the frightening. One can't stop shouting "Victory for the forces of democratic freedom!" while ejaculating during sex. An abuser seeks counseling for the sake of his own self-esteem. Another makes the case that a woman can actually benefit from rape or incest ("Her idea of herself and what she can live through and survive is bigger now."). A man with a disfigured arm relates how he uses his deformity to persuade women to sleep with him. He preys on their guilt ("Sometimes they get me crying too"), and he refers to his shriveled appendage as the Asset."

Wallace says he's uneasy discussing the book. "I said I'd be happy to talk to you, but I have no idea what to say, simply because there isn't really an agenda with this book, except for a certain amount of technical, formal stuff that I don't know if I want to talk about and I don't think people really want to hear about."

By the time of our conversation, Wallace had relented on his prohibition against photos. So when I pull up to the Cracker Barrel, I have a photographer in tow. Wallace is immediately recognizable: A husky, unshaven fellow in a leather jacket and a University of Iowa jersey sits in a rocking chair on the restaurant's front porch. Wallace frets that the restaurant's manager will object to our taking pictures inside and refuses to pose near an antique Coke machine. "No one will believe that," he says. After the photographer snaps a few shots, Wallace relaxes.

"I don't know if you've ever enjoyed Cracker Barrel before," he says, leading the way inside. The restaurant is fronted by a gift shop, with shelves full of ceramic figurines and jars of jams and sauces. The air is thick with the smell of soap and potpourri. A variety of farm implements hang from the ceiling. A mechanical toy pig grunts, "Let me out of here."

"It's easy to make fun of," he says, "but the food is really pretty good."

Our table is in the middle of a teeming dining room, halfway between the kitchen and the toilet. Wallace, whose new book includes an acknowledgment to "the staff and management of Denny's 24-Hour Family Restaurant," feels at home in such places. He opens a tiny cardboard box and places a pile of toothpicks on the table. He explains that he's trying to stop smoking, and chewing toothpicks beats his previous solution—chewing tobacco.

"We're attempting a new regime here," he says. "You guys get in a toothpick mood, please feel free to partake. I think it's easy to stop smoking; it's just hard not to commit a felony after you stop. I have like one-tenth the temper speed that I used to. I have road rage, phone rage. If I was snappish with you, I apologize. My girlfriend said I was, and then I snapped at her for telling me that I was."

As we peruse the menu, Wallace advises, "Get something nice and generic—there's no way you can go wrong." He says he's ordering the meatloaf dinner, though he objects when I attempt to follow suit. "If you get the meatloaf and don't like it, you could blame me."

Normal Life

Wallace grew up in downstate Illinois, the son of schoolteachers. His father is a philosophy professor at the University of Illinois at Urbana-Champaign; his mother teaches English. He says he has a younger sister but hesitates when it comes to discussing his background in detail: "It was a very kind of quiet, semi-nerdy life in a mid-sized academic town in Illinois. I don't mind telling you about it. I'm just highly aware that it's not very interesting or dramatic."

He graduated summa cum laude from Amherst College in 1985, having studied philosophy, his father's subject. He turned to fiction writing in his senior year, when he helped published a humor magazine and earned money doing term papers for hire. "It was really good training for writing in different voices and styles—you'll get kicked out if you get caught," he says.

Wallace ended up getting his master's degree in fine arts from the University of Arizona. "Then I sort of drifted for a while," he says. "I lived in Boston and New York for like five years before I moved back." He came to Bloomington-Normal to take a part-time job at Dalkey Archive Press, which had made its reputation resurrecting out-of-print works by early-modern writers, including Gertrude Stein and Louis-Ferdinand Celine.

"I don't do well in big cities," Wallace says. "It's not the cities' fault—it's mine. I can't stand noise, and I like to choose how many people are within a hundred feet of me at any given time. A lot of my college friends are in New York, and when they come here, they can't stay more than a few days. It creeps them out—it's very boring. But I'm alarmingly happy. I just want to be left alone to eat my meatloaf.

"I have a lot of advantages. I live in small town. If anybody wants to talk to me, they have to drive a long way and come to shitty restaurants."

By the time he moved back to Illinois, Wallace had already published two well-received books: the 1987 novel *The Broom of the System* and the 1989 short-story collection *Girl with Curious Hair.* But for better or for worse, his reputation may now rest on his big book—*Infinite Jest.* Fans found his digressive method perfectly captured a world saturated by data, while his detractors claimed he was reckless in his plotting and loquacious to a fault. Yet his verbosity came as part and parcel of a potent world view—the new realities of media hype and information overload have not exactly made people happier.

Wallace's editor at Little, Brown, Michael Pietsch, has said he was initially intimidated by the sheer size of the novel. "I had no clue how the characters connected, except they were either doing drugs or playing tennis," he admitted in one interview. Eventually Pietsch decided to turn the book's length into a dare: "Have you finished David Foster Wallace's gargantuan masterpiece?" A Little, Brown sales representative told me, "We put more effort and money behind marketing that book than we ever had before . . . and it paid off."

"It's a good book," Wallace says, a little defensively. "But it's a difficult long book and there's no reason why it should have gotten that kind of attention. Much of the attention was hype attention rather than literary attention, and so it didn't get to me all that much. The book is partly about hype and sort of the spiritual consequences of hype, and then the book itself became an object of hype. For a while I was amused by the irony, and then it just kind of made me feel empty."

He doesn't expect to receive the same attention for *Brief Interviews with Hideous Men.* "I kind of hope that this will just be a normal mid-list book," he says. "Maybe you, a couple other people will want to talk about it, and that will be it. I don't know that I'm quite up for another circus.

Brief Interviews

In *Brief Interviews with Hideous Men* Wallace was obviously concerned with form. The book's architecture may come off as somewhat precious and picky: titles recur, characters carefully dissect their own emotions, every idea or feeling is fastidiously annotated. ("I've got to keep myself amused," he says. "It's late at night when I'm typing.")

One story is split in half: "Adult World I" concerns a young, sexually naïve newlywed; "Adult World II" continues her story, but the narrative breaks down into a diagram as the main character becomes more sophisticated and alienated from her passions and Wallace allows the reader a glimpse into the very mechanics of storytelling. "There's a certain amount of formal stunt pilotry in the book," he explains. "I as a reader don't like stunt pilotry if it doesn't have much of a reason. The big reason to have 'Adult World II' in outline form is that for myself as a reader I don't buy epiphanies done dramatically anymore. You know: 'She gazed out the window. Suddenly, the revelation hit her face.' I begin wincing when I'm reading shit like that. I don't think readers can buy epiphanies anymore . . . I like stuff that's moving, but I don't want to be perceived as manipulative, and I don't like to be manipulative. So some of the stories that look the weirdest at least were designed to try to access emotional stuff in a different way. It's maybe easier to swallow. Or, to be more honest, it's easier for me to write about, where I don't feel like I'm being that, you know, *Bridges of Madison County* guy.

"We're real good at recognizing when somebody's fumbling at our emotions like they were a bra," he says, pulling his hands to his chest, his fingers clenched in an arthritic grip. The diners at the next table sing "Happy Birthday."

The waiter sets down our plates—slabs of meat and mashed potatoes smothered in brown gravy. Wallace eagerly picks up a fork and inquires about the photographer's breaded shrimp. "I've never had it," he says. "I've come close a couple times."

Wallace says he's been surprised by the reaction the new book has received so far. "Some friends who've read the thing have come back and said, 'Man, there has got to be a part of you that's a pretty serious misogynist because you do misogyny pretty well.' I don't know what to tell them. If you do a convincing thing about a serial killer, does that mean you have murder in your heart? Well, maybe, I guess . . . More than the average person? I don't know."

He sighs and shakes his head. "There's no denying it—this is pretty sad. One of my friends said, 'Everyone is so completely fucking doomed in this,' because they are. They have a reasonable sense of what's going on and they're very self-aware. God knows they're self-conscious. And yet they're trapped."

He rejects criticism that his work is unnecessarily complicated: "I don't have any strong feelings about that, unless if somebody says, 'You know, Dave, I read your book and it seems like it required all this hard work just basically for the sake of saying, "Hey fuck you, reader, I can make you work hard."' Then I know with that reader I have failed. Then I really feel that they think I'm a putz. And I hate books where, you know, those books where you get halfway through and you get the sense that the author is so stupid that he thinks he can fool you into thinking that the book is really sophisticated and profound just because it's difficult. It's an epidemic in academic writing. And it happens about half the time in avant-garde writing. And it's the thing I most fear as a writer because it's the thing I most hate as a reader. And I'm sure I'm guilty of it sometimes."

Wallace says he continues teaching part-time not for the money—he only makes seventeen thousand dollars a year doing it—but because "it is real good for my work. If I am by myself for like a week, I get weird. Teaching forces me to talk to other people." He glances at the photographer's shrimp. "Is that all right? Not a little heavy on the breading?"

The 1991 edition of *Contemporary Authors* shows a twentysomething Wallace, looking earnest, or at least clean shaven. Under "Religion," it says "Catholic," and after "Politics" it lists the "Communist Party of the United States." Seven years later, his entry lists no religion or political persuasion.

Wallace explains that he tried to join the Catholic Church twice, once in the mid-'80s and again in the early '90s. "I've gone through RCIA (Right of Christian Initiation for Adults) a couple of times, but I always flunk the period of inquiry. They don't really want inquiries. They really just want you to learn responses," he says. "My parents are atheists of the '60s brand. You know, religion for them equals central suppression from authority. But their parents—so my grandparents—were very, very religious. My grandmother was basically raised in a convent. . . . I think religion kind of skips a genera-tion. Most of my best friends are religious in a way that's cool, where you don't even know it for several years. They're not the type to show up at your door with a pamphlet under their arms. You know, I enjoy church and I en-joy being part of a larger thing. I think it's just not in my destiny to be part of an institutional religion, because it's not in my nature to take certain things on faith."

He peers once again at the photographer's dinner. "Could I just have one shrimp?" he asks.

"America is one big experiment in what happens when you're a wealthy, privileged culture that's pretty much lost religion or spirituality as a real informing presence. It's still a verbal presence—it's part of the etiquette that our leaders use, but it's not inside us anymore, which in one way makes us very liberal and moderate and we're not fanatics and we don't tend to go around blowing things up. But on the other hand, it's very difficult to think that the point of life is to double your salary so that you can go to the mall more often. Even when you're making fun and sneering at it, there's a real dark emptiness about it."

Wallace sits up straight in his chair and pushes his plate away. "That's simply my opinion as a private citizen—I don't know that it has all that much to do with the stuff that I write about."

A Supposedly Fun Thing

Wallace turns to the photographer. "This has got to be boring for you," he says. "Try this game." He picks up a triangular piece of wood with pegs jammed into several holes. It's been provided by the restaurant, right next to the salt and pepper shakers. "I want to see if somebody else can do this. It's sort of like checkers. You try to jump one thing over another thing. Whatever you jump, you can take out. The object is to be left with only one.

"I am not good at this. All I've figured out is that you have got to keep the fuckers close together, or else things get very dicey." He notices our reluctance. "It will be fun."

Instead, we order dessert.

"Should we talk about you guys' jobs now?" Wallace asks.

Finally, the check comes.

"Well, this hasn't hurt at all," he says. "It was easy."

Back in the gift shop, Wallace says, "The thing to realize is how fast this will move across everybody's brain but yours and mine. You'll care about the story, and I'll care about the story. Everybody else, like people in dentist offices . . ." He shakes his head but then thinks better of it. "That doesn't mean you don't have an obligation to the truth." I thank him for the advice. The piece is supposed to be short.

"How long?"

A couple thousand words.

"Oh, Christmas! Just take out all the articles."

We walk out into the parking lot, and Wallace puts his hand on my shoulder.

"I'll be interested to see what you do with it." He smiles. "Compression has never been my forte."

Mischief: A Brief Interview
with David Foster Wallace

Chris Wright/1999

From *Boston Phoenix*, 3–10 June 1999. © 1999 by the Phoenix Media/Communications Group. Reprinted by permission.

Don't expect to find any rakishly charming Don Juans in David Foster Wallace's new collection of fiction, *Brief Interviews with Hideous Men*. More neurotic than erotic, the book delves (with some glee, we might add) into the mire of modern romance through a series of fictional Q&As. With characteristic flair, Wallace subverts the form by omitting the questions, marking their absence with a Q. We caught up with Wallace in New York, a day after he read to a packed house at the Harvard Film Archive, and found him to be tired and full-bladdered, but not at all hideous. In the spirit of his book, however, we adopted the *Brief Interview* format for our ten-minute discussion.

Q:
A: What do you mean?

Q:
A: Not suffering fools gladly is a euphemism for being hostile and snapping at people, and I can't remember ever having done that.

Q:
A: Yes, no. The thing is, sometimes you're concerned with Q&As being boring, so it's tempting to make sport of people just to keep things interesting. That can be mean. I think I perhaps do that.

Q:
A: I think, um, the car crash is less important than turning to your friends and seeing the expressions on their faces. And them seeing the expression on your face. I'm more a reactor than a spectator. Does that make any sense?

Q:
A: No, I'm glad you're being honest. We left [Boston] at six o'clock this morning. I feel that people are asking perfectly reasonable questions and I'm just ranting. Feel free to cut out major nouns.

Q:
A: Between you and me, it'll be closer to fifteen, 'cause the next guy's not calling till 5:30. Actually fourteen, 'cause I need to piss.

Q:
A: I don't think it's really quite the same as being unable to walk down the street without girls trying to tear your shirt off.

Q:
A: No, the test is actually how many of them read it.

Q:
A: That's very nice of you, and I applaud your discernment and all that. The stuff that I cut my teeth on, the stuff that I really like to read, struck me as being challenging but also just fun as hell. I think a lot of avant-garde stuff in the U.S. has lost touch with the fun—you know, has flown up its own butt.

Q:
A: Say the quote again.

Q:
A: Ha!

Q:
A: At first when people said that about *Infinite Jest* it hurt my feelings. All writers want everybody to love them. But, you know, for me to do what I do and have some people like it—that's going to have to be enough. When reviewers structure entire reviews around how fatigued they were when they

tried to slog through the book—yeah, that hurts my feelings, and I think they're being peckerheads.

Q:

A: Oh no, I'm not talking about you.

Q:

A: Attention is not the same thing as affection. I've finally figured that out. Anyway, my bladder begs. Is this gonna be enough? Okay. I apologize for any incoherence. Feel free to edit it however you like.

Behind the Watchful Eyes
of Author David Foster Wallace

Mark Shechner/2000

From *Buffalo News*, 10 September 2000. © 2000 by Mark Shechner and the *Buffalo News*.
Reprinted by permission.

From a certain point of view, that of raw Mozartian virtuosity, Wallace might honestly be called the best young writer in America. For pungent phrase, performative strategy, unpredictability, hurricane force, risk-for-risk's-sake bravado, and back-of-the-envelope improvisation, he stands out among his contemporaries. Young as novelists go, thirty-eight, Wallace has published five books: *The Broom of the System* (novel, 1987), *Girl with Curious Hair* (stories, 1989) a massive novel *Infinite Jest* (1996), a collection of essays and commissioned travel pieces, *A Supposedly Fun Thing I'll Never Do Again* (1997), and a grab bag of stories and psychiatric interviews, *Brief Interviews with Hideous Men* (1999). Reviewing *Infinite Jest* in 1996, I described it as "a Godzilla of a novel, 1079 pages of drug and rehab lore, high-tech razzle-dazzle, social comedy, hallucination, millenarian prophecy, terrorist hugger mugger, paramilitary simulation, psychic dysfunction and neural calamity, and tennis." *Interviews* is a mixture of strange short stories and apparently transcribed interviews, surveillance reports on romantically challenged men who may be under a therapist's care or under police custody or under lock and key.

Born in Ithaca, New York, and raised in Champaign-Urbana, Illinois, Wallace is the son of academic parents, his father being a professor of philosophy at the University of Illinois. He has called his childhood uneventful, and he writes of having been a youthful tennis prodigy. But there have been lost years, about which Wallace does not speak, though they pop up in his writing through his fascination with the worlds of mortal pain, powerful obsession, neural trauma, and addiction.

To have read any of Wallace's work is to encounter a feverish and Joyce-like grapple with language, a deep psychological penetration into extreme mental states, a doctor's knowledge of arcane pharmacology, a finely tuned awareness of elaborate maneuver, a theoretical sophistication about film, television, and video, and an outrageous sense of humor. (When the father of the main character of the novel *Infinite Jest* commits suicide by poaching his head in the family microwave, his older son comes into the house saying, "Something smells delicious.")

I spoke to Wallace by telephone on August 15 and explained my rule that we talk only about writing, not personal matters, and that he was free to direct the interview as he liked.

WALLACE: My rule is that no really interesting question can be broached and answered in a forum this fast, and so after a whole lot of head clutching about these things what I do is rant in response to questions and then offer the questioner the freedom he wants anyway, which is to edit my answers any way he wants. Concision is not my strength.

SHECHNER: One thing I admire in your writing is point-blank observation, the watching and the listening. You write in "E Unibus Plurum" essay (about television and its creation of reality, in *Fun Thing*): "Fiction writers tend to be oglers. They tend to lurk and to stare. They are born watchers. They are the ones on the subway about whose nonchalant stare there is something creepy, somehow. Almost predatory. This is because human situations are writers' food. Fiction writers watch other humans sort of the way gapers slow down for car wrecks: they covet a vision of themselves as witnesses."
WALLACE: This is not particularly new. There is the anecdote about all Jane Austen's friends being terrified to talk around her because they knew they would end up in a book. I'm not sure how fiction and poetry work, but part of it is that really we notice a lot more than we notice we notice. A particular job of fiction is not so much to note things for people but rather to wake readers up to how observant they already are, and that's why for me as a reader the descriptions or just toss offs that I like the most are not the ones that seem utterly new but the ones that have that eerie "good Lord I've noticed that too but have never even taken a moment to articulate to myself."

SHECHNER: That puts me in mind of a character in E. L. Doctorow's *The Book of Daniel*, who refers to himself as a "criminal of perception," as though watching people is an act of cruelty. You remind me of the great literary lurkers, like Vladimir Nabokov or Saul Bellow. Do you think of your observing as cruel?

WALLACE: It depends on whether it is based on something real and what the purpose is. The culture since the mid-'70s and early '80s has become much more conscious of the phenomenon of watching and the arrangements between performers and audiences. While there is nothing different in the act of watching, I think public behavior now is much more conscious of being watched, and there is an element of display that changes the equation between the watcher and the watched, eliminating the last bits of voyeurism that used to be attached to aesthetic watching.

SHECHNER: In a number of places, particularly in *Hideous Men*, you've got characters involved in erotic situations who are also at the same time acting out scenes from books or films. There's a young woman in a piece called "Think." It is a bedroom situation, and the man imagines that her expression is from the Victoria's Secret catalog. "She is, he thinks, the sort of woman who'd keep her heels on if he asked her to. Even if she'd never kept heels on before she'd give him a knowing, smoky smile, Page 18. . . . The languid half-turn and push of the door are tumid with some kind of significance; he realizes she's replaying a scene from some movie she loves."

WALLACE: That's complicated, because that's the guy watching her and interpreting, more or less guessing, that she is putting on a performance, so there is an extra element of creepiness. The whole watching/being watched, display/reception of display stuff gets complicated and probably creepier when you are in a sexual situation. *Brief Interviews* is the only book in which I've explored that kind of sexuality.

SHECHNER: In *Brief Interviews* and elsewhere, you show a fascination with the symptomatic life, the involuntary life, such as the vignette in *Brief Interviews* in which a character, at the moment of orgasm, cries out, "Victory for the forces of Democratic Freedom," or the man who abandons a woman, claiming that he wants to put to rest her fear that he will abandon her. So much of this sounds like excerpts from a therapist's notebook, or as if a fly on the wall of an analyst's office heard it all and was reporting it back as a comedy of neurosis. How did these scenarios get developed in your mind?

WALLACE: That cycle of interviews is hard to talk about briefly, although for the purposes of your questions I would say that these are not events taking place but events that are being related to an interlocutor, and in fact a hostile one, so that there is a blur between how much of the stuff is involuntary and how much is the rhetoric of the presentation, because as far as I can see the one thing that most of these men have in common is an unconscious genius for self-presentation and self-defense. They try to anticipate how they are going to be interpreted and head it off, which seems to me to be not all the different from ordinary discourse between the sexes.

SHECHNER: Many people have remarked on the grim authenticity of the story, "The Depressed Person," who bores her therapist into suicide, but the story—actually it is an interview—that stands out in my mind is with the man in Peoria Heights, Illinois, whose father was a washroom attendant in a fancy hotel, who, for six days a week, stood there amid the "rococo fixtures and scalloped basins" and the horrible sounds and odors, dutifully and politely handing out towels.

WALLACE: I don't know where that came from, but I do know that I tried to read that out loud once and will never do it again.

[We shift momentarily to the novel *Infinite Jest*, and I mention to Wallace that what I appreciate is its reports back from a recognizable world: meetings of the Boston AA, for example, various psychologically profiled characters, who, however they may have been invented, had also to be observed. I mention Kate Gompert, a catatonic, and Tony Kraus, an epileptic who suffers a visionary seizure in the book.]

WALLACE: You don't mind weird stuff. So long as there is a neural event going on that placates your realism fears, you'll take it, because that seizure scene is extremely weird and consists mostly of hallucinations. I get very different responses from readers. Some people are neurologically disposed to like very pomo, avant-gardie—let's-just-play-games-here-stuff—and some people are disposed to need stuff that is grounded and plausible, and once you can persuade them of your ability to do that, you can more or less do what you want.

SHECHNER: On the subject of pomo and the fictional avant garde of the '70s, in some interviews you've indicated a double relationship to it. On the one hand, it seems to be a source of influence, while on the other hand you want to place some distance between yourself and writers like Barth, Pynchon, Barthelme, Burroughs.

WALLACE: I don't know about distance. I do know that my parents read a lot and I read a lot when I was growing up, and what we liked was probably not all that different from what you liked. We like to be moved, and yet, for someone who is trying to be a fiction writer in the year 2000, the conventions of what was called Realism don't seem all that real anymore, or are more difficult to swallow. Some things in the writers you've mentioned seem to me more "real" than Dickens or Anne Tyler or pick your realist. On the other hand, some of what gets called pomo can get so occluded and conscious of itself as text or hall of mirrors, that its only appeal is intellectual and cerebral. I don't dismiss the idea that there is something of value in that; it just isn't what turns me on. I don't particularly consider myself a member of either camp, though it is interesting to watch members of different camps who talk about you contort things so that you end up being a friendly force.

SHECHNER: Whom do you read these days with pleasure? Who among your contemporaries is something that you would want the rest of us to read?

WALLACE: The answer, first of all, depends on how long you have, but to take a broad swipe, the three people who are at the top of the food chain just now are Don DeLillo, Cynthia Ozick, and Cormac McCarthy, all of whom are either in their fifties or their sixties. People around my age whom I'm a big fan of include George Saunders, who writes for the *New Yorker* a lot, and Richard Powers—the way he can combine and transfigure data is just incredible—Joanna Scott [whom I remind Wallace lives nearby in Rochester], Denis Johnson, though more of his earlier work in poetry than the later work that is getting so much attention now. There is a San Francisco writer named William T. Vollmann, who is very prolific. He has a book of stories called *The Rainbow Stories* that will raise hair on parts of your body that don't have hair.

SHECHNER: I had read before that you were a fan of Cynthia Ozick's. That is surprising to me; you seem so different.

WALLACE: We're both politically active Jewish females. I don't see the problem. [Laughter on both sides.] When I was in high school I read a lot of Malamud, because that is what my parents had around, and afterward I read Ozick, including some Ozick that is written in the margins of Malamud, and it blew the top of my skull off. I think Ozick is an immortally good pure prose writer, but I think it is also the fact that I'm about the goyist gentile anybody's ever met, and I can feel in my nerve endings the kind of stuff she is writing about. In reading her I feel an utter erasure of difference, which does not happen to me with a lot of other writers from different cultural backgrounds. I can appreciate the peering across the chasm at another culture, but with Ozick that chasm just vanishes. Her *Bloodshed and Three Novellas*, if you haven't read it, is fine.

SHECHNER: Do you want to say anything about work in progress? And are you going to read from anything new when you are here?
WALLACE: I'm going to read from whatever they tell me.

[I mention to Wallace that I respond to his verbal density, and that I get from his work a rare sentence-by-sentence pleasure that normally I get only from music. He responds:]

WALLACE: I think people write the way their brain voices sound to them.

SHECHNER: I've always thought of writing as a kind of artificial discipline, in which you write a sentence ten times before it sounds like your natural voice.
WALLACE: But very often that ten times is meant to serve a kind of mimesis. I don't find that fiction is meant to be read out loud. Fiction is meant to be read inwardly, to march along with people's mental circuitry, and the voice we hear in our heads is very different from our larynx sound.

We agree to call the interview to a close, though I'm brimming to ask over and over the question that I've already ruled out of bounds: "Where does all this stuff come from?" But invention and the portion of life it comes from are the writer's secrets. We readers have to content ourselves with the product, which in the case of David Foster Wallace, is spectacular.

Conversation with David Foster Wallace and Richard Powers

John O'Brien/2000

O'BRIEN: Most of the questions are about relationships, fortunately not personal ones. First is relationship to your readers. How much do you take your reader into account, how much do you think about your reader as you're writing? How often are you afraid that you may be stepping over the boundary with readers, expecting too much from them or demanding too much? David, this is a subject you and I have discussed many times, actually.

WALLACE: One of many reasons for being terrified about this sort of venue is that a lot of the stuff, it sort of feels like it's not in my interests to think about—think-think. I know that if stuff is going well, it feels like I'm talking to somebody, or like there's somebody there, and I think it's somebody rather suspiciously like me. And I know it's a very charitable way to put it, "Are you making too high demands on stuff." I know I run into problems with irritation thresholds, cost-benefit flux, and all kinds of stuff. I guess the deal I've made with myself is that I don't think about it a whole lot when I'm working but I've gathered a little set of three or four readers—only one of whom is a relative—who have graciously been reading for me for fifteen years and are fairly blunt about when irritation thresholds or gratuitousness thresholds are being exceeded. I think I lean on them in the respect that it allows me not really to think about it very much when I'm doing it, which of course doesn't yield a very interesting answer.

O'BRIEN: I'll come back to our ongoing argument about this.

WALLACE: Hence embedding the thing about the outside readers, which is the only nugget I really have to offer.

O'BRIEN: Rick?

POWERS: This came up at breakfast. Michael Silverblatt had used a line with regard to another writer—that his books would have been much better had he completely discounted their effect, or ceased to think about their effect on his readership. It was such a strange and wonderful formulation that I've been turning it over in my head all day. I guess, finally, it seems to me almost inconceivable that you would not be gauging the effect of the work upon some receiver. The question is, who? It's not a question of whether you're writing without mindfulness, or creating a transmission without a reception, the question is: who is the ideal reader? Is this a stable configuration or is this perpetually reinvented in the light of the many, many needs that a novel will present? I think it's a good exercise, at various points in the creative process, to reach out towards something antithetical to your own ideal reception. I mean, I agree with David, in some ways my ideal reader does look like me, at least during the first draft, the invention part of the process. I think, at different moments in revision, I will work hard to see what this would look like to someone who is very much not me.

O'BRIEN: If it's pleasing you, do you assume it's going to please others?

POWERS: That's a horrible assumption! The assumption that pleasure can be calculated at all in advance is a very difficult one.

WALLACE: Although if it's pleasing enough you just don't care. Which is nice. And then if, by chance, people do like it, it seems like this wonderful bit of frosting.

POWERS: Can you do that? You can get to a level of personal pleasure where you essentially . . .

WALLACE: I thought implicitly we were talking early drafts and stuff here, then there's the horrible dash of cold water when you realize someone else is going to see this.

O'BRIEN: So the next level of this, or maybe it's pre-level: relationship with editors. To what degrees are they helps, hindrances, learning from . . .

POWERS: You know, I can honestly say that I do not think of my current editor as a reader at all. I don't say that to be flip, because I know that his reading will have everything to do with what happens to the book as it attempts to make its way in the world. And I'm always surprised by what he has to say. I simply don't conceive of him as an active presence in the making.

O'BRIEN: Does he have a lot to say and do you pay attention?

POWERS: You know, John told us in the van on the way here that one of his favorite pedagogical techniques when a student asks him a question that he doesn't want to answer is to answer something else.

O'BRIEN: I mentioned that, huh?

POWERS: I think that's varied quite a bit from book to book. I think it would be pretty rare in commercial publishing now to get a real hands-on Max-Perkins read from a literary editor.

WALLACE: We're very different in this respect. Again this is going to sound like real editorial sucking up. I've got an editor who has made the last four things that he's worked on with me better, and he's not part of the first screen of readers because he's an authority figure and duh duh duh . . . it's weird . . . I'll spend nine months sending him letters begging him for editorial help, then by the time he gets the manuscript I'll be done with it. It will have gone to other readers, I will have worked out my response to that. So what he gets I am so reptilianly attached to that the poor guy gets all these letters, which I'm sure he just throws away, and then we begin to fight about the manuscript. He hasn't been my editor all through all the books but he's been the editor on the last four. The last fiction book—Rick and I were just talking—*Brief Interviews with Hideous Men*, the order of the things that I had sent him was utterly different than the order that's in the book. He made the arrangement that's in the book and it's about 450 percent better—I've already convinced you?—than what it was. I'm just grateful, and I know that I'm unusual and the guy puts up with a lot of neuroses and mixed messages, but I've actually come to lean on him. Which I'm not supposed to say, because then if the editor knows he's got you then . . .

O'BRIEN: Well this has been a semi-argument between us, and the first form of it was my insisting that the writer didn't owe anything to the reader except to write as well as he or she could and forget about the reader. Then you convinced me of the opposite using, I think, a story from Michael Pietsch that nobody had an obligation to buy a book. [They might] pick it off a shelf in a bookstore, but they weren't obligated to go on. So having convinced me of that, next time we talked about it you took the opposite position, and proceeded to convince me of the opposite . . .

WALLACE: And where do we stand now?

O'BRIEN: Well I've used your first argument many times with authors I've dealt with—that it's much more like a conversation that you're having and neither an editor nor a reader has any obligation to continue to listen unless you're being interesting.

WALLACE: Obviously both *obligation* and *interesting* would take a lot of unpacking that I don't think anybody here is interested in.

POWERS: I don't get what that would mean—a writer owes nothing to the reader.

O'BRIEN: Do what he or she feels as though they want to do, and whatever group of readers there may be, small or large, they're going to get it or they won't get it.

WALLACE: This was my original position?

O'BRIEN: No—that was mine—and you argued against it.

WALLACE: Good for me.

POWERS: The way that I would try to reconcile those positions is to say, "do whatever you think you feel is necessary" means locate in this process a, or a series of, ideal readers.

WALLACE: Well, there's even a more basic—and this is probably . . . who cares if it's boring—Rick and I have been talking a lot about teaching and there's this fundamental difference that comes up in freshman comp and haunts you all the way through teaching undergrads: there is a fundamental difference between expressive writing and communicative writing. One of the biggest problems in terms of learning to write, or teaching anybody to write, is getting it in your nerve endings that the reader cannot read your mind. That what you say isn't interesting simply because you, yourself, say it. Whether that translates to a feeling of obligation to the reader I don't know, but we've all probably sat next to people at dinner or on public transport who are producing communication signals but it's not communicative expression. It's expressive expression, right? And actually it's in conversation that you can feel most vividly how alienating and unpleasant it is to feel as if someone is going through all the motions of communicating with you but in actual fact you don't even need to be there at all. Could this be a third different point . . .

O'BRIEN: I'll think about this one. What about relationship with reviewers? Most writers go through various stages—they pay attention, read them seriously at the beginning, grow to hate them, stop reading them or drive themselves crazy by continuing to read them. Do either of you read them? Do you read them all? Does somebody edit them for you?

POWERS: Does Michael do that for you?

WALLACE: No—it's not that full service.

POWERS: I do read them. I don't believe the good ones, I agonize over the bad ones. A review can say, "This is the most astonishing book I've read for years and years. I wish that it had had a few more peaks and not so many valleys," and I'd be worried about the little cavil. But I think saying that, I would also say at the same time I am entirely indifferent to them. There are two paradoxical modes: one in which I really want a kind of return communication in the face of what I've just been doing for the last three years; and the second, which is somewhat indifferent to that and capable, rightly or wrongly, of convincing myself that there are other more satisfying conversations going on there, I'm just not hearing the return.

O'BRIEN: When they get to the part of the "however" are you more inclined to believe that?

POWERS: I don't think my visceral belief in the moment of reading the review ever filters into the writing process. I simply don't think you can write more than one novel in this country and not have managed to create a fundamental imperviousness to reception.

O'BRIEN: David?

WALLACE: Oh . . . well . . . I don't read them as a matter of practice. I'm fairly disciplined as long as they're in the organ. If somebody mails it to me very often I slip up and read them, and I'm not indifferent to them and they are extremely upsetting to me. It's not that they shouldn't exist—I have an analogy but it's somewhat off-color: we got to go and listen to a research presentation at the Santa Fe Institute this afternoon, and afterwards there was a restroom break, and people were using the restroom. There I was in a stall and there are two guys out in the bathroom and one says "who were those guys?," "I don't know, a couple of writers. . ." And right away, I was in the position that I am in when I'm contemplating reading a review, which is that it's incredibly tempting to want to listen to this, but it messes you up every time because it's a special communication between the reviewer who is talking to potential book buyers or people who bought the book and want to get their own reactions checked and it is not a communication that includes the author, I don't think.

POWERS: Oh, it can. There are good faith reviews and there are bad faith reviews.

WALLACE: For me, and could you poke holes in this?—yes—would I prefer that you didn't?—yes—because this is a protection mechanism. I've just decided that this is like people talking about you somewhere and you're in a position to eavesdrop, and if you do, by all means go ahead and do, but we all know what happens, right? Sitcom plots revolve around what happens. Is it a shaky idea? Yeah. Would I prefer to be impervious to them? Yeah—I'm not. It just helps me to pretend that they're not going on. Though the Japanese lady haunts my dreams.

O'BRIEN: Neither of you has to answer this one—is there any sense of reviewers waiting in the bushes after your first few novels to suggest that you're not as good as others have thought you've been? I can answer it for you?

POWERS: You mean the same reviewer who has received you well early on has decided . . .

O'BRIEN: Not the same ones, but others.

POWERS: Can I rephrase the question and say "does the reviewing process become a different thing at different stages in a career?" which, I guess, in some ways suggests that the act of reviewing isn't a good-faith process because it's reviewing a narrative about you rather than the words between the covers.

WALLACE: What are your thoughts on reviewers, John?

O'BRIEN: Generally? Dumb. Self-indulgent. More talking about themselves . . .

POWERS: Don't pull any punches.

O'BRIEN: I don't have to worry about the reviewers, so I can't even identify the daily reviewer for the *New York Times* as the prime example of such things. What about scholarly articles? Now, given the state of academia there haven't been a great number written on either of you—do you read them and how do they effect you? Do you take them seriously? The ones who are really attempting to do something more serious than what a 500-, 700-word book review can do.

WALLACE: God's honest truth: sometimes people send them to me, I've read a few—don't understand them. Can't follow the argument. Cannot see in my version of the text any of the stuff they see—sometimes they're very impressive in a kind of I-wonder-what-on-earth-he's-talking-about way. So those I don't have any problem with. And it's not a joke—that is the cold truth—I do not understand them.

O'BRIEN: Richard—you've had some of these.

POWERS: Yeah, and I enjoy reading them in the way that I enjoy reading scholarly articles about other contemporary novels—they seem part of a conversation that daily reviewing can't afford to be or doesn't have the time or the energy to be—part of an ongoing conversation about what books do and what has come before.

O'BRIEN: Do they seem to be less about you than reviews might be?

POWERS: Clearly.

O'BRIEN: Why do you write? A lot of people don't write. You two do write. A number of other people do write. Why? Why not stop?

WALLACE: Sounds good to me.

POWERS: Yeah, I never thought of that . . .

WALLACE: John, is there some way to rephrase it so it's less cruel? That's such a general question that it's difficult not just to babble.

O'BRIEN: So, is it compulsive? There's no choice?

POWERS: In a sense, any answer to that question is going to be a narrative overlay. It's going to be a fabrication, and it's going to be an attempt to add to the narrative explanation of self that the writing is anyway. I write out of pleasure, and every morning I can't believe I'm getting away with this, and that sort of deep puritanical sense that this is a zero-sum game leads me to believe that I've got twenty lean years to come. But you write to enhance your pleasure in life and to increase your sense of where you are, where you've been dropped down.

WALLACE: You really get up every morning and you feel just incredibly lucky?

POWERS: What other career affords you that advantage?

WALLACE: Oh, I'm not arguing. I'm just in awe. I would like to be that healthy between my ears. And this isn't a set-up or anything. Sometimes yeah, and sometimes, my god, it's like the back of my hand is stapled to my forehead.

POWERS: You're not saying that I'd rather be piling boxes up?

WALLACE: No. I mean Jon Franzen's got a real good one about this, because he gets asked this a lot. He says "yeah, there's the bullshit narrative overlay, and then the truth is: because there's nothing else I want to do." My own narrative overlay is just something that I've always liked that's in—except this is going to make it sound nobler and more compulsive than it is—but there's this thing in Oliver Sacks. It might be in *The Man Who Mistook His Wife for a Hat*, about, I think, it's a bag lady who was tourettic, and I bet other people remember this. She'd stand on a street corner in maybe New York, LA, or something, you know thousands of passers-by, and she'd just stand there and wouldn't do anything. But then after maybe five or ten minutes, after a certain number of passers-by had gone by, she would go back into an alley and express somehow every face and—according to Sacks—it was eerie. It wasn't just the faces it was the people who go by, and then she would go back out there and stand. And I resonate with something about that, though I wouldn't claim that it was some Romantic "some are just driven, and born, and compelled to do it." But there is a kind of . . .

POWERS: As a sort of footnote to that, and as a response to Franzen's formulation, for me there are plenty of other things that I would love to spend time doing. Writing is the only place where you can do them all.

O'BRIEN: Are you coming down on the side—and I've heard a lot of writers say this, David—that they wish they didn't have to do it? That it's a painful process.

WALLACE: Half the time, yeah; but then the other half of the time you're like "how could I ever, ever have stopped thanking the ceiling for being able to do this." I want, and again—narrative overlay, whatever—I was in a restaurant, this was years ago, and overheard two guys talking about how hard their jobs were and how they felt like their creativity was one thing, but then there was the constant pressure. The industry was always changing, and they couldn't rely on their sense of what the person they were making their stuff for was going to think, and they were terrified that they were going to get fired but also praying they were going to get fired because they just couldn't take this. And, I don't do this often, but I eventually, because I figured they were part of the few, the proud—they were upholsterers. Furniture upholsterers. And I swear to God, word-for-word, the conversation was, I don't know. So I guess I sort of think that there's not anything within a certain kind of broad genus of certain kinds of jobs—we were talking about this with scientists at the Santa Fe Institute—I don't think it's substantively different, at least for me, than most other jobs would be. If you are the sort of person who could be grateful in any sort of job, then I wish I were you.

POWERS: I've heard that on this question of agony that it genders strongly. That women novelists tend to be filled with religious gratitude, and men like to bitch and moan.

O'BRIEN: What's the pleasure of writing? What pleasure do you derive?

WALLACE: Except the weird thing is it's both at the same time, and the weird thing for me, having done it for a while, is that I almost can't imagine one without the other.

POWERS: Getting in touch with your inner-feminine side . . .

WALLACE: I don't think that I've had any problem getting in touch with my inner-feminine side.

O'BRIEN: So tell me your pleasure.
POWERS: For me it's connection—the pleasure of an expansive, long-ranging dinner conversation with people who do all sorts of things and being able to come back to that, night after night, and pick up threads and follow them. There's a voyeuristic pleasure, there's a synthetic pleasure, but primarily it's the pleasure of being able to live in a frame of time that the rest of life conspires to annihilate.

O'BRIEN: So it's the time that you're writing?

POWERS: Ideally, and on the very best days, it's no time at all, it's simply breaking the constraints of time and physical constraint.

WALLACE: That's a beautiful way to put it. My experience of it is just that the good days are when you look up and it's just way later than you thought it could be.

POWERS: Way later by the clock and in some sort of inner . . .

WALLACE: When it goes well, there's a way that you're tired that's just a really good way. Just a really good kind of tired.

Approaching Infinity

Caleb Crain/2003

From *Boston Globe*, 26 October 2003. © 2003 by Caleb Crain. Reprinted by permission.

If there were another superpower anymore, it would probably classify David Foster Wallace's *Everything and More: A Compact History of* ∞ (W. W. Norton) as a Sputnik-level threat to its national security. After all, America's intellectual vigor must be fearsome if a publisher is willing to bet that its citizens will voluntarily, recreationally, and in reasonably large numbers read a book with sentences like this:

> Cantor shows that P's first derived set, P', can be "decomposed" or broken down into the union of two different subsets, Q and R, where Q is the set of all points belonging to first-species derived sets of P', and R is the set of all points that are contained in *every single* derived set of P', meaning R is the set of just those points that all the derived sets of P' have in common.

Everything and More is not for lightweights. The book has a hero: the nineteenth-century German mathematician Georg F. L. P. Cantor, who spent the last twenty years of his life in and out of mental hospitals. But it is less Cantor's story than the story of the problem he solved, which led him to pioneer set theory and to discover the mathematical rules that govern infinity—which, it turns out, comes in different sizes.

The forty-one-year-old Wallace is probably the most important novelist of his generation, and he has fans who will follow him even into differential equations. He is the author of two story collections, a book of essays, and the 1079-page, 388-footnote novel *Infinite Jest*, which is set in Greater Boston (in 1989 Wallace spent a semester as a graduate student in philosophy at Harvard), and is concerned with Alcoholics Anonymous, wheelchair-bound terrorists from Quebec, and a tennis prodigy whose late father directed a film so entertaining that it melts the minds of its viewers.

A year ago Wallace left his longtime home in central Illinois to become the Roy Edward Disney Professor in Creative Writing at Pomona College in California. Last Friday he was in New York, and he met with Ideas in his hotel room to discuss infinity, Whitey Bulger, and Platonists (people who believe that math's concepts exist independent of the mathematicians who think them). Before the interview began, Wallace, who recently quit smoking, served Ideas a glass of club soda and himself a nicotine patch.

IDEAS: A few years ago, you reviewed two novels about math for the magazine *Science* and took them to task for not having thought through who their audience was.

WALLACE: They were really dreadful books. One of them would take time to define very simple stuff like addition but would then throw around really high-level math terms.

IDEAS: How do you address the question of audience in your book?

WALLACE: Oh, it's so much more fun criticizing how other people have done it. There was this book by Amir Aczel, which was about Georg Cantor's mental illness, and certain supposed connections between infinity and mental illness, and infinity and the kabbalah. Obviously I wanted to do something different, and the only way I could think of was to talk about where the math actually came from. The idea is, if the book works right, you finish it with a better idea of not just how Cantorian transfinite set theory works but actually why it was a big deal and why it's beautiful and amazing. A couple of people have already said to me, "Gosh, good book but it's really *hard*," thinking that's a compliment, and it's not. Does it seem halfway clear to you?

IDEAS: The Uniqueness Theorem lost me.

WALLACE: It's the hardest part of the book. The idea is, if you can show that all the different series that a function expands to are equivalent, then it is just one series.

IDEAS: I pretty much followed the rest.

WALLACE: My fondest hope is that the average reader has more or less your experience. I'm hoping that even a reader who hasn't had a semester of college math will be able to follow enough to get why this stuff is a big deal and why it was beautiful, in a more substantive way than "A madman in an institution created this heavy-duty concept." My justification for the parts that are hard is that at least it's not just giving the reader pablum and abetting certain romantic but flabby ideas about madness and genius and certain mathematical concepts being so forbidden that they drive people crazy.

IDEAS: In your book, you draw a distinction between solutions that are technically correct and those that are intellectually satisfying. For example, you say that the first-year calculus answer to Zeno's paradox is correct but "semi-impoverished." [Zeno claimed that it's impossible to walk across, say, a hotel room, because you would first have to walk halfway across, then halfway across the remaining quarter-length, etc., and there would always be some space left between you and the other side of the room.]
WALLACE: I think I'm working out some of my own anger. I was very frustrated in college math classes, because they just wouldn't *tell* you why this stuff was important. If you ever had Zeno's dichotomy in a calc class and you saw the calc solution, you don't walk away bathed in relief at the resolution to the paradox, because they strip all the interesting context away. If you're just given "a over 1 minus r" in a math class, I'd say that's semi-impoverished. OK, I can solve that, but I still don't understand how I walked out of the room.

IDEAS: Your book convinced me that irrational numbers can't possibly exist. I don't know what I was thinking, accepting them as real.
WALLACE: You mean, mathematically real or physically real?

IDEAS: Physically real.
WALLACE: But *are* numbers physically real?

IDEAS: I had thought they were, in some way.
WALLACE: So you're a bit of a Platonist then.

IDEAS: That was my next question for you.
WALLACE: We're brainwashed into being Platonists in elementary school, because it's the easiest way to think about numbers. Nobody wants to tell a fourth-grader the metaphysics of the integer 3, so we've got this idea that 3 is this thing. These are not things. Even if you're a Platonist—that is, even if you believe that numbers are real in some metaphysical sense, the way trees and Calebs are real, as opposed to mathematically real—the reason you're

convinced of it is we never really think about it. Well, if they are, where are they? What do they look like? What is 3? It's like the speculations that little children have, or adolescents who smoke a lot of pot at 3 o'clock in the morning.

IDEAS: A character in *Infinite Jest* describes "Marijuana Thinking" in a way that reminded me of how you talk about a certain kind of math-philosophical abyss in this book.
WALLACE: The stuff that drives us crazy is the really, really, really basic stuff. What are numbers? What exactly are these three dimensions we're sitting in? Stuff that it's embarrassing to talk about out loud because it sounds like pot-smoking "Oouhh, oouhh, oouhh," but in some sense, this is what mathematicians—and back in the Greeks, philosophers, because there was no difference at the time—this is what they did.

IDEAS: So, even though you've resisted the brainwashing, are you a Platonist? Do you think mathematical concepts exist?
WALLACE: Personally, yeah, I'm a Platonist. I think that God has particular languages, and one of them is music and one of them is mathematics. That's not something I can defend. It's just something I've felt in my tummy since I was a little kid, but how exactly to try to make sense of that and to fit it in any kind of a working philosophy, much less cross the street to buy a loaf of bread, is a different matter.

IDEAS: Was it hard to write about the abstract, without plots or bodies?
WALLACE: You know, in a weird way, there's really only one basic problem in all writing—how to get some empathy with the reader. And that problem is a jewel on which there are many facets. And this is a somewhat different facet—how to take this very, very abstract stuff, boil it down so that it fits in a pop book, and give the reader enough of the real story so that you're not lying to him, but also to make it clear enough so that it's not just understandable but halfway enjoyable for somebody who hasn't studied math for twenty years. It's really not completely different from the question, how do you get a reader to inhabit the consciousness of a character who, say, isn't a hero or isn't a very nice guy, and feel that person's humanity and something of his 3-D contours while not pretending that he's not a monster.

IDEAS: What are you teaching now at Pomona?
WALLACE: I got hired to teach writing, but they're also letting me teach

some literature classes. Last spring I did eclectic modern—Christina Stead's *The Man Who Loved Children*, Joan Didion's *Play It as It Lays*, and Richard Brautigan's *In Watermelon Sugar*. The kind of books that are big but you know college students are never going to get them in a class.

IDEAS: Do you miss Boston?
WALLACE: I miss parts of Brighton and Allston and the Back Bay very much. But I lived there for only three years and I moved away only a decade ago. I'll go back at some point. Sure. Ride the B Line.

IDEAS: A friend of mine thinks that *Infinite Jest* should be understood as a Boston novel.
WALLACE: I think a lot of the dialect in there probably doesn't make much sense if you don't know Boston. Boston made a big impression on me, because linguistically it's very different than where I'm from.

IDEAS: Was the character Whitey Sorkin inspired by Whitey Bulger?
WALLACE: I don't think Whitey Sorkin's supposed to be an isomorphically unique mapping of Whitey Bulger, but when I was in Boston, there were rumors that Whitey had it fixed so that his people won the lottery. I mean, at least in the parts of Boston in which I was moving, Whitey was a creature of myth.

IDEAS: The Greek epigraph to *Everything and More*—where's it from?
WALLACE: It's made up. "It is not what's inside your head, it's what your head's inside." It's a gag. I think the editor thought it was some really esoteric ancient Greek. I got a big kick out of it. It was a big deal to get him to get the diacriticals right.

IDEAS: In *Everything and More*, once some of the technical questions about infinity are answered, a new abyss opens up with Gödel's incompleteness theorem.
WALLACE: Infinity was the great albatross for math—really, ever since calculus. [The nineteenth-century mathematicians] Karl Weierstrass, Richard Dedekind, and Cantor close all those holes, and it's beautiful, and at the same time they open what turns out to be a much worse one, as [the twentieth-century mathematician and logician] Kurt Gödel demonstrated. Gödel is able to come up with a theorem that says, "I am not provable." And it's a theorem, which means that, by definition, math is either not consistent

or it's not complete. Packed in. He is the devil, for math. After Gödel, the idea that mathematics was not just a language of God but a language we could decode to understand the universe and understand everything—that doesn't work anymore. It's part of the great postmodern uncertainty that we live in.

IDEAS: What fiction are you working on now?

WALLACE: Just this morning, I delivered the post-editing draft of a book of stories. All but a couple have been in magazines, although not all under my name. I don't think any of the stories have footnotes, which I'm rather proud of. Got that monkey off my back. I think one story maybe has a couple of asterisk footnotes. You know, there are so few of them that you can use asterisks.

To the Best of Our Knowledge: Interview with David Foster Wallace

Steve Paulson/2004

PAULSON: I want to start by talking about one particular story, "The Soul Is Not a Smithy." How would you describe this story?
WALLACE: As longer than I intended it to be? A little kid with attention problems in school is not attending on a very dramatic day for him, where his teacher kind of has a psychotic breakdown.

PAULSON: His substitute teacher starts writing "Kill Them" over and over on the blackboard, and then when these kids in the fourth grade start realizing what he's doing—that he's basically lost his marbles—they panic.
WALLACE: Yes.

PAULSON: But your narrator who is reflecting back on that time, his mind was actually elsewhere because he had been staring out the window watching other strange stuff.
WALLACE: Yeah, it's weird because the narrator is partly narrating as a child and partly as an adult. But mainly his big concern is how boring and meaningless his life has been and how he's missed the one really dramatic thing that ever happened to him. It's actually more interesting than that— I'm not making it sound very . . .

PAULSON: It's actually a fascinating story, and I think fascinating partly because it takes a turn somewhere else, really near the end, and it becomes about a child's fear of the adult world and what seems to be this boy's fear of becoming like his own father, who is an insurance actuary. I wonder if you

127

could read a passage from the story, I'm thinking maybe starting around page 103 or so.

WALLACE: So I should start now?

PAULSON: Yes.

[Wallace reads a section from pages 103–6 of *Oblivion*, beginning "For my own part . . ." and ending ". . . dreamed in the real world."]

PAULSON: That's wonderful, thank you. So evocative, and I have to say that when I first read that passage it seemed like something right out of Kafka—the nightmare quality of the ordinary world—does that have any resonance for you?

WALLACE: Well, no. It's a weird story because the story started out really surreal and parts of this [section] are actually the climax, but the climax is much more plain, everyday realistic than surreal, so it ended up kind of like inverted Kafka for me. It's a very strange piece, I think.

PAULSON: Did you have that kind of dread when you were a kid?

WALLACE: I think that in a country where we have it as easy as we do, one of our big dread vectors is boredom. I think little edges of despair and soul-level boredom appear in things like homework or particularly dry classroom stuff. I can remember the incredible soaring relief when certain teachers said we were going to watch a movie in grade school. And it wasn't just a hedonistic "oh-we're-going-to-have-fun." It was a relief from some kind of terrible burden, I thought. So, I don't know. Maybe.

PAULSON: Did you look at what your parents were doing, your father, in particular, and think, "Oh my god, I don't want to become like that"?

WALLACE: I don't know, both my parents were teachers so they always got pale and haunted looking when there were big stacks of papers to grade. But I think a lot of this has more to do with friends' parents, and friends who have become kind of office workers. I just got interested in the reality of boredom, which is something that I think is a hugely important problem and yet none of us talk about it because we all act like it's just sort of something that we have to get through, which I suppose we do.

PAULSON: It's funny because as I was reading that I was thinking back to my own childhood, and my father was a professor and after dinner he would typically go on up into his study and close the door. And I don't know what he did but I remember thinking when I was pretty little that this doesn't seem like fun to have to do this, night after night, and I didn't want to become like that. Of course, I sort of have become like that because I go home, and I have my own homework as well. I'm wondering if that at all resonated for you?

WALLACE: One of my little family stories that Mom always tells is that on the day in second grade, when we all had to talk about what our father's did for a living, I said my father didn't do anything for a living. He just stayed home and wrote on yellow paper, because he was a professor, too. I know that part of what interested me in this story was trying to remember what I thought about what my parents did when I was a child. Because when you're a child I don't think you're aware of how incredibly easy you have it, right? You have your own problems and you have your own burdens and chores and things you have to do, but, yeah, I think my intuitions were very much like yours. When they went into these quiet rooms and had to do things that it wasn't obvious they wanted to do, I think there was a part of me that felt that something terrible was coming. But also, of course, now that we're putatively grown up there's also a lot of really, really interesting stuff and sometimes you sit in quiet rooms and do a lot of drudgery and at the end of it is a surprise or something very rewarding or a feeling of fulfillment.

PAULSON: That's the life of a writer, isn't it?

WALLACE: Yeah, but it's also probably the life of a radio-host, and probably, in many cases, the life of office workers, who we think of as having very boring, dry jobs. Probably all jobs are the same and they're filled with horrible boredom and despair and quiet little bits of fulfillment that are very hard to tell anyone else about. That's just a guess.

PAULSON: You know what I find interesting about what we've been talking about, and also the passage you've just read? Your public image as a writer—you're typically described as one of the leading figures of the postmodern hip ironic generation of writers in their thirties and early forties, but I read somewhere that you really think of yourself as a realist.

WALLACE: These various classifications are important for critics, right? You have to form different things into groups or you have to talk about a trillion different particulars. I don't know very many writers who don't think of themselves as realists, in terms of trying to convey the way stuff tastes and feels to you. I mean, a lot of stuff that's capital-R Realism just seems to me somewhat hokey, because obviously realism is an illusion of realism, and the idea that small banal details are somehow more real or authentic than large or strange details has always seemed to me to be just a little bit crude. But this was an interesting piece to write because during the real payoff part of it it did become extremely realistic and small and filled with banal details. The truth of the matter is that when you're in an interview you have to say all kinds of stuff; I don't really know what I am and I don't think very many writers have any idea what they are. You just try to do stuff that seems alive to you.

PAULSON: I'm wondering, particularly for people of our generation—I think we're roughly around the same age, we're both in our early forties—whether there's a certain cultural landscape that you feel most compelled to write about.

WALLACE: I know that when I was in graduate school those of us who used to write about what used to be called pop culture or advertizing or television were really scorned by our older professors, who saw that stuff as kind of vapid and banal, and lacking a kind of platonic timelessness. And I remember it was a really big source of conflict because in lots of ways we just didn't get what they were saying. I mean, this was our world and our reality, the same way the Romantics' world was trees and babbling brooks and mountains and blue skies. So, yeah, I'm forty-two, and if there's something that's distinctive about our generation it's that we've been steeped in media and marketing since the time we were very, very small. And it's kind of a grand experiment because no other generation in the history of the world has been that mediated. What implications that has, I don't know, but I know it affects what seems urgent and worth writing about and what kind of feels real in my head when I'm working on it.

PAULSON: Isn't that also complicated, though, because the danger of writing about mass culture or pop culture is that it's going to seem shallow? In fact, you wrote an essay about this some years back, about the risk of just being clever, and I guess how do you say something original about this world that in so many ways is really pretty shallow?

WALLACE: The way to answer is with a platitude, but some platitudes are kind of deep. For me, art that's alive and urgent is art that's about what it is to be a human being. And whether one is a human being in times of enormous profundity and depth and challenge, or one is trying to be a human being in times that appear to be shallow and commercial and materialistic, really isn't all that relevant to the deeper project. The deeper project is: what is it to be human? There are certain paradoxes and there are certain hazards involved in writing about this world because a lot of commercial culture is itself based on kinds of art, at least sort of pop art, and there's the danger of being sucked into it, and simply trying, for instance, to do something that seems very hip and clever and thinking the job has been done then. I've certainly done stuff like that, and realized only later with horror that what I did was, in fact, just regurgitated the same stuff that I've been hearing since I was four or five. There's another side to it, though, I think, that part of this division into postmodern experimentalists and realists is—at least for people like me, I'm forty-two and I grew up, I don't know how many afterschool specials and Hallmark network things I've seen—a lot of what is quote unquote conventionally Realistic ends up seeming hokey to me. The resolutions seem contrived, everything seems a little bit too convenient and platitudish, and the ultimate goal of it is to sell me something. And there's a part of me, I think, that recoils from that, and that's a problem because some Realistic stuff really is alive and urgent, but the model and the form has been so exhaustively mined for commercial reasons that I think for a lot of us about our age, we're looking for different, less commercial forms, in which to talk about the urgent, moving stuff. I'm not sure whether that makes any sense, but that's pretty much the truth the way I see it.

PAULSON: I think the other piece of that is a lot of this commercial world, whether it's movies or advertizing, it's pretty compelling—it's entertaining—and I suppose, from a writer's perspective, you might feel that if you want to write about this stuff, you have to be entertaining, too.
WALLACE: There's that danger, the other danger is, to reprise an early twentieth-century painting thing, where once there was photography the interest in mimesis in painting really disappeared and everything got really abstract—it's a real problem. I don't have a TV anymore, but when I'm doing something like this and I'm on the road I watch TV in hotels and I'm appalled by how good the commercials have gotten. They're fascinating, they're funny, they're hip, they've got trunk lines into my high-school level anxieties and desires in a way that the commercials I grew up with never did. What it is, is the hip, cynical, cool people I went to college feeling intimidated by are now making two million dollars a year, figuring out how to do this stuff. And they've gotten very, very good at it.

PAULSON: I have to ask you about another one of your stories, "The Suffering Channel," which among other things deals with a new kind of reality TV show that shows real-life episodes of torture and murder and rape and all of that. Is that sort of your vision of what might happen in some dystopian future?

WALLACE: I don't know that it's that, I think that, to the extent that I understand reality TV, it has a certain logic, and it's not hard to take that kind of logic to its extreme. I think celebrity autopsy, while childhood friends of the celebrity sit around talking about whether or not this celebrity was a good person while his or her organs are being excised would be the terminus of that logic. But the question is how far we go? The inhibition of shame on the part both of the contestants and on the part of the people who put together the show—at some point people have figured out that even if viewers are sneering or talking about in what poor taste stuff is, they're still watching, and that the key is to get people to watch, and that that's what's remunerative. Once we lost that shame hobble, only time will tell how far we'll go.

PAULSON: Your essays and your fiction are famous for various things—for their footnotes, for various digressions on all kinds of odd bits of information, obscure bits of science and philosophy—are you just drawn to this kind of thing, do you just have a hunger to know about the world?

WALLACE: I don't know if it's that so much as a lot of it really does come back to trying to do something that feels real to me. And—I don't really know what the interior of anybody else is like—I often feel very fragmented, as if I have a symphony of different voices, and voice-overs, and factoids, going on all the time and digressions on digressions on digressions, and I know that people who don't much care for my stuff see a lot of the stuff as just sort of vomiting it out. That's at least my intent, what's hard is to seem very digressive and bent in on yourself and diffracted and yet also have there be patterns and significances about it, and it takes a lot of drafts, but it probably comes out just looking like, you know, a manic mad monologue or something. I don't know that I'm more interested in trivia or factoids than anyone else—I know that they sort of bounce around within my head an awful lot.

PAULSON: I came across a quote from the novelist Zadie Smith, who said, "It's not the writer's job to tell us how somebody felt about something, it's to tell us how the world works." Do you agree with that?

WALLACE: Well, what you've got there is a very clever statement on one side of this division between capital-R Realism and something more experimental or postmodern with a kind of social agenda. Probably if you backed me into a tight corner what I'd say is ultimately there's no difference between those two things, although they're different as philosophies via which to proceed in the project. But if you could articulate well enough what something felt like to somebody, you would have a fantastic template for how the world worked. That might be a kind of solipsistic view, but I sort of think it's mine. But also, Zadie is very clever and what she calls a wind-up merchant, and I think part of her saying that is just to get people revved up.

PAULSON: But you're also suggesting it's sort of the way science is going, as the study of consciousness gets more and more complicated, to some degree it's all in our mind anyway, I mean, how we perceive the world, so maybe there really isn't this distinction between the world out there and how we make sense of it in our own minds?

WALLACE: Yeah, but the other tricky thing is that the only way we can talk to each other about this is with language, and in language, built in is the idea of this distinction you just presented to me, so maybe there is nothing outside the mind. If there is nothing outside the mind, it's really not a very big deal that there isn't. But when we talk to each other about it, there automatically becomes a big deal. So, language, and the way we have to communicate with each other and process the world through words I think is the wild card in all this, and I don't totally understand it. So the answer just kind of tails off, I'm afraid.

PAULSON: You were a philosophy student at one point, weren't you?
WALLACE: I was.

PAULSON: Does that impulse still stay with you?
WALLACE: Oh, I think at the time that I was studying philosophy it was the beginning of the infiltration by kind of continental deconstruction on analytic philosophy and the world was full of recursion, and involution, and things bending back on themselves, and various incarnations of Gödel's proof, and I think some of that kind of affected me at a spinal level. I really like recursions, and I really like contradictions and paradoxes and statements that kind of negate themselves in the middle. But at this point in my life it seems to me to be more of a tic than anything really all that important.

PAULSON: I mentioned this essay that you wrote, I think it was back in 1993, about writing and what various fiction writers are up to, and one point

you made is that irony tyrannizes us. The implicit message of irony is "I don't really mean what I'm saying" and you went on to suggest that the next generation of rebel writers might ditch irony in favor of sincerity, I think I'm quoting here, "who treat of plain old untrendy human troubles and emotions . . . with reverence and conviction. Who eschew self-consciousness and hip fatigue."
WALLACE: Yeah?

PAULSON: Is that a critique of your own kind of writing?
WALLACE: I don't know that it's that. The thing even sounds dated to me now. I think it's less that than an articulation of the thing you were asking me about before: you know, what is it like to be working really hard on this stuff at age forty-two having been marketed to all your life. Because you want your art to be hip and seem cool to people, you want people to like the stuff, but a great deal of what passes for hip or cool is now highly, highly commercially driven. And some of it is important art. I think *The Simpsons* is important art. On the other hand, it's also—in my opinion—relentlessly corrosive to the soul, and everything is parodied, and everything's ridiculous. Maybe I'm old, but for my part I can be steeped in about an hour of it, and I sort of have to walk away and look at a flower or something. If there's something to be talked about, that thing is this weird conflict between what my girlfriend calls the "inner sap"—the part of us that can really wholeheartedly weep at stuff—and the part of us that has to live in a world of smart, jaded, sophisticated people and wants very much to be taken seriously by those people. I don't know that it's that irony tyrannizes us, but the fashions that are so easy to criticize but are so incredibly powerful and authentic-seeming when we're inside them, tyrannize us. I don't know that it's ever been any different. That probably makes absolutely no sense. That was my experiment at telling the truth.

PAULSON: That makes total sense. But can you hold those two impulses simultaneously?
WALLACE: No, but I think my personal opinion—and what I tell my students—if there's suffering involved in art, or however you want to say it, right now this is the form of the suffering: to be the battleground for the war between those two kinds of impulses. Neither of which are stupid, neither of which are wrong, but it's not at all clear to me how to marry them and I don't think it's been at all clear since about the 1950s. I just think it's where we're at.

PAULSON: Is that what you're trying to do in your fiction—to get at those two impulses within the same work, the same story?

WALLACE: For the purposes of this conversation I'll say yes, but sitting in a bright, quiet room in front of the paper it's much more, uhhh does this make me want to throw up? Does this seem real? Is this the sort of thing the person would say? It's much more boneheaded and practical than that. You realize this, right? There's something very artificial about once the book's all through galleys and now I'm engaging in critical discourse about it—I might be right, but it's very different than what it's like to actually do the things. The stuff that's in my mind as I'm doing it is far less sophisticated than this.

The Connection: David Foster Wallace

Michael Goldfarb/2004

GOLDFARB: Here are some things we know about author David Foster Wallace. He is from the Midwest, but currently lives in Southern California. He knows more about mathematics than most of us, and he's a tennis player of some quality. And for better or worse, for richer or poorer, whether he wants to be or not, he has been handed the mantle of writer of his generation, the person among his peers most likely to write the great American novel. His last novel was *Infinite Jest*, a thousand-page excursion into twelve-step programs, terrorism, and other stuff, and it was published in 1996. His latest work is a collection of stories, some short others not so short, called *Oblivion*. The stories show an interest in the work world of media, and also the panicked world of ordinary life where substitute teachers go barking mad and babies suffer accidents that boggle their parents' minds. We're talking about the work and worldview of David Foster Wallace in this hour. With me in the studio is David Foster Wallace. Hi.

WALLACE: Hello.

GOLDFARB: It's nice to meet you because I have been reading you in a variety of different places for a while now, and it's nice to have you face to face with me. First of all, just out of curiosity, when did you move to Southern California?

WALLACE: I moved there in the summer of 2002. I got a really good teaching job that was just un-turn-downable.

GOLDFARB: And you're living in LA?

WALLACE: I live between Los Angeles and San Bernardino.

GOLDFARB: And is it a place that's kind of begun to work on your imagination in a different way than being in downstate?

WALLACE: I think for the most part I'm just trying to adjust. It's both very beautiful weather-wise and very, very urban. The place I live in is essentially one great big stripmall.

GOLDFARB: Just the perfect environment. A stripmall, presumably, where every single item that's visible to the naked eye has already been pretested and preplotted by marketing men.

WALLACE: I smell a segueway here.

GOLDFARB: Yes, thank you David, you're very helpful. The thing that struck me in the book is how interested you are in the world of work, that nobody else is interested in. Just in the last hour we were talking about gender inequality in the workplace, talking about Walmart. But you're interested in the way that the work of media, of marketing goes on. It's something that comes across in the book. Where did that come from?

WALLACE: I don't know. I know that I'm now forty-two, and grew up watching a lot of television and being part of a heavily mediated culture. I think that one of the things that interest me is the fact that, though it does compose our generation's reality, we don't often think of it as a human product—the product of human choices, and human thought, and human work. And I think you're right. I think a lot of people aren't interested in the behind-the-scenes stuff about media, as much as I am, although on the other hand, I don't have any particular experience of it, and a lot of the behind-the-scenes stuff that I do is made up.

GOLDFARB: Yeah, well it's called fiction.

WALLACE: There we go.

GOLDFARB: The first story in this collection, *Oblivion*, is set in a focus group, and it's imagined, obviously. Why don't you tell us a bit about the story and maybe read us a bit?

WALLACE: This is a long one, called "Mister Squishy," that originally I'd done pseudonymously as part of a cycle, and the rest of the cycle kind of died. It started out to be a kind of twelve-angry-men jury story—but set in a focus group—and then I got more and more interested in the facilitator, the statistician who's kind of in charge of the focus group. The focus group is together testing a made-up snack cake called *Felonies!®* that is due to be distributed soon, and there's a lot of marketing and focus group nomenclature in the story. If the story's got a movement, I guess, it's that it starts out really heavily on the technical stuff about how focus-group testing and marketing works and as it goes on gets more and more interested in the facilitator as a traditional third-person schlemiel.

GOLDFARB: I like the way in the story it says "the dark and exceptionally dense and moist-looking snack cakes"—this is on a table in a focus group room—"inside the packaging were *Felonies!®*, a risky and multivalent trade name meant both to connote and to parody the modern health-conscious consumer's sense of vice/indulgence/transgression." That is exactly the way they talk about these things, people who are bringing new products to market, with all of the energy and intensity and sense of profundity that people write philosophy, as if they're making some great discovery about how we know what we know.

WALLACE: It's really quite remarkable. I mean, I went to school with people who are now making huge salaries as kind of scholars of demography in New York, and for advertizing agencies. And, yeah, they're very smart, well-educated people who are putting in full-time hard work on figuring out stuff that presents to us as vapid or ephemeral.

GOLDFARB: Read a bit from the story, set it up first.

WALLACE: Oh boy. I think this is a part of the story where we're moving from the mechanics of the focus group more into the personal bio and woes of the facilitator, whose name is Terry Schmidt. There's a certain amount of nomenclature in here, *Team Δy* is the focus group firm that's being used by the advertizing agency of *RSB*, which is Reesemeyer Shannon Belt, which is a made-up name, and *TFG* stands for Targeted Focus Group. Here's the part she marked. Sorry, *GRDS* is Group Response Data Summary, which is the group form that this focus group fills out.

[Wallace reads a single, long sentence from pages 31–33 of *Oblivion*, beginning "At various intervals . . ."]

GOLDFARB: Now, there's a world in that, and it's a single sentence, which is one of the reasons why she—our senior producer—marked that off for reading. A first quick question: that is one single sentence that you've just read. Now, you do that on purpose or the words just came out and you just said "well, we'll just keep going to the end"?

WALLACE: Well, it looks a little more diarrhetic reading it out loud than it probably did on the page. Yeah, I think a simple deal is that, this is a weird story because it switches in and out of a more omniscient third-person narrator into the consciousness of this Terry Schmidt. The closer stuff is to Terry Schmidt, the more run-on it gets, because his thoughts sort of tumble. The whole story isn't like this, but, yeah, there are some long sentences.

GOLDFARB: It's a question of the style of the story, in other words, when we come to it as readers you keep going through it and you wonder, after a while, because we're used to sentences of a certain length, or punctuated in a certain way. This is all part of the process, the interaction between the page and the reader. But the other thing about this story, and I come back to the theme of work, maybe I'm over-generalizing here, but most American writers of fiction just avoid it. And here we are, a society notorious throughout the world for living to work as opposed to working to live, working to earn enough money to enjoy life. And yet it isn't something that hooks people in, and my own theory is that it's partially because people don't want to think about what goes on in marketing seminars.

WALLACE: Why do you suppose they don't?

GOLDFARB: I don't know, I'm asking you. To me it's a frightening thing. I just think that a lot of writers don't want to deal with the world of work, possibly because they haven't experienced it first-hand, possibly because it's just too terrifying to contemplate.

WALLACE: I prefer the terrifying explanation because it's sexier than that people find it boring, or you know they work all day and then the last thing they want to do when they come home and put their feet up is hear about somebody else's work. Probably this is very crude, but when you were talking about most writing avoiding the world of work, it would seem to me that a fair amount of commercial fiction emphasizes people's work, but it's always sexy, dangerous police or FBI or that kind of work. And literary fiction maybe emphasizes more domestic life, and the interior life and stuff. It's not clear to me that the two are all that distinguishable. I hear the music, I'm probably supposed to trail off here in meaningful way.

GOLDFARB: You're so well educated.

WALLACE: Media savvy!

GOLDFARB: That's what it said in all the reviews.

[short break]

GOLDFARB: We went out talking about work and its place in American fiction. When you're not writing fiction, David, do you think much about how real things are that are coming into your world? Do you try and play games in your own head to get to some kind of pure form of the idea of a thing, shedding all of the conditioning that's coming to you—you're forty-two—from watching television, from anything else that's gone on, to some kind of pure, almost mathematical notion of what is real?

WALLACE: Do I drift along as a Platonist? I don't know that I regard media or marketing or the degree of saturation that you and I and all of us have with this stuff as necessarily evil. I mean, one of the hallmarks of postmodernism is that it's not at all clear anymore that there's some kind of platonic truth that rests behind people's interpretations of the truth, and particularly paid people's enforced interpretations of the truth. One of the things that interests me, though, is just how little we think of the fact that so much of what we voluntarily turn on and see and hear and listen to are actually human products designed by human people. I'm not a particular Luddite. I'm not particularly opposed to media. I just think it's weird that we don't often talk or think about the agenda behind a lot of this stuff. I mean, I've got a whole little story about this if you want to hear, but it's going to take like two minutes to tell.

GOLDFARB: You know something? We have the best part of an hour yet, so tell it.

WALLACE: I was thinking about this because we had some kind of public argument about this in San Francisco. I was in grad school studying writing in the mid-eighties, and there were some of us who used pop elements in some of our stories—brand names, celebrities—and our professors, who were, you know, twenty-to-thirty years older than us, strongly, strongly opposed this. Their belief was that literary fiction, like most serious art, was supposed to be timeless, and pop elements were vapid and trivial. Literary short stories were supposed to be part of high culture, which was really kind of the antidote for low culture. We had a very interesting intergenerational argument about this at school, because the kids my age—I was in my early twenties at the time—we just didn't get it. Media and marketing and corporate and celebrity stuff were part of our reality every bit as much as cars and highways and skies were part of our professors' reality. But as I've grown older I've realized, I think, that there is a big difference. The Romantics— skies and babbling brooks and nature and all that stuff—those aren't human products. Much of the media world that I and we live in is a human product, made by human beings with agendas and fears and desires, and that there's an odd resistance to thinking in any but the most reductive—these are evil people trying to manipulate us—terms of what the human reality of making all this stuff is like. I don't know if that makes any sense.

GOLDFARB: It does. The thing is that you were talking about the generational difference, and you're growing now to an understanding, at least, of where your professors were coming from. I also wonder if it's an educational difference: that if you get at the elementary and secondary level, even before you get to college, a certain kind of high culture, canonical education, that it allows you to be more skeptical about the pop thing earlier on, and that you can make a distinction.

WALLACE: I think that's probably true, and probably one reason why allowing corporations to subsidize educational materials or to move their advertising into high school cafeterias is a bit scary, because those are educating children in a very specific way that's tailored to the interests of the corporation. On the other hand, I don't know that it takes a great deal of special liberal arts education to be skeptical of the media, if by skeptical you mean realizing that this isn't reality, but this is, in fact, a certain version put out by human beings who have an interest. I think what it depends upon is a willingness to pay a certain kind of attention, and I think it's probably a certain kind of attention that people younger than me—people who are now in their twenties and thirties—are actually more accustomed to doing. I've had younger readers who don't quite understand what the big deal is, why I make such a big deal of this. I think it's harder for those of us who are older to do it.

GOLDFARB: Attention must be paid. Because you come from the Midwest, you stayed in the Midwest even after you became a celebrity . . .

WALLACE: With quotation marks . . .

GOLDFARB: I try to do that vocally, since we're not looking at a page. But do you regard this as a Midwestern view: media culture has homogenized America—that's also a cliché—but is this the view of someone who grew up in the Midwest as opposed to someone who grew up in Manhattan?

WALLACE: Well I think it's certainly the view of somebody who both read and watched a lot of TV, and is very used to being on his side of the screen. The sort of celebrity that I'm writing about and thinking about has a great deal more cultural energy and dollars attached to it than the kind of celebrity of being a semi-well-known literary-fiction writer, I don't know what the numbers are for how many Americans are interested in literary fiction, but it's not high.

GOLDFARB: It isn't high, in fact, earlier this week we did an hour on the marketing fact that only 44 percent of men read fiction. That to me was kind of astonishing because I figured everybody was reading at least detective novels, but apparently men aren't reading fiction at all. In the world of public radio, you assume that you're operating at the high end of people who are reading and so we can have this kind of conversation, but in the rest of America one isn't sure. When you travel around the country on a tour like this, what impressions do you have about people reading, about standards of conversation?

WALLACE: Oh boy, in a literary fiction reading you're going to get about as many people as the venue can hold, and it doesn't seem like a very good reflection of the culture as a whole. I mean, I don't tour all that much. I don't talk directly to all that many readers. My sense is that, in terms of the audience I'm interested in, there are still plenty of smart, sophisticated readers who are willing to put in a little extra work. But I also think that it's understandable, particularly maybe for men, who typically have to sit all day and do kind of boring jobs. . . . Reading requires solitude and extended periods of a kind of unusual sort of attention and most of my friends aren't writers or aren't all that educated and what they want when they get out of work is they want stimulation. They want entertainment, which TV and movies and the internet are far better suited for than literary arts.

GOLDFARB: Diana is calling from Raleigh, North Carolina.

DIANA: My question is, without this writer's informative, intellectual, high-culture writing, why is it that we find it so hard for the masses to be exposed to this? It's been so long for me.

GOLDFARB: It's been so long for you down there in Raleigh to hear a conversation like this?

DIANA: I'm outside of Raleigh, as an NPR listener, but something to read . . .

GOLDFARB: Okay, let me put that question, Diana, to David Foster Wallace.

WALLACE: Well, I'm not totally sure what your question means, there's hundreds of good literary fiction and poetry volumes that get published every year. It's true that they don't get marketed and advertised as heavily as commercial stuff for the simple reason that it doesn't make as much money, there aren't as many people who are interested in it. But the sense I get is that people who are interested, and are willing to dig around on the internet or to go to bookstores and look, have never found there to be any shortage of quality literary stuff of all different sorts. Am I answering your question?

DIANA: Well I agree with exactly what you said. What I guess it is, is the varied topics that you write about. Didn't quite make myself clear. It's so exciting because it just hits, hits, hits on so many different things, and I'm not exposed to your writing and I'm very excited about going to my independent bookstore and looking you up.

WALLACE: Or a library.

DIANA: I've got an English degree, and I'm working as a substitute teacher right now, while I'm working on getting my certification. So my curiosity is very high about substitute teachers gone mad.

GOLDFARB: It's a very, very interesting story.

DIANA: I look forward to reading it.

GOLDFARB: The book is *Oblivion*, thank you, Diana. Amy is calling from Chapel Hill, North Carolina.

AMY: Hi. I have a question for David Foster Wallace. I read *Infinite Jest*—I put in the effort, as it were—and what you've been saying in some of this conversation today made me think about a question about the idea of material that's put out by humans, talking about corporate output and being influenced by products, and so forth. The kind of just media-saturated existence. And what I wanted to ask you about is the very last sentence of that book. It struck me that it took the entire book to get to that very last moment. It was like a last gasp. It was actually kind of a moment of redemption, I was really shocked by it.

WALLACE: You're talking about the last sentence of the main text?

AMY: Yeah, of *Infinite Jest*, not the last sentence of the footnotes.

WALLACE: I like it as a last sentence, so obviously I'm going to agree with you.

GOLDFARB: Amy, you don't have it memorized do you? What is it?

AMY: I don't have it in front of me. It's a character—one of the myriad characters you've been following—and I was actually feeling resentful toward the end because I realized there was no way you'd be tying up all the stories you'd begun. I couldn't believe that I'd gone that far and wasn't going to get a neat bow on everything.

WALLACE: Yeah, I got hate mail about that.

AMY: I forgave you, though, at the end because it was just clear that that wasn't what you wanted, and it was all fine, you know. But it was so violent and surreal for so much of the time, so much suffering, and the very last sentence I was literally shocked by it, because it brought it to—it's going to sound a little corny—a truly human moment. It took a ten-pound book to get that one sentence.

GOLDFARB: David, Amy was talking about the experience of getting through the book. As a writer, do you like getting that kind of very specific feedback from readers?

WALLACE: Well, sure. That book, there's a certain amount of stuff that I do that plays a little game where it's hard, but I'm trying to make it seductive or natural—like a two-page sentence. If I do it right, yes it's a long sentence, but you can track it grammatically and syntactically. I get worried when people draw attention to it, because I feel like if they're able to notice it, I'm not doing the job entirely well. I don't know that all of *Infinite Jest* is a support structure for the last sentence, but I, too, like the last sentence. And I didn't want to wrap various plots up neatly within the frame of the book, I think, largely because a lot of commercial entertainments that I grew up with use that and it's not entirely real. It's a kind of falsely satisfying way to wrap up various things that happen, and now I'm just maundering on.

GOLDFARB: So you're consciously aware that there's an element in your work that is in response to the neatly wrapped-up two-hour, three-act structure of a Hollywood movie, or even six episodes of *The Sopranos*. As an artist, what you're trying to do is avoid that?

WALLACE: Well, I've got that wrapped up as a nice soundbyte answer because I've been asked a whole, whole lot why, after making the reader kind of climb this big hill does *Infinite Jest* not wrap up. That book, actually, for me does resolve, but it resolves sort of outside the right-frame of the picture. You can get a pretty good idea, I think, of what happens. I think, for the most part, I'm just like all writers. I want to do stuff that feels real to me, and so stuff that's been very heavily used in commercial entertainments, that are very neat and slick and sophisticated are probably going to strike me as not real, and I'm going to avoid them. And probably in some cases that's a problem because there are certain types of artworks that should wrap up neatly. The visceral knee-jerk—oh god, if it's ever been done in a commercial thing, I shouldn't do it—is probably something of a limitation, I hope I don't have that all the time.

GOLDFARB: You were talking about your friends who aren't writers and they come home from work and they're watching stories. Stories, which is what people used to read 150 years ago, and now you have stories told to you, you said passively watching them on television.

WALLACE: Except before that 150 years ago, stories were things we told each other. So there's a neat coming full-circle about the whole thing. They weren't originally told to us by someone whose entire agenda was to acquire our attention so that he could deliver messages to us that were for the sake of somebody who was giving him money. So there's a bit of an odd spin on it now.

GOLDFARB: And also the stories took on this extra life throughout the day in other places, because the people who appear in these stories are also on billboards, talking about something else, wholly unrelated to the story in which you saw them. But I mean, when you're writing, are there moments where you say, "You know, I could resolve this situation very easily, but no I'm not going to do it because that's the way they would do it in Hollywood"?

WALLACE: Here's what's hard about talking about this: the truth—at least for me—is not nearly as sophisticated or interesting as the kind of question you've just posited. It's usually a tummy thing: does this feel real? Does this make me want to puke? Does this seem fake or contrived or not? And there's not a whole lot of cerebration, at least for me, going on.

[short break]

GOLDFARB: We can talk about writing, David, or you can just read some of your writing, that might work also.

WALLACE: Okay. Another thing that's been selected is part of a story called "Good Old Neon," that's basically a story about a lot of different kinds of loneliness.

[Wallace reads part of a paragraph, from pages 150–51 of *Oblivion*, beginning "Once again, I'm aware . . ." and ending at "It's not really like that."]

WALLACE: That last part was a separate sentence, by the way.

GOLDFARB: That's an interesting technical stylistic point.

WALLACE: It's just that she's picked all the really long, run-on sentences that we read out loud.

GOLDFARB: But this one is particularly good, because it seems to me to about the process of consciousness before it forms itself into language. Do you think that language is the endpoint of the process of formulating a thought?

WALLACE: There's a whole, very heavy debate to get into here. There are schools of thought, some of which I find persuasive, that argue that there really is no meaningful reality outside language. That language creates in a very complicated way what we call reality—that would be your poststructural . . .

GOLDFARB: One of the reasons I didn't complete a Ph.D. in philosophy—I just didn't want to have that conversation for professional purposes.

WALLACE: The stuff is incredibly abstract and abstruse, partly because it's dealing with the paradox that we're attempting to talk metaphysically about language using nothing but language, which sets up certain paradoxes that your readers may not find all that interesting but are really, really kind of tough.

GOLDFARB: Well, we'll challenge them. Tell us some of the paradoxes that they set up.

WALLACE: The basic paradox, which is one that's handled more facilely in mathematical logic, is that it's very, very difficult to talk about a language within that language. Kurt Gödel's famous "I am lying" paradox—I'm sorry that's not even Gödel, that comes out of Ancient Greece—is the first instance of this fact. This is making the story that I read from seem very cerebral—this is actually supposed to be kind of the saddest story in the book—but one of the things about the narrator is, he's had enough sort of education to drive himself crazy with the surface of these certain paradoxes. The philosophy of the whole stuff is very interesting; I don't really keep up that much with it.

GOLDFARB: David is on the line from Boston.

DAVID: Earlier in the show you touched, very briefly, on the question of truth in the postmodern era. And I think we live in a very, I don't know what you'd call it, where truth is up for grabs. I just would like you to elaborate a little bit more on where you were going with that thought.

GOLDFARB: Okay David, that's a good question.

WALLACE: I think you were talking about the truth thing. Were I to weigh in, I guess I would say that to an extent I agree with you, and I think this is an interesting legacy of postmodern skepticism. The idea that everything is spin. That there is no truth. That you can derive one truth even about the day's events from, say, Fox News, and another from the great liberal conspiracy of the *New York Times* and CNN—is, I think, both liberating and exciting and also extremely scary.

GOLDFARB: David?

DAVID: Your latter point has me in the same paradoxical, ambivalent, situation. It has me very scared as well, and I'm not sure there's an easily reconcilable way out.

GOLDFARB: Thank you for your call.

WALLACE: An astute call, I think.

GOLDFARB: It is. But truth, at the personal level—it used to be that an artist said "I want to create the truth out of my experience of life." Are you operating there or is that just a concept that adds extra weight to the process?

WALLACE: Well, that's a bit of a Romantic thing. The thing about it is, it is true because when you're doing stuff like this so much of it is tummy-truth, as opposed to head-truth—does this feel true or not? The interesting thing for me, this is a very Romantic—capital R—idea of truth that as far as I can tell comes from Nietzsche, that all truth is perspectival. It seems to me that one of the ingenious things that particularly the right in America has been able to do is to inject this kind of skepticism into public debate. Where if you or I proffer something that seems absolutely true—that, I don't know, justice for the homeless might be an imperative—they can say, "Well, that appears to you to be true only because you've been conditioned by a liberal conspiracy within academia and the media in order to think that way." And, rhetorically, it is very difficult to come up with an effective, concise rebuttal to that, because anything you say can be said to be a further product of the conditioning of your perspective. It is scary, I agree with David. But it is also really exciting because I don't know that there's been a rhetorization of the debate in quite this way in America ever before, and I think that any time capital-A Authority is brought into question is exciting. Also it seems to me to have a huge capacity for danger.

GOLDFARB: Jennifer is calling from Durham, North Carolina.

JENNIFER: I wanted to ask you about your sense of maturing as a writer. You mentioned earlier things that you see differently now than you did when you were in school, and I recently went back and reread "A Supposedly Fun Thing I'll Never Do Again," which is an essay I loved. And I still loved it but—being not in my mid-thirties but now I'm closer to forty—my experience of it was, not exactly that it was sarcastic, but that it was funny at the expense, in some places, of people or things. And I'm wondering if you think there is a trajectory from something like sarcasm for a writer to something more generous, and—if so—if there's an edge that gets lost?

WALLACE: That is an uncomfortably good question. You're referring to a long essay I did about a cruise ship that was funny, and I rather liked it when I first did it. And now, about ten years later, particularly with respect to certain people I met on the cruise, when I read sections of it I wince because it seems cruel. I know I don't do as much nonfiction as I used to as a writer, and I think part of it is that I don't have the heart or stomach to say even truthful things that might hurt somebody's feelings. I doubt that is artistically all that promising, although it might make me maybe a slightly better human being. I think I'm going through the standard arc that just about everybody goes through, in that my interest in intellectual and cerebral and clever stuff—although it's not like I'm not interested in that, but I was very, very interested in that when I was a really young writer—and the older I get the more what's magical about art becomes for me the idea of stuff that's moving. And I don't necessarily just mean sad but has a very complicated emotional resonance as opposed to an intellectual or kind of meta-artistic resonance, ooh, which sounds like a very egg-headed answer. Actually I thought your question was dead on.

GOLDFARB: Jennifer?

JENNIFER: Your response is just pretty much what I would have expected, and it actually excites me about reading your new work. I mean, I think especially if we age with the writers we like then I will be in the same place that you are now, and I was in the same place you were when I first read something that was perhaps more biting.

WALLACE: Imagine it from the writer's point of view, though. The writer's point of view is that I'm pretty good at being a smartass, but what if this new stuff that affects me a lot more, what if I can't do that as well? And it's probably the same conflict I'll have in my fifties or my sixties, it ends up being kind of scary.

JENNIFER: Well that's what all artists have to face if they grow.

WALLACE: Well, you're a smart person.

GOLDFARB: David, you're teaching now—earlier we were talking about your experiences as a student—do you think the people that you're teaching are different than you were when you were in your early twenties and taking a degree in writing?

WALLACE: Well, I teach undergrads and, yeah. Although I don't have children, I'm going through my version of the-older-you-get-the-smarter-your-parents-get thing, because I hear leaving my mouth certain things that professors said to me and I thought was just a sign that they didn't recognize, you know, my genius and that I could transcend all of that stuff. So, it sounds like a cliché, but the fact of the matter is the good thing about teaching is that you learn more than anybody else in the classroom.

GOLDFARB: We had Evan Wright on the other day, *Generation Kill*, and he thought there was a fundamental difference between the marines that were fighting in Iraq, say, and the marines that would have fought in Vietnam, and it had to do with the way the kids he was observing had been involved in video games and all the media stuff we talked about earlier. Do you get that talking to the young writers? Whereas you were just fighting to have pop references respected in a high-cultural sense, do they think it's a fight worth fighting or are they just used to that's the way it is?

WALLACE: I mean, this is still a big split in fiction, and there's a lot of really good, vibrant, capital-R Realistic fiction that doesn't engage very much with features of the culture that you also couldn't have found a hundred and a hundred and fifty years ago. What I notice more with my students, sort of the way Evan notices video games as operant conditioning helping people be better killers, is that their attention spans are shorter but also more agile. There are more flash-cuts in their stuff. The differences, to me, seem really to be far more technical than spiritual.

Interview with David Foster Wallace

Didier Jacob/2005

JACOB: You were born in a place where people are not very interested in foreign literature, and perhaps not even interested in American literature. What led you to love literature, and to want to become a writer?

WALLACE: I assume that your "born in a place where . . . literature" refers to the entire U.S.A., not to the specific region where I was born. If I'm right, then your real question is "How, given most Americans' lack of interest in literature, does America produce any literary writers?" Obviously, one could ask the same question about how any Americans become classical musicians, or sculptors, or ballet dancers. It is true that serious art dos not interest many Americans to the same degree that it interests many Europeans. But it's also dangerous to try to characterize a whole nation as "a place where people are not very interested . . . ," because then, by the question's logic, the only artistic vocations that Americans pursued would be commercial film and television, popular music, and video games. For only these mainstream commercial art forms "interest very many people" here, which is sad, and for Europeans it may be further evidence of what philistines Americans are. But the U.S.A. is also a nation of extraordinary diversity and myriad different cultural interests and enthusiasms. There may be comparatively few living Americans who care enough about serious fiction and poetry to buy books and to read and think about literature, but there are enough to keep literature alive—just as there are enough to keep classical music alive, and ballet, etc. ("Alive" here means available for those who are interested in it.)

In some respects, the comparatively small audience for serious culture is a good thing. It is true that one cannot become wealthy or a big star in the U.S.A. as a dancer, or composer, or poet. But this means that only those who are truly devoted to these forms will pursue them as a career. Young people who primarily wish to make huge amounts of money, or to be big celebrities, go into film, TV, pop music, or the Internet. This situation has certain advantages. Huge amounts of money and fame deform artists, deform art—we have all seen this happen many times, to many different musicians and actors who "hit it big"—and the fact that there is no real money or fame in serious culture here helps keep these vocations purer, cleaner. At least that's one way to see the situation. In another respect, of course, it's sad and scary. Serious art is where difficult, complex questions get made urgent and human and real; and the political climate in the U.S.A. right now is so ugly, unreflective, selfish, jingoistic, and materialistic that serious art has probably never been needed more. But serious art makes people uncomfortable—it is meant to—and large portions of our populace seem willing to go to great lengths now to avoid being uncomfortable; and we have elected leaders who are weak and short-sighted enough to be willing to exploit that fact. So these are also very dark, frightening times . . . though you in France hardly need me to tell you that. For serious writers and artists, though, I think that the mainstream neglect and lack of interest is ultimately a good thing—good for the art, I mean.

JACOB: How would you summarize your entire life, from birth to the summer of 2005?
WALLACE: Taken literally, this question is impossible to answer. My best guess is that the question is meant to be humorous, or to set up the respondent to say something funny or piquant in answer. Unfortunately, whenever I feel pressure to say something funny or piquant, my mind fills with the same roaring static as an off-air TV channel, and I can think of nothing to say. This is just one reason why I am not a very good subject for an interview.

JACOB: How do you mix journalism and literature? Are the two forms very different or very similar? Are the works and ideas of Hunter Thompson, for example, important to you?
WALLACE: I'm not really sure that I do "mix journalism and literature." I tend to think more in terms of fiction versus nonfiction. I am not a journalist; I have no training in journalism, and I have never worked for a newspaper or any news organization. But I do write both fiction and nonfiction, "nonfiction" meaning primarily essays and articles. A lot of U.S. writers do this, partly because we need income from magazines, and most American magazines publish a great deal more nonfiction than fiction or poetry. Nobody here is quite sure how to classify the writing that results when novelists

and poets write nonfiction for magazines. Because there is some really great nonfiction written by American novelists/poets—Cynthia Ozick comes to mind, and Tobias Wolff, Joan Didion, Jonathan Franzen, William T. Vollmann, Denis Johnson, and Louise Glück are other good examples—it's gaining a certain literary respectability here. In fact, in U.S. academia, there is a movement now that wants to include essays and literary journalism as a "fourth genre" alongside fiction, poetry, and drama, to be studied in literature courses and also taught in the creative writing workshops that are so popular in our colleges. There's also been a big American publishing trend for the last decade in which poets and novelists produced memoirs: Tobias Wolff's *This Boy's Life* and Mary Karr's *The Liar's Club* are two of the more famous recent autobiographies. I don't know how many of these memoirs get published in French; some are very good, others trashy and exploitative.

I myself got into serious nonfiction mostly for financial reasons. In the early 1990s, I was writing a long piece of fiction, and I had no job and very little money, and an editor I knew at *Harper's* magazine gave me a couple of "experiential essay" assignments so that I could make enough money to stay alive. I turned out to enjoy the genre, and people have liked some of the articles, and I've continued doing nonfiction pieces even when I didn't need the income to survive. My main problem as a nonfiction writer is that, if I get interested enough in something to write about it, it tends to become very detailed and complex for me, and the articles I turn in to the magazines are usually much longer than they can publish. So what appears in American magazines is usually just a small portion of the actual article I wrote; the rest gets edited out. The best thing about collecting the pieces into books (I'm supposed to have the second such collection coming out soon in the U.S.; we're editing the galleys right now) is that I get to publish the "director's cuts" of the articles, the ones I actually wrote rather than the heavily edited magazine versions.

For me, there is only one difference between fiction and what you call "journalism." But it's a big difference. In nonfiction, everything has to be true, and it also has to be documented, because magazines have fact checkers and lawyers who are very thorough and completely devoid of any sense of humor, and the magazines are very afraid of being sued. The editorial process for nonfiction is very long and involved and tedious. That's probably the real reason why I don't do more nonfiction: the writing is fun, but the editing and fact-checking is usually irksome.

Regarding your example: For complicated reasons that I won't bore you with, I am not very interested in Hunter S. Thompson. In brief, he seems to me to be far more interested in developing himself as a charismatic persona and as a heroic symbol of decadent nihilism and rage than he is in writing honest or powerful nonfiction. His book on the Hell's Angels is an exception, but most of his work bores me; it seems naive and narcissistic. Maybe this will annoy your readers; maybe Thompson is an icon in France (like J. Lewis?). If so, I can assure you that I do not pretend to speak for all American readers . . . but I personally find a great deal more pleasure and value in the "works and ideas" of nonfiction writers like Swift, Montaigne, Lamb, Orwell, Baldwin, Dillard, and Ozick than in those of Hunter Thompson or Tom Wolfe. I do, however, have intelligent, discerning friends who disagree with me: *De gustibus non est disputandum.*

JACOB: Could you describe a typical writing day, how you describe the Illinois State Fair or a tennis tournament?
WALLACE: I don't quite understand how the two clauses in your question fit together. I have no typical "writing day." For one thing, the process is very different depending on whether something is fiction or nonfiction, and on whether or not there is a deadline. I tend to be very slow and to do many different drafts before something is finished. When there is a deadline (which there often is for a nonfiction piece commissioned by a magazine), the whole process has to be speeded up, which usually means I do nothing else in my life for a month. I should add, regarding your question's second clause, that the time spent at an event like the IL State Fair or the Du Maurier Open does not really count as writing time. All I do at these events is walk around, smoke too many cigarettes, fill notebooks with observations, and worry about how I can possibly write anything coherent about an event that is so detailed and complex. The actual writing time starts when I get home and have to start organizing the notes into an article.

JACOB: What would you prefer to do: play tennis, go to the cinema, write a thousand-page novel, chat with your fellow writers, or do nothing at all?
WALLACE: I'm afraid this is another question I don't entirely understand. Do you mean "prefer to do" at any given moment? Well, it depends. The truth is probably this: Sometimes I enjoy writing very much; at other times, it seems impossibly difficult and unpleasant, and I go to great lengths to avoid doing it. I am not very disciplined or (a current U.S. vogue word) "structured" about work. If I'm truly interested in something I'm working on, if it seems truly alive to me and I am able to forget my own fears, then I spend far more time writing than I spend doing anything else, simply be-

cause it's what I'd most prefer to be doing. If I'm not very interested, or if I'm in a period when I'm too frightened and self-conscious to be able to enjoy trying to write, then I spend a great deal of time avoiding work and doing other things. Some of these things are on your list; some are not.

JACOB: Which writer, living or dead, interests you the most, and which one would you most like to talk to? Pynchon? Hemingway? Salinger? (or Shakespeare, or somebody else . . .)

WALLACE: I am not very curious about the lives or personalities or other writers. The more I like someone's work, the less I want personal acquaintance to pollute my experience of reading her. I have briefly met some of the U.S. writers I admire—Cormac McCarthy, for example, and Don DeLillo, and Annie Dillard—and they all seemed like fine, pleasant people. But I found that I did not want to "chat" with them. In fact, I did not like even hearing them speak. In their books, each of these writers to me has a very distinctive "voice," a kind of sound on the page, and it has nothing to do with their actual larynx or nasality or timbre. I do not want to be hearing their "real" voice in my head when I'm reading. I'm not sure whether this makes sense, but it's the truth. There are, on the other hand, some writers I exchange letters with, and this I enjoy very much. Because the consciousness in the letters feels to me much more like the consciousness I admire in the work. I hope this is at least a partial answer to your question.

JACOB: A tennis player can dream of having Agassi's legs, Connor's spirit, or McEnroe's vocabulary, and so on. As a writer, what parts of another writer's work would you dream of being able to borrow—the rhythms of Don DeLillo, for example? Russell Banks's characters? Pynchon's titles?

WALLACE: I would have been better at answering this question in my twenties, when there was very little difference between my admiring some writer's particular ability and my wishing to appropriate that ability for myself. I notice this same tendency in students and younger writers—many of them spend a lot of time imitating writers they admire, and they are often not even aware that what they're doing is an imitation, because when you're young your sense of yourself is fluid and the possibilities seem infinite. For myself, as I get older and see myself more clearly (at least I think I do), I have come to accept that there are certain things I do quite well and others I don't do well . . . and still other things that it would be absurd for me to try. Examples: I admire Cormac McCarthy's ability to use antiquated, ornate English in ways that don't seem silly or stilted, but I have no illusion that I could do the same. I admire the conciseness and lucidity of DeLillo and Ozick, but I have accepted the fact that I will never be very lucid or concise in my own work. As far as I can see, at age forty-three, those vestiges of envy and desire for appropriation that survive in me have to do with larger, more amorphous qualities. The abilities of writers like St. Paul, Rousseau, Dostoevsky, and Camus to render so fully, passionately, the spiritual urgencies they felt as, saw as reality continue to fill me with an awe that is almost despair: To be able to be such a person! But what are envied and coveted here seem to me to be qualities of human beings—capacities of spirit—rather than technical abilities or special talents.

Just Asking . . . David Foster Wallace

Christopher John Farley/2008

From *Wall Street Journal*, 31 May 2008. © 2008 by Dow Jones & Co. Reprinted by permission.

David Foster Wallace, author of the novel *Infinite Jest*, was asked by *Rolling Stone* magazine to cover John McCain's presidential campaign in 2000. That assignment became a chapter in his essay collection *Consider the Lobster* (2005); the essay has now been issued as a stand-alone book, *McCain's Promise*. In a phone interview, Mr. Wallace said he came away from the experience marveling at "how unknowable and layered these candidates are." Mr. Wallace also answered questions via email about presidential hopefuls, the youth vote, and smiley faces.

WSJ: So why would a novelist want to travel around on a campaign bus?
Mr. Wallace: What made the McCain idea interesting to me was that I'd seen a tape of his appearance on Charlie Rose at some point the previous year, in which he spoke so candidly and bluntly about stuff like campaign finance and partisan ickiness, stuff I'd not heard any national-level politician say. There was also the fact that my own politics were about 179 degrees from his, so there was no worry that I'd somehow get seduced into writing an infomercial.

Q: Have you changed your mind about any of the points that you made in the book?
A: In the best political tradition, I reject the premise of your question. The essay quite specifically concerns a couple weeks in February 2000 and the situation of both McCain [and] national politics in those couple weeks. It is heavily context-dependent. And that context now seems a long, long, long time ago. McCain himself has obviously changed; his flipperoos and weaselings on Roe v. Wade, campaign finance, the toxicity of lobbyists, Iraq time-

tables, etc., are just some of what make him a less interesting, more depressing political figure now—for me, at least.

Q: You write that John McCain, in 2000, had become "the great populist hope of American politics." What parallels do you see between McCain in 2000 and Barack Obama in 2008?
A: There are some similarities—the ability to attract new voters, Independents; the ability to raise serious money in a grassroots way via the Web. But there are also lots of differences, many too obvious to need pointing out. Obama is an orator, for one thing—a rhetorician of the old school. To me, that seems more classically populist than McCain, who's not a good speechmaker and whose great strengths are Q&As and small-group press confabs. But there's a bigger [reason]. The truth—as I see it—is that the previous seven years and four months of the Bush Administration have been such an unmitigated horror show of rapacity, hubris, incompetence, mendacity, corruption, cynicism, and contempt for the electorate that it's very difficult to imagine how a self-identified Republican could try to position himself as a populist.

Q: In the book, you talk about why many young people are turned off by politics. What do you think could get young people to the voting booth this election?
A: Well, it's a very different situation. If nothing else, the previous seven years and four months have helped make it clear that it actually matters a whole, whole lot who gets elected president. A whole lot. There's also the fact that there are now certain really urgent, galvanizing problems—price of oil, carbon emissions, Iraq—that are apt to get more voters of all ages and education levels to the polls.

Q: You're known for writing big, complex books. Your novel *Infinite Jest* is 1,079 pages long, but *McCain's Promise* is a trim 124 pages. What made you decide to drop a few weight classes for this release?
A: The truth is that this book is really a magazine article whose subject just turned out to be too big and thorny and multiramified to be doable at article length.

Q: I have an advance copy of *Infinite Jest* that your publishing house sent me in 1996. It's signed—apparently—by you and there's a little smiley face under your name. I've always wondered—did you actually draw that smiley face?

A: One prong of the Buzz plan [for *Infinite Jest*] involved sending out a great many signed first editions—or maybe reader copies—to people who might generate Buzz. What they did was mail me a huge box of trade-paperback-size sheets of paper, which I was to sign; they would then somehow stitch them into these "special" books. You've probably had the weird epileptoid experience of saying a word over and over until it ceases to denote and becomes very strange and arbitrary and odd-feeling—imagine that happening with your own name. That's what happened. Plus it was boring. So boring that I started doing all kinds of weird little graphic things to try to stay alert and engaged. What you call the "smiley face" is a vestige of an amateur cartoon character I used to amuse myself with in grade school. I must have made thousands over that weekend in '95.

The Lost Years and Last Days
of David Foster Wallace

David Lipsky/2008

Article by David Lipsky From *Rolling Stone* issue dated, October 30, 2008. © Rolling Stone LLC 2008. All Rights Reserved. Reprinted by Permission.

He was the greatest writer of his generation—and also its most tormented. In the wake of his tragic suicide, his friends and family reveal the lifelong struggle of a beautiful mind.

He was six-feet-two, and on a good day he weighed two hundred pounds. He wore granny glasses with a head scarf, points knotted at the back, a look that was both pirate-like and housewife-ish. He always wore his hair long. He had dark eyes, soft voice, caveman chin, a lovely, peak-lipped mouth that was his best feature. He walked with an ex-athlete's saunter, a roll from the heels, as if anything physical was a pleasure.

David Foster Wallace worked surprising turns on nearly everything: novels, journalism, vacation. His life was an information hunt, collecting hows and whys. "I received 500,000 discrete bits of information today," he once said, "of which maybe twenty-five are important. My job is to make some sense of it." He wanted to write "stuff about what it feels like to live. Instead of being a relief from what it feels like to live." Readers curled up in the nooks and clearings of his style: his comedy, his brilliance, his humaneness.

His life was a map that ends at the wrong destination. Wallace was an A student through high school, he played football, he played tennis, he wrote a philosophy thesis and a novel before he graduated from Amherst, he went to writing school, published the novel, made a city of squalling, bruising, kneecapping editors and writers fall moony-eyed in love with him. He published a thousand-page novel, received the only award you get in the nation for being a genius, wrote essays providing the best feel anywhere of what

161

it means to be alive in the contemporary world, accepted a special chair at California's Pomona College to teach writing, married, published another book and, last month, hanged himself at age forty-six.

"The one thing that really should be said about David Foster Wallace is that this was a once-in-a-century talent," says his friend and former editor Colin Harrison. "We may never see a guy like this again in our lifetimes— that I will shout out. He was like a comet flying by at ground level."

His 1996 novel, *Infinite Jest*, was Bible-size and spawned books of interpretation and commentary, like *Understanding David Foster Wallace*—a book his friends might have tried to write and would have lined up to buy. He was clinically depressed for decades, information he limited to family and his closest friends. "I don't think that he ever lost the feeling that there was something shameful about this," his father says. "His instinct was to hide it."

After he died on September 12, readers crowded the Web with tributes to his generosity, his intelligence. "But he wasn't Saint Dave," says Jonathan Franzen, Wallace's best friend and the author of *The Corrections*. "This is the paradox of Dave: The closer you get, the darker the picture, but the more genuinely lovable he was. It was only when you knew him better that you had a true appreciation of what a heroic struggle it was for him not merely to get along in the world, but to produce wonderful writing."

David grew up in Champaign, Illinois. His father, Jim, taught philosophy at the University of Illinois. His mother, Sally, taught English at a local community college. It was an academic household—poised, considerate— language games in the car, the rooms tidy, the bookcase the hero. "I have these weird early memories," Wallace told me during a series of interviews in 1996. "I remember my parents reading *Ulysses* out loud to each other in bed, holding hands and both lovin' something really fiercely." Sally hated to get angry—it took her days to recover from a shout. So the family developed a sort of interoffice conflict mail. When his mother had something stern to say, she'd write it up in a letter. When David wanted something badly— raised allowance, more liberal bedtime—he'd slide a letter under his parents' door.

David was one of those eerie, perfect combinations of two parents' skills. The titles of his father's books—*Ethical Norms, Particular Cases*—have the sound of Wallace short-story titles. The tone of his mother's speaking voice contains echoes of Wallace's writing voice: Her textbook *Practically Painless English*, sounds like a Wallace joke. She uses phrases like "perishing hot" for very hot, "snoof" for talking in your sleep, "heave your skeleton" for go to bed. "David and I both owe a huge debt to my mother," says his sister, Amy, two years younger. "She has a way of talking that I've never heard anywhere else."

David was, from an early age, "very fragile," as he put it. He loved TV, and would get incredibly excited watching a program like *Batman* or *The Wild Wild West*. (His parents rationed the "rough" shows. One per week.) David could memorize whole shows of dialogue and predict, like a kind of plot weatherman, when the story was going to turn, where characters would end up. No one saw or treated him as a genius, but at age fourteen, when he asked what his father did, Jim sat David down and walked him through a Socratic dialogue. "I was astonished by how sophisticated his understanding was," Jim says. "At that point, I figured out that he really, really was extraordinarily bright."

David was a big-built kid; he played football—quarterback—until he was twelve or thirteen, and would always speak like an athlete, the disappearing G's, "wudn't," "dudn't," and "idn't" and "sumpin." "The big thing I was when I was little was a really serious jock," Wallace told me. "I mean, I had no artistic ambition. I played citywide football. And I was really good. Then I got to junior high, and there were two guys in the city who were better quarterbacks than me. And people started hitting each other a lot harder, and I discovered that I didn't really love to hit people. That was a huge disappointment." After his first day of football practice at Urbana High School, he came home and chucked it. He offered two explanations to his parents: They expected him to practice every day, and the coaches did too much cursing.

He had also picked up a racket. "I discovered tennis on my own," Wallace said, "taking public-park lessons. For five years. I was seriously gonna be a pro tennis player. I didn't look that good, but I was almost impossible to beat. I know that sounds arrogant. It's true." On court, he was a bit of a hustler: Before a match, he'd tell his opponent, "Thank you for being here, but you're just going to cream me."

By the time he was fourteen, he felt he could have made nationals. "Really be in the junior show. But just at the point it became important to me, I began to choke. The more scared you get, the worse you play." Plus it was the seventies—Pink Floyd, bongs. "I started to smoke a lot of pot when I was fifteen or sixteen, and it's hard to train." He laughed. "You don't have that much energy."

It was around this time that the Wallaces noticed something strange about David. He would voice surprising requests, like wanting to paint his bedroom black. He was constantly angry at his sister. When he was sixteen, he refused to go to her birthday party. "Why would I want to celebrate her birthday?" he told his parents.

"David began to have anxiety attacks in high school," his father recalls. "I noticed the symptoms, but I was just so unsophisticated about these matters. The depression seemed to take the form of an evil spirit that just haunted David." Sally came to call it the "black hole with teeth." David withdrew. "He spent a lot of time throwing up junior year," his sister remembers. One wall of his bedroom was lined with cork, for magazine photos of tennis stars. David pinned an article about Kafka to the wall, with the headline THE DISEASE WAS LIFE ITSELF.

"I hated seeing those words," his sister tells me, and starts to cry. "They seemed to sum up his existence. We couldn't understand why he was acting the way he was, and so of course my parents were exasperated, lovingly exasperated."

David graduated high school with perfect grades. Whatever his personal hurricane was, it had scattered trees and moved on. He decided to go to Amherst, which is where his father had gone, too. His parents told him he would enjoy the Berkshire autumn. Instead, he missed home—the farms and flat horizons, roads stretching contentedly nowhere. "It's fall," David wrote back. "The mountains are pretty, but the landscape isn't beautiful the way Illinois is."

Wallace had lugged his bags into Amherst the fall of 1980—Reagan coming in, the seventies capsized, preppies everywhere. He brought a suit to campus. "It was kind of a Sears suit, with this Scotch-plaid tie," says his college roommate and close friend Mark Costello, who went on to become a successful novelist himself. "Guys who went to Amherst, who came from five prep schools, they always dress a notch down. No one's bringing a suit. That was just the Wallace sense that going East is a big deal, and you have to not embarrass us. My first impression was that he was really very out of step."

Costello came from working-class Massachusetts, seven kids, Irish-Catholic household. He and Wallace connected. "Neither of us fit into the Gatsby-ite mold," Costello says. At Amherst David perfected the style he would wear for the rest of his life: turtleneck, hoodie, big basketball shoes. The look of parking-lot kids who in Illinois were called Dirt Bombs. "A slightly tough, slightly waste-product-y, tennis-playing persona," Costello says. Wallace was also amazingly fast and good company, even just on a walk across campus. "I'd always wanted to be an impressionist," Wallace said, "but I just didn't have an agile enough vocal and facial register to do it." Crossing a green, it was The Dave Show. He would recount how people walked, talked, held their heads, pictured their lives. "Just very connected to people," Costello recalls. "Dave had this ability to be inside someone else's skin."

Observing people from afar, of course, can be a way of avoiding them up close. "I was a complete just total banzai weenie studier in college," Wallace recalled. "I was really just scared of people. For instance, I would brave the TV pit—the central TV room—to watch *Hill Street Blues*, 'cause that was a really important show to me."

One afternoon, April of sophomore year, Costello came back to the dorm they shared and found Wallace seated in his chair. Desk clean, bags packed, even his typewriter, which weighed as much as the clothes put together.

"Dave, what's going on?" Costello asked.

"I'm sorry, I'm so sorry," Wallace said. "I know I'm really screwing you."

He was pulling out of college. Costello drove him to the airport. "He wasn't able to talk about it," Costello recalls, "He was crying, he was mortified. Panicky. He couldn't control his thoughts. It was mental incontinence, the equivalent of wetting his pants."

"I wasn't very happy there," Wallace told me later. "I felt kind of inadequate. There was a lot of stuff I wanted to read that wasn't part of any class. And Mom and Dad were just totally cool."

Wallace went home to hospitalization, explanations to his parents, a job. For a while, he drove a school bus. "Here he was, a guy who was really shaky, kind of Holden Caulfield, driving a school bus through lightning storms," Costello recalls. "He wrote me a letter all outraged, about the poor screening procedures for school-bus drivers in central Illinois."

Wallace would visit his dad's philosophy classes. "The classes would turn into a dialogue between David and me," his father remembers. "The students would just sit looking around, 'Who is this guy?'" Wallace devoured novels—"pretty much everything I've read was read during that year." He also told his parents how he'd felt at school. "He would talk about just being very sad, and lonely," Sally says. "It didn't have anything to do with being loved. He just was very lonely inside himself."

He returned to Amherst in the fall, to room with Costello, shaky but hardened. "Certain things had been destroyed in his head," Costello says. "In the first half of his Amherst career, he was trying to be a regular person. He was on the debate team, the sort of guy who knows he's going to be a success." Wallace had talked about going into politics; Costello recalls him joking, "No one is going to vote for somebody who's been in a nuthouse." Having his life fall apart narrowed his sense of what his options were—and the possibilities that were left became more real to him. In a letter to Costello he wrote, "I want to write books that people will read 100 years from now."

Back at school junior year, he never talked much about his breakdown. "It was embarrassing and personal," Costello says. "A zone of no jokes." Wallace regarded it as a failure, something he should have been able to control. He routinized his life. He'd be the first tray at the dining hall for supper, he'd eat, drink coffee dipped with tea bags, library study till 11, head back to the room, turn on *Hawaii Five-O*, then a midnight gulp from a scotch bottle. When he couldn't turn his mind off, he'd say, "You know what? I think this is a two-shot night," slam another and sleep.

In 1984, Costello left for Yale Law School; Wallace was alone senior year. He double-majored—English and philosophy, which meant two big writing projects. In philosophy, he took on modal logic. "It looked really hard, and I was really scared about it," he said. "So I thought I'd do this kind of jaunty, hundred-page novel." He wrote it in five months, and it clocked in at seven hundred pages. He called it *The Broom of the System*.

Wallace published stories in the Amherst literary magazine. One was about depression and a tricyclic anti-anxiety medication he had been on for two months. The medication "made me feel like I was stoned and in hell," he told me. The story dealt with the in-hell parts:

> You are the sickness yourself . . . You realize all this . . . when you look at the black hole and it's wearing your face. That's when the Bad Thing just absolutely eats you up, or rather when you just eat yourself up. When you kill yourself. All this business about people committing suicide when they're "severely depressed;" we say, "Holy cow, we must do something to stop them from killing themselves!" That's wrong. Because all these people have, you see, by this time already killed themselves, where it really counts. . . . When they "commit suicide," they're just being orderly.

It wasn't just writing the novel that made Wallace realize his future would lie in fiction. He also helped out friends by writing their papers. In a comic book, this would be his origin story, the part where he's bombarded with gamma rays, bitten by the spider. "I remember realizing at the time, 'Man, I'm really good at this. I'm a weird kind of forger. I can sound kind of like anybody.'"

Grad school was next. Philosophy would be an obvious choice. "My dad would have limbs removed without anesthetic before ever pushing his kids about anything," Wallace said. "But I knew I was gonna have to go to grad school. I applied to these English programs instead, and I didn't tell any-body. Writing *The Broom of the System*, I felt like I was using 97 percent of me, whereas philosophy was using 50 percent."

After Amherst, Wallace went to the University of Arizona for an MFA. It was where he picked up the bandanna: "I started wearing them in Tucson because it was a hundred degrees all the time, and I would perspire so much I would drip on the page." The woman he was dating thought the bandanna was a wise move. "She was like a sixties lady, a Sufi Muslim. She said there were various chakras, and one of the big ones she called the spout hole, at the very top of your cranium. Then I began thinking about the phrase 'Keep-ing your head together.' It makes me feel kind of creepy that people view it as a trademark or something—it's more a recognition of a weakness, which is that I'm just kind of worried that my head's gonna explode."

Arizona was a strange experience: the first classrooms where people weren't happy to see him. He wanted to write the way he wanted to write— funny and overstuffed and nonlinear and strange. The teachers were all "hardass realists." That was the first problem. Problem two was Wallace. "I think I was kind of a prick," he said. "I was just unteachable. I had that look— 'If there were any justice, I'd be teaching this class'—that makes you want to slap a student." One of his stories, "Here and There," went on to win a 1989 O. Henry Prize after it was published in a literary magazine. When he turned it in to his professor, he received a chilly note back: "I hope this isn't representative of the work you're hoping to do for us. We'd hate to lose you."

"What I hated was how disingenuous it was," Wallace recalled. "'We'd hate to lose you.' You know, if you're gonna threaten, say that."

Wallace sent his thesis project out to agents. He got a lot of letters back: "Best of luck in your janitorial career." Bonnie Nadell was twenty-five, work-ing a first job at San Francisco's Frederick Hill Agency. She opened a letter from Wallace, read a chapter from his book. "I loved it so much," Nadell says. It turned out there was a writer named David Rains Wallace. Hill and Nadell agreed that David should insert his mother's maiden name, which is how he became David Foster Wallace. She remained his agent for the rest of his life. "I have this thing, the nearest Jewish mother, I will simply put my arms around her skirt and just attach myself," Wallace said. "I don't know what it means. Maybe sort of WASP deprivation."

Viking won the auction for the novel, "with something like a handful of trading stamps." Word spread; professors turned nice. "I went from border-line ready-to-get-kicked-out to all these tight-smiled guys being, 'Glad to see you, were proud of you, you'll have to come over for dinner.' It was so delicious: I felt kind of embarrassed for them, they didn't even have integrity about their hatred."

Wallace went to New York to meet his editor, Gerry Howard, wearing a U2 T-shirt. "He seemed like a very young twenty-four," Howard says. The shirt impressed him. "U2 wasn't really huge then. And there's a hypersincerity to U2, which I think David was in tune with—or that he really wanted to be sincere, even though his brain kept turning him in the direction of the ironic." Wallace kept calling Howard—who was only thirty-six—"Mr. Howard," never "Gerry." It would become his business style: a kind of mock formality. People often suspected it was a put-on. What it was was Midwestern politeness, the burnout in the parking lot still nodding "sir" to the vice principal. "There was kind of this hum of superintelligence behind the 'aw, shucks' manner," Howard recalls.

The Broom of the System was published in January of 1987, Wallace's second and last year at Arizona. The title referred to something his mother's grandmother used to say, as in, "Here, Sally, have an apple, it's the broom of the system." "I wasn't aware David had picked up on that," his mother says. "I was thrilled that a family expression became the title of his book."

The novel hit. "Everything you could hope for," Howard says. "Critics praised it, it sold quite well, and David was off to the races."

His first brush with fame was a kind of gateway experience. Wallace would open the *Wall Street Journal*, see his face transmuted into a dot-cartoon. "Some article like 'Hotshot's Weird New Novel,'" he said. "I'd feel really good, really cool, for exactly ten seconds. Probably not unlike a crack high, you know? I was living an incredibly American life: 'Boy, if I could just achieve X, Y, and Z, everything would be OK.'" Howard bought Wallace's second book, *Girl with Curious Hair*, a collection of the stories he was finishing up at Arizona. But something in Wallace worried him. "I have never encountered a mind like David's," he says. "It functioned at such an amazingly high level, he clearly lived in a hyperalert state. But on the other hand, I felt that David's emotional life lagged far behind his mental life. And I think he could get lost in the gap between the two."

Wallace was already drifting into the gap. He won a Whiting Writers' Award—stood on a stage with Eudora Welty—graduated Arizona, went to an artists' colony, met famous writers, knew the famous writers were seeing his name in more magazines ("absolutely exhilarating and really scary at the same time"), finished the stories. And then he was out of ideas. He tried to write in a cabin in Tucson for a while, then returned home to write—Mom and Dad doing the grocery shopping. He accepted a one-year slot teaching philosophy at Amherst, which was strange. Sophomores he had known were now his students. In the acknowledgments for the book he was completing, he thanks "The Mr. and Mrs. Wallace Fund for Aimless Children."

He was balled up, tied up. "I started hating everything I did," he said. "Worse than stuff I'd done in college. Hopelessly confused, unbelievably bad. I was really in a panic, I didn't think I was going to be able to write anymore. And I got this idea: I'd flourished in an academic environment— my first two books had sort of been written under professors." He applied to graduate programs in philosophy, thinking he could write fiction in his spare time. Harvard offered a full scholarship. The last thing he needed to reproduce his college years was to reactivate Mark Costello.

"So he comes up with this whole cockamamie plan," Costello recalls. "He says, 'OK, you're going to go back to Boston, practice law, and I'm going to go to Harvard. We'll live together—it'll be just like the house we had at Amherst.' It all ended up being a train wreck."

They found an apartment in Somerville. Student ghetto: rickety buildings, outdoor staircases. Costello would come home with his briefcase, click up the back stairs, David would call out, "Hi, honey, how was your day?" But Wallace wasn't writing fiction. He had thought course work would be a sideline, but professors expected actual work.

Not writing was the kind of symptom that presents a problem of its own. "He could get himself into places where he was pretty helpless," Costello says. "Basically it was the same symptoms all along: this incredible sense of inadequacy, panic. He once said to me that he wanted to write to shut up the babble in his head. He said when you're writing well, you establish a voice in your head, and it shuts up the other voices. The ones that are saying, 'You're not good enough, you're a fraud.'"

"Harvard was just unbelievably bleak," Wallace said. It became a substance marathon: drinking, parties, drugs. "I didn't want to feel it," he said. "It was the only time in my life that I'd gone to bars, picked up women I didn't know." Then for weeks, he would quit drinking, start mornings with a ten-mile run. "You know, this kind of very American sports training—I will fix this by taking radical action." Schwarzenegger voice: "If there's a problem, I will train myself out of it. I will work harder."

Various delays were holding up the publication of his short-story collection *Girl with Curious Hair*. He started to feel spooked. "I'm this genius writer," he remembered. "Everything I do's gotta be ingenious, blah, blah, blah, blah." The five-year clock was ticking again. He'd played football for five years. Then he'd played high-level tennis for five years. Now he'd been writing for five years. "What I saw was, 'Jesus, it's the same thing all over again.' I'd started late, showed tremendous promise—and the minute I felt the implications of that promise, it caved in. Because see, by this time, my ego's all invested in the writing. It's the only thing I've gotten food pellets from the universe for. So I feel trapped: 'Uh-oh, my five years is up, I've gotta move on.' But I didn't want to move on."

Costello watched while Wallace slipped into a depressive crisis. "He was hanging out with women who were pretty heavily into drugs—that was kind of alluring to Dave—skanking around Somerville, drinking himself blotto."

It was the worst period Wallace had ever gone through. "It may have been what in the old days was called a spiritual crisis," he said. "It was just feeling as though every axiom of your life turned out to be false. And there was nothing, and you were nothing—it was all a delusion. But you were better than everyone else because you saw that it was a delusion, and yet you were worse because you couldn't function."

By November, the anxieties had become locked and fixed. "I got really worried I was going to kill myself. And I knew that if anybody was fated to fuck up a suicide attempt, it was me." He walked across campus to Health Services and told a psychiatrist, "Look, there's this issue. I don't feel real safe."

"It was a big deal for me, because I was so embarrassed," Wallace said. "But it was the first time I ever treated myself like I was worth something."

By making his announcement, Wallace had activated a protocol: Police were notified, he had to withdraw from school. He was sent to McLean, which, as psychiatric hospitals go, is pedigreed: Robert Lowell, Sylvia Plath, Anne Sexton all put in residences there; it's the setting for the memoir *Girl, Interrupted*. Wallace spent his first day on suicide watch. Locked ward, pink room, no furniture, drain in the floor, observation slot in the door. "When that happens to you," David said, smiling, "you get unprecedentedly willing to examine other alternatives for how to live."

Wallace spent eight days in McLean. He was diagnosed as a clinical depressive and was prescribed a drug, called Nardil, developed in the 1950s. He would have to take it from then on. "We had a brief, maybe three-minute audience with the psychopharmacologist," his mother says. Wallace would have to quit drinking, and there was a long list of foods—certain cheeses, pickles, cured meats—he would have to stay away from.

He started to clean up. He found a way to get sober, worked very hard at it, and wouldn't drink for the rest of his life. *Girl with Curious Hair* finally appeared in 1989. Wallace gave a reading in Cambridge; thirteen people showed up, including a schizophrenic woman who shrieked all the way through his performance. "The book's coming out seemed like a kind of shrill, jagged laugh from the universe, this thing sort of lingering behind me like a really nasty fart."

What followed was a phased, deliberate return to the world. He worked as a security guard, morning shift, at Lotus software. Polyester uniform, service baton, walking the corridors. "I liked it because I didn't have to think," he said. "Then I quit for the incredibly brave reason that I got tired of getting up so early in the morning."

Next, he worked at a health club in Auburndale, Massachusetts. "Very chichi," he said. "They called me something other than a towel boy, but I was in effect a towel boy. I'm sitting there, and who should walk in to get their towel but Michael Ryan. Now, Michael Ryan had received a Whiting Writers' Award the same year I had. So I see this guy that I'd been up on the fucking rostrum with, having Eudora Welty give us this prize. It's two years later—it's the only time I've literally dived under something. He came in, and I pretended not very subtly to slip, and lay facedown, and didn't respond. I left that day, and I didn't go back."

He wrote Bonnie Nadell a letter; he was done with writing. That wasn't exactly her first concern. "I was worried he wasn't going to survive," she says. He filled in Howard, too. "I contemplated the circumstance that the best young writer in America was handing out towels in a health club," Howard says. "How fucking sad."

Wallace met Jonathan Franzen in the most natural way for an author: as a fan. He sent Franzen a nice letter about his first novel, *The Twenty-Seventh City*. Franzen wrote back, they arranged to meet in Cambridge. "He just flaked," Franzen recalls. "He didn't show up. That was a fairly substance-filled period of his life."

By April of 1992, both were ready for a change. They loaded Franzen's car and headed for Syracuse to scout apartments. Franzen needed "somewhere to relocate with my wife where we could both afford to live and not have anyone tell us how screwed up our marriage was." Wallace's need was simpler: cheap space, for writing. He had been researching for months, haunting rehab facilities and halfway houses, taking quiet note of voices and stories, people who had fallen into the gaps like him. "I got very assertive research- and finagle-wise," he said. "I spent hundreds of hours at three halfway houses. It turned out you could just sit in the living room—nobody is as gregarious as somebody who has recently stopped using drugs."

He and Franzen talked a lot about what writing should be for. "We had this feeling that fiction ought to be good for something," Franzen says. "Basically, we decided it was to combat loneliness." They would talk about lots of Wallace's ideas, which could abruptly sharpen into self-criticism. "I remember this being a frequent topic of conversation," Franzen says, "his notion of not having an authentic self. Of being just quick enough to construct a pleasing self for whomever he was talking to. I see now he wasn't just being funny—there was something genuinely compromised in David. At the time I thought, 'Wow, he's even more self-conscious than I am.'"

Wallace spent a year writing in Syracuse. "I lived in an apartment that was seriously the size of the foyer of an average house. I really liked it. There were so many books, you couldn't move around. When I'd want to write, I'd have to put all the stuff from the desk on the bed, and when I'd want to sleep, I would have to put all the stuff on the desk."

Wallace worked longhand, pages piling up. "You look at the clock and seven hours have passed and your hand is cramped," Wallace said. He'd have pens he considered hot—cheap Bic ballpoints, like batters have bats that are hot. A pen that was hot he called the orgasm pen.

In the summer of 1993, he took an academic job fifty miles from his parents, at Illinois State University at Normal. The book was three-quarters done. Based on the first unruly stack of pages, Nadell had been able to sell it to Little, Brown. He had put his whole life into it—tennis, and depression, and stoner afternoons, and the precipice of rehab, and all the hours spent with Amy watching TV. The plot motor is a movie called *Infinite Jest*, so soothing and perfect it's impossible to switch off: You watch until you sink into your chair, spill your bladder, starve, die. "If the book's about anything," he said, "it's about the question of why am I watching so much shit? It's not about the shit. It's about me: Why am I doing it? The original title was *A Failed Entertainment*, and the book is structured as an entertainment that doesn't work"—characters developing and scattering, chapters disordered— "because what entertainment ultimately leads to is 'Infinite Jest,' that's the star it's steering by."

Wallace held classes in his house, students nudging aside books like *Compendium of Drug Therapy* and *The Emergence of the French Art Film*, making jokes about Mount Manuscript, David's pile of novel. He had finished and collected the three years of drafts, and finally sat down and typed the whole thing. Wallace didn't really type; he input the giant thing twice, with one finger. "But a really fast finger."

It came to almost 1,700 pages. "I was just terrified how long it would end up being," he said. Wallace told his editor it would be a good beach book, in the sense that people could use it for shade.

It can take a year to edit a book, re-edit it, print it, publicize it, ship it, the writer all the time checking his watch. In the meantime, Wallace turned to nonfiction. Two pieces, published in *Harper's*, would become some of the most famous pieces of journalism of the past decade and a half.

Colin Harrison, Wallace's editor at *Harper's*, had the idea to outfit him with a notebook and push him into perfectly American places—the Illinois State Fair, a Caribbean cruise. It would soak up the side of Wallace that was always on, always measuring himself. "There would be Dave the mimic, Dave the people-watcher," Costello says. "Asking him to actually report could get stressful and weird and complicated. Colin had this stroke of genius about what to do with David. It was a much simpler solution than anyone ever thought."

In the pieces, Wallace invented a style writers have plundered for a decade. The unedited camera, the feed before the director in the van starts making choices and cuts. The voice was humane, a big, kind brain tripping over its own lumps. "The *Harper's* pieces were me peeling back my skull," Wallace said. "You know, welcome to my mind for twenty pages, see through my eyes, here's pretty much all the French curls and crazy circles. The trick was to have it be honest but also interesting—because most of our thoughts aren't all that interesting. To be honest with a motive." He laughed. "There's a certain persona created, that's a little stupider and schmuckier than I am."

The cruise-ship piece ran in January 1996, a month before David's novel was published. People photocopied it, faxed it to each other, read it over the phone. When people tell you they're fans of David Foster Wallace, what they're often telling you is that they've read the cruise-ship piece; Wallace would make it the title essay in his first collection of journalism, *A Supposedly Fun Thing I'll Never Do Again*. In a way, the difference between the fiction and the nonfiction reads as the difference between Wallace's social self and his private self. The essays were endlessly charming, they were the best friend you'd ever have, spotting everything, whispering jokes, sweeping you past what was irritating or boring or awful in humane style. Wallace's fiction, especially after *Infinite Jest*, would turn chilly, dark, abstract. You could imagine the author of the fiction sinking into a depression. The nonfiction writer was an impervious sun.

The novel came out in February of 1996. In *New York Magazine*, Walter Kirn wrote, "The competition has been obliterated. It's as though Paul Bunyan had joined the NFL, or Wittgenstein had gone on *Jeopardy!* The novel is that colossally disruptive. And that spectacularly good." He was in *Newsweek*, *Time*. Hollywood people appeared at his readings, women batted their eyelashes, men in the back rows scowled, envied. A FedEx guy rang his bell, watched David sign for delivery, asked, "How's it feel to be famous?"

At the end of his book tour, I spent a week with David. He talked about the "greasy thrill of fame" and what it might mean to his writing. "When I was twenty-five, I would've given a couple of digits off my non-use hand for this," he said. "I feel good, because I wanna be doing this for forty more years, you know? So I've got to find some way to enjoy this that doesn't involve getting eaten by it."

He was astonishingly good, quick company, making you feel both wide awake and as if your shoes had been tied together. He'd say things like, "There's good self-consciousness, and then there's toxic, paralyzing, raped-by-psychic-Bedouins self-consciousness." He talked about a kind of shyness that turned social life impossibly complicated. "I think being shy basically means being self-absorbed to the point that it makes it difficult to be around other people. For instance, if I'm hanging out with you, I can't even tell whether I like you or not because I'm too worried about whether you like me."

He said one interviewer had devoted tons of energy to the genius question. "That was his whole thing. 'Are you normal?' 'Are you normal?' I think one of the true ways I've gotten smarter is that I've realized that there are ways other people are a lot smarter than me. My biggest asset as a writer is that I'm pretty much like everybody else. The parts of me that used to think I was different or smarter or whatever almost made me die."

It had been difficult, during the summer, to watch his sister get married. "I'm almost thirty-five. I would like to get married and have kids. I haven't even started to work that shit out yet. I've come close a few times, but I tend to be interested in women that I turn out to not get along very well with. I have friends who say this is something that would be worth looking into with someone that you pay."

Wallace was always dating somebody. "There were a lot of relationships," Amy says. He dated in his imaginative life too: When I visited him, one wall was taped with a giant Alanis Morissette poster. "The Alanis Morissette obsession followed the Melanie Griffith obsession—a six-year obsession," he said. "It was preceded by something that I will tell you I got teased a lot for, which was a terrible Margaret Thatcher obsession. All through college: posters of Margaret Thatcher, and ruminations on Margaret Thatcher. Having her really enjoy something I said, leaning forward and covering my hand with hers!"

He tended to date high-strung women—another symptom of his shyness. "Say what you want about them, psychotics tend to make the first move." Owning dogs was less complicated: "You don't get the feeling you're hurting their feelings all the time."

His romantic anxieties were full-spectrum, every bit of the mechanics individually examined. He told me a joke:

What does a writer say after sex?

Was it as good for me as it was for you?

"There is, in writing, a certain blend of sincerity and manipulation, of trying always to gauge what the particular effect of something is gonna be," he said. "It's a very precious asset that really needs to be turned off sometimes. My guess is that writers probably make fun, skilled, satisfactory, and seemingly considerate partners for other people. But that the experience for them is often rather lonely."

One night Wallace met the writer Elizabeth Wurtzel, whose depression memoir, *Prozac Nation,* had recently been published. She thought he looked scruffy—jeans and the bandanna—and very smart. Another night, Wallace walked her home from a restaurant, sat with her in her lobby, spent some time trying to talk his way upstairs. It charmed Wurtzel: "You know, he might have had this enormous brain, but at the end of the day, he still was a guy."

Wallace and Wurtzel didn't really talk about the personal experience they had in common—depression, a substance history, consultations at McLean—but about their profession, about what to do with fame. Wallace, again, had set impossible standards for himself. "It really disturbed him, the possibility that success could taint you," she recalls. "He was very interested in purity, in the idea of authenticity—the way some people are into the idea of being cool. He had keeping it real down to a science."

When Wallace wrote her, he was still curling through the same topic. "I go through a loop in which I notice all the ways I am self-centered and careerist and not true to standards and values that transcend my own petty interests, and feel like I'm not one of the good ones. But then I countenance the fact that at least here I am worrying about it, noticing all the ways I fall short of integrity, and I imagine that maybe people without any integrity at all don't notice or worry about it; so then I feel better about myself. It's all very confusing. I think I'm very honest and candid, but I'm also proud of how honest and candid I am—so where does that put me?"

Success can be as difficult to recover from as failure. "You know the tic big-league pitchers have," his mother says, "when they know that they've pitched a marvelous game—but gee, can they do it again, so they keep flexing that arm? There was some of that. Where he said, 'OK. Good, that came out well. But can I do it again?' That was the feeling I got. There was always the shadow waiting."

Wallace saw it that way too. "My big worry," he said, "is that this will just up my expectations for myself. And expectations are a very fine line. Up to a certain point they can be motivating, can be kind of a flamethrower held to your ass. Past that point they're toxic and paralyzing. I'm scared that I'll fuck up and plunge into a compressed version of what I went through before."

Mark Costello was also worried. "Work got very hard. He didn't get these gifts from God anymore, he didn't get these six-week periods where he got exactly the 120 pages he needed. So he found distraction in other places." He would get engaged, then unengaged. He would call friends: "Next weekend, Saturday, you gotta be in Rochester, Minnesota, I'm getting married." But then it would be Sunday, or the next week, and he'd have called it off.

"He almost got married a few times," Amy says. "I think what ultimately happened is he was doing it more for the other person than himself. And he realized that wasn't doing the other person any favors."

Wallace told Costello about a woman he had become involved with. "He said, 'She gets mad at me because I never want to leave the house. "Honey, let's go to the mall." "No, I want to write." "But you never do write." "But I don't know if I'm going to write. So I have to be here in case it happens."' This went on for years."

In 2000, Wallace wrote a letter to his friend Evan Wright, a *Rolling Stone* contributor: "I know about still having trouble with relationships. (Boy oh boy, do I.) But coming to enjoy my own company more and more—most of the time. I know about some darkness every day (and some days, it's all dark for me)." He wrote about meeting a woman, having things move too easily, deciding against it. "I think whatever the pull is for me is largely composed of wanting the Big Yes, of wanting someone else to want you (Cheap Trick lives). . . . So now I don't know what to do. Probably nothing, which seems to be the Sign that the universe or its CEO is sending me."

In the summer of 2001, Wallace relocated to Claremont, California, to become the Roy Edward Disney Chair in Creative Writing, at Pomona College. He published stories and essays, but was having trouble with his work. After he reported on John McCain's 2000 presidential campaign for this magazine, he wrote his agent that it would show his editor that "I'm still capable of good work (my own insecurities, I know)."

Wallace had received a MacArthur "genius" award in 1997. "I don't think it did him any favors," says Franzen. "It conferred the mantle of 'genius' on him, which he had of course craved and sought and thought was his due. But I think he felt, 'Now I have to be even smarter.'" In late 2001, Costello called Wallace. "He was talking about how hard the writing was. And I said, lightheartedly, 'Dave, you're a genius.' Meaning, people aren't going to forget about you. You're not going to wind up in a Wendy's. He said, 'All that makes me think is that I've fooled you, too.'"

Wallace met Karen Green a few months after moving to Claremont. Green, a painter, admired David's work. It was a sort of artistic exchange, an interdisciplinary blind date. "She wanted to do some paintings based on some of David's stories," his mother says. "They had a mutual friend, and she thought she would ask permission."

"He was totally gaga," Wright recalls. "He called, head over heels, he was talking about her as a life-changing event." Franzen met Green the following year. "I felt in about three minutes that he'd finally found somebody who was up to the task of living with Dave. She's beautiful, incredibly strong, and a real grown-up—she had a center that was not about landing the genius Dave Wallace."

They made their debut as a couple with Wallace's parents in July 2003, attending the Maine culinary festival that would provide the title for his last book, *Consider the Lobster.* "They were both so quick," his father says. "They would get things and look at each other and laugh, without having to say what had struck them as funny." The next year, Wallace and Green flew to his parents' home in Illinois, where they were married two days after Christmas.

It was a surprise wedding. David told his mother he wanted to take the family to what he called a "high-gussy" lunch. Sally Wallace assumed it was Karen's influence. "David does not do high gussy," she says. "His notion of high gussy is maybe long pants instead of shorts or a T-shirt with two holes instead of eighteen." Green and Wallace left the house early to "run errands," while Amy figured out a pretext to get their parents to the courthouse on the way to the lunch. "We went upstairs," Sally says, "and saw Karen with a bouquet, and David dressed up with a flower in his buttonhole, and we knew. He just looked so happy, just radiating happiness." Their reception was at an Urbana restaurant. "As we left in the snow," Sally says, "David and

Karen were walking away from us. He wanted us to take pictures, and Jim did. David was jumping in the air and clicking his heels. That became the wedding announcement."

According to Wallace's family and friends, the last six years—until the final one—were the best of his life. The marriage was happy, university life good, Karen and David had two dogs, Warner and Bella, they bought a lovely house. "Dave in a real house," Franzen says, laughing, "with real furniture and real style."

To Franzen's eye, he was watching Wallace grow up. There had been in David a kind of purposeful avoidance of the normal. Once, they'd gone to a literary party in the city. They walked in the front door together, but by the time Franzen got to the kitchen, he realized Wallace had disappeared. "I went back and proceeded to search the whole place," Franzen recalled. "He had walked into the bathroom to lose me, then turned on his heels and walked right back out the front door."

Now, that sort of thing had stopped. "He had reason to hope," Franzen said. "He had the resources to be more grown-up, a wholer person."

And then there were the dogs. "He had a predilection for dogs who'd been abused, and unlikely to find other owners who were going to be patient enough for them," Franzen says. "Whether through a sense of identification or sympathy, he had a very hard time disciplining them. But you couldn't see his attentiveness to the dogs without getting a lump in your throat."

Because Wallace was secure, he began to talk about going off Nardil, the antidepressant he had taken for nearly two decades. The drug had a long list of side effects, including the potential of very high blood pressure. "It had been a fixture of my morbid fear about Dave—that he would not last all that long, with the wear and tear on his heart," Franzen says. "I worried that I was going to lose him in his early fifties." Costello said that Wallace complained the drug made him feel "filtered." "He said, 'I don't want to be on this stuff for the rest of my life.' He wanted to be more a member of the human race."

In June of 2007, Wallace and Green were at an Indian restaurant with David's parents in Claremont. David suddenly felt very sick—intense stomach pains. They stayed with him for days. When he went to doctors, he was told that something he'd eaten might have interacted with the Nardil. They suggested he try going off the drug and seeing if another approach might work.

"So at that point," says his sister Amy, with an edge in her voice, "it was determined, 'Oh, well, gosh, we've made so much pharmaceutical progress in the last two decades that I'm sure we can find something that can knock out that pesky depression without all these side effects.' They had no idea that it was the only thing that was keeping him alive."

Wallace would have to taper off the old drug and then taper on to a new one. "He knew it was going to be rough," says Franzen. "But he was feeling like he could finally *afford* a year to do the job. He figured that he was going to go on to something else, at least temporarily. He was a perfectionist, you know? He wanted to be perfect, and taking Nardil was not perfect."

That summer, David began to phase out the Nardil. His doctors began prescribing other medications, none of which seemed to help. "They could find nothing," his mother says softly. "Nothing." In September, David asked Amy to forgo her annual fall-break visit. He wasn't up to it. By October, his symptoms had become bad enough to send him to the hospital. His parents didn't know what to do. "I started worrying about that," Sally says, "but then it seemed OK." He began to drop weight. By that fall, he looked like a college kid again: longish hair, eyes intense, as if he had just stepped out of an Amherst classroom.

When Amy talked to him on the phone, "sometimes he was his old self," she says. "The worst question you could ask David in the last year was 'how are you?' And it's almost impossible to have a conversation with someone you don't see regularly without that question." Wallace was very honest with her. He'd answer, "I'm not all right. I'm trying to be, but I'm not all right."

Despite his struggle, Wallace managed to keep teaching. He was dedicated to his students: He would write six pages of comments to a short story, joke with his class, fight them to try harder. During office hours, if there was a grammar question he couldn't answer, he'd phone his mother. "He would call me and say, 'Mom, I've got this student right here. Explain to me one more time why this is wrong.' You could hear the student sort of laughing in the background. 'Here's David Foster Wallace calling his mother.'"

In early May, at the end of the school year, he sat down with some graduating seniors from his fiction class at a nearby cafe. Wallace answered their jittery writer's-future questions. "He got choked up at the end," recalls Bennett Sims, one of his students. "He started to tell us how much he would miss us, and he began to cry. And because I had never seen Dave cry, I thought he was just joking. Then, awfully, he sniffled and said, 'Go ahead and laugh—here I am crying—but I really am going to miss all of you.'"

His parents were scheduled to visit the next month. In June, when Sally spoke with her son, he said, "I can't wait, it'll be wonderful, we'll have big fun." The next day, he called and said, "Mom, I have two favors to ask you.

Would you please not come?" She said OK. Then Wallace asked, "Would your feelings not be hurt?"

No medications had worked; the depression wouldn't lift. "After this year of absolute hell for David," Sally says, "they decided to go back to the Nardil." The doctors also administered twelve courses of electroconvulsive therapy, waiting for Wallace's medication to become effective. "Twelve," Sally repeats. "Such brutal treatments," Jim says. "It was clear then things were bad."

Wallace had always been terrified of shock therapy. "It scares the shit out of me," he told me in 1996. "My brain's what I've got. But I could see that at a certain point, you might beg for it."

In late June, Franzen, who was in Berlin, grew worried. "I actually woke up one night," he says. "Our communications had a rhythm, and I thought, 'It's been too long since I heard from Dave.'" When Franzen called, Karen said to come immediately: David had tried to kill himself.

Franzen spent a week with Wallace in July. David had dropped seventy pounds in a year. "He was thinner than I'd ever seen him. There was a look in his eyes: terrified, terribly sad, and far away. Still, he was fun to be with, even at 10 percent strength."

Franzen would sit with Wallace in the living room and play with the dogs, or step outside with David while he smoked a cigarette. "We argued about stuff. He was doing his usual line about, 'A dog's mouth is practically a disinfectant, it's so clean. Not like human saliva, dog saliva is marvelously germ-resistant.'" Before he left, Wallace thanked him for coming. "I felt grateful that he allowed me to be there," Franzen says.

Six weeks later, Wallace asked his parents to come to California. The Nardil wasn't working. It can happen with an antidepressant; a patient goes off, returns, and the medication has lost its efficacy. Wallace couldn't sleep. He was afraid to leave the house. He asked, "What if I meet one of my students?"

"He didn't want anyone to see him the way he was," his father says. "It was just awful to see. If a student saw him, they would have put their arms around him and hugged him, I'm sure."

His parents stayed for ten days. "He was just desperate," his mother says. "He was afraid it wasn't ever going to work. He was suffering. We just kept holding him, saying if he could just hang on, it would straighten. He was very brave for a very long time."

Wallace and his parents would get up at six in the morning and walk the dogs. They watched DVDs of *The Wire*, talked. Sally cooked David's favorite dishes, heavy comfort foods—pot pies, casseroles, strawberries in cream.

"We kept telling him we were so glad he was alive," his mother recalls. "But my feeling is that, even then, he was leaving the planet. He just couldn't take it."

One afternoon before they left, David was very upset. His mother sat on the floor beside him. "I just rubbed his arm. He said he was glad I was his mom. I told him it was an honor."

At the end of August, Franzen called. All summer long he had been telling David that as bad as things were, they were going to be better, and then he'd be better than he'd ever been. David would say, "Keep talking like that— it's helping." But this time it wasn't helping. "He was far away," Franzen says.

A few weeks later, Karen left David alone with the dogs for a few hours. When she came home that night, he had hanged himself.

"I can't get the image out of my head," his sister says. "David and his dogs, and it's dark. I'm sure he kissed them on the mouth, and told them he was sorry."

Index